LACAN'S RETURN TO ANTIQUITY

Lacan's Return to Antiquity is the first book devoted to the role of classical antiquity in Lacan's work. Oliver Harris poses a question familiar from studies of Freud: what are Ancient Greece and Rome doing in a twentieth-century theory of psychology? In Lacan's case, the issue has an additional edge, for he employs antiquity to demonstrate what is radically *new* about psychoanalysis. It is a tool with which to convey the revolutionary power of Freud's ideas by digging down to the philosophical questions beneath them. It is through these questions that Lacan allies psychoanalysis with the pioneering intellectual developments of his time in anthropology, philosophy, art and literature.

Harris begins by considering the role of Plato and Socrates in Lacan's conflicted thoughts on teaching, writing and the process of becoming an intellectual icon. In doing so, he provides a way into considering the uniquely challenging nature of the Lacanian texts themselves and the live performances behind them. Two central chapters explore when and why myth is drawn upon in psychoanalysis, its threat to the discipline's scientific aspirations, and Lacan's embrace of its expressive potential. The final chapters explore Lacan's defence of tragedy and his return to Ovidian themes. These include the unwitting voyeurism of Actaeon and the fate of Narcissus, a figure of tragic metamorphosis that Freud places at the heart of infantile development.

Lacan's Return to Antiquity brings to Lacan studies the close reading and cross-disciplinary research that has proved fruitful in understanding Freud's invention of psychoanalysis. It will appeal to psychoanalysts and advanced students studying in the field, being of particular value to those interested in the roots of Lacanian concepts, the evolution of his thought, and the cultural context of his work. What emerges is a more nuanced, self-critical figure, a corrective to the reputation for dogmatism and obscurity that Lacan has attracted. In the process, new light is thrown on enduring controversies, from Lacan's pronouncements on feminine sexuality to the opaque drama of the seminars themselves.

Oliver Harris is a novelist and academic. He holds an MA in Shakespeare Studies from UCL, and a PhD on classical myth and psychoanalysis from the London Consortium (Birkbeck). He has taught at Birkbeck, London Metropolitan University and Cambridge Institute of Continuing Education.

'This book makes a compelling case for returning, with Lacan, to antiquity, and by doing so Oliver Harris shows the reader how it is possible to open up and thereby also lay anew the foundations for an innovative reading of Lacanian psychoanalysis. *Lacan's Return to Antiquity* accomplishes its task with clarity and energy, bringing a writer's craft to bear on telling us what we should already have known, and thereby striking a conceptual blow après-coup for antiquity with Lacan.'

– **Ian Parker**, psychoanalyst, Professor of Management, University of Leicester

'Much like Freud, Lacan had a lifelong "compulsion for antiquity", although in his case it was definitely more focused on hommelettes than on statuettes. In this brilliantly researched and masterfully written book, Oliver Harris explains why the study of Plato and Aristotle is as important for the development of Lacan's thought as the reading of Freud himself, and he shows how key Lacanian notions cannot be fully understood without a return to classical antiquity. Avoiding the Bacchic frenzy that often accompanies the contemporary Lacan-cult, this book stands out as a new beacon, which will cast its light on the roots of Lacanian psychoanalysis for many years to come.'

– **Dany Nobus**, Professor of Psychoanalytic Psychology and Pro-Vice-Chancellor, Brunel University London; chair of the Freud Museum London

'The exploration of Lacan's engagement with the Classics sheds a novel and appealing light on his thinking. In this sparkling study, Oliver Harris shows how fruitful for Lacan's ideas, no less than for Freud's, were the writings of classical authors from the Presocratics and Plato to Plautus and Ovid. The deep-rooted connections of ancient myth, philosophy and literature with Lacan's insights into sexuality, creativity and fantasy allow Harris to present an original and engaging exploration of key texts for both psychoanalysis and the Classics.'

– **Armand D'Angour**, Associate Professor of Classics, Oxford University

LACAN'S RETURN TO ANTIQUITY

Between nature and the gods

Oliver Harris

LONDON AND NEW YORK

First published 2017
by Routledge
2 Park Square, Milton Park, Abingdon, Oxon OX14 4RN

and by Routledge
711 Third Avenue, New York, NY 10017

Routledge is an imprint of the Taylor & Francis Group, an informa business

© 2017 Oliver Harris

The right of Oliver Harris to be identified as author of this work has been asserted by him in accordance with sections 77 and 78 of the Copyright, Designs and Patents Act 1988.

All rights reserved. No part of this book may be reprinted or reproduced or utilised in any form or by any electronic, mechanical, or other means, now known or hereafter invented, including photocopying and recording, or in any information storage or retrieval system, without permission in writing from the publishers.

Trademark notice: Product or corporate names may be trademarks or registered trademarks, and are used only for identification and explanation without intent to infringe.

British Library Cataloguing in Publication Data
A catalogue record for this book is available from the British Library

Library of Congress Cataloging in Publication Data
Names: Harris, Oliver, 1978- author.
Title: Lacan's return to antiquity : between nature and the gods / Oliver Harris.
Description: Abingdon, Oxon ; New York, NY : Routledge, 2016. | Includes bibliographical references and index.
Identifiers: LCCN 2016001406 (print) | LCCN 2016009826 (ebook) | ISBN 9781138820371 (hardback) | ISBN 9781138820388 (pbk.) | ISBN 9781315743929 (ebook)
Subjects: LCSH: Lacan, Jacques, 1901-1981. | Psychoanalysis and philosophy. | Civilization, Classical.
Classification: LCC BF109.L23 H37 2016 (print) | LCC BF109.L23 (ebook) | DDC 150.19/5092--dc23
LC record available at http://lccn.loc.gov/2016001406

ISBN: 978-1-138-82037-1 (hbk)
ISBN: 978-1-138-82038-8 (pbk)
ISBN: 978-1-315-74392-9 (ebk)

Typeset in Bembo
by Integra Software Services Pvt. Ltd.

CONTENTS

Acknowledgements   *vi*

Introduction: The meaning of a return   1
1   'Surprised by truth': Socrates, Plato and the Lacanian seminar   9
2   The myth of sexual reproduction   52
3   Creation and castration: Making something out of nothing   91
4   Exploiting tragedy: Psychoanalysis, fate and free will   125
5   Unknown pleasures: Orgasms and epistemology   163

Index   *203*

ACKNOWLEDGEMENTS

I'd like to thank Steve Connor for sharing his knowledge, irreverence and intellectual excitement, offering supervision with equal measures of support and trust. The London Consortium provided an astonishing academic environment in which to enjoy three years of research: thank you to all who made it happen, friends and faculty. More broadly, it was a privilege to be part of Birkbeck's inspiring nocturnal community. Big thanks to Matt Taunton, without whose encouragement I would never have found my way there, and who has offered continuing support over the years.

Dany Nobus provided insight and expertise when it was needed most. Parveen Adams was generous with both conversation and resources at a seminal stage. Lionel Bailly contributed multiple suggestions and a most uplifting interrogation as part of the final examination. A very large thank you to Ian Parker, who not only saved the day but proved to be an invaluable person to meet, lending assistance ever since. Not least of his contributions was an introduction to Armand D'Angour, who shared his classical knowledge with generosity and tolerance. Needless to say, any errors remain my own.

The Arts and Humanities Research Council fully funded the PhD on which this book is based. With an invitation to the conference, 'Classical Myth and Psychoanalysis', Vanda Zajko and Ellen O'Gorman provided the opportunity to share work with an incredible group of people at a formative moment. At the other end of the process, Kristopher Spring responded with enthusiasm, stamina and sharp-eyed attention to a somewhat chaotic manuscript.

I am grateful to Oxford University Press for permission to reproduce parts of my essay, 'The Ethics of Metamorphosis', from *Classical Myth and Psychoanalysis: Ancient and Modern Stories of the Self*, and to the Random House Group, WW Norton, Polity Press and the State University of New York Press for allowing use of the quotations that stand at the head of chapters 1 and 2.

A belated but important thank you to everyone in the UCL English Department for starting off the adventure. Special thanks to Henry Woudhuysen for two unforgettable years of supervision, as well as words of encouragement at more than one difficult moment of transition; and thank you to René Weis for his inspirational scholarly passion and for offering a warm welcome back to UCL as I embarked on a very privileged year studying Shakespeare.

Thank you to my parents, Charles and Elaine, for wholehearted support every step of the way. Final, inestimable thanks to my wife, Emily Kenway, for putting up with more years of *tuches* and *homelettes* than any partner should have to endure. Maybe Aristophanes was right after all.

INTRODUCTION

The meaning of a return

Lacan's career was devoted to re-engineering the shock of psychoanalysis. For a generation that had seen Freud's theory become fashionable to the point of cliché, he sought to make it unfamiliar again, even threatening. As such, one might expect him to shake off Freud's fascination with Ancient Greece and Rome as itself antiquated, a dusty Victorian crutch for a new way of thinking. Yet, of all Freud's disciples, it is Lacan who turns to classical antiquity with the greatest passion. In his 30 years of teaching he draws on the work of Homer, Heraclitus, Herodotus, Democritus, Parmenides, Epicurus, Theophrastus, Anaxagoras; the Schools of the Stoics, the Skeptics and Pythagoras; the dramatists Sophocles, Euripides and Aristophanes. From Rome, he discusses works by Lucretius, Ovid, Plautus, Plutarch, Pliny, Cicero, Longus and Livy. By far the greatest attention is given to the trio of Socrates, Plato and Aristotle; combined, there are 31 entries for Plato and Aristotle in the index of the *Écrits*. By way of comparison, there are ten entries for Lévi-Strauss, six for Roman Jakobson and eight for Ferdinand de Saussure.

This is not the Lacan of popular or scholarly imagination. There are books devoted to Lacan and science, Lacan and politics, Lacan and philosophy, but no extended study of Lacan and classical antiquity. In attempting to fill this gap, this book makes two broad arguments: one relating to the role of this classicism in Lacan's teaching, the other to the value of approaching his work in this way.

Freud's classical references provided Lacan with the entry point he needed to revise psychoanalysis under the cover of orthodoxy. Lacan (2007) considered Freud's allusions to Greek philosophy and declared that they bear witness to 'a properly metaphysical apprehension of what were pressing problems for him' (p. 319). 'Problems', especially those elided by other analysts, are what Lacan seized upon: what exactly is the unconscious? Does libido have a physical existence? Why did Freud formulate a death drive? Confronted head on, these questions reveal the deeper, metaphysical implications of psychoanalysis, questions of ontology and epistemology, that allowed Lacan to express the value of Freud's thought in new ways.

By far the most pressing question, and the one underlying all others, concerns the intellectual status of psychoanalysis itself. Is it a science? Or more like art, or even religion? Ancient Greece, where we find myth, science, philosophy and drama confronting each other self-consciously for the first time, is a powerful precedent for a discipline whose problems are never entirely separable from the question of its own genre. The question of what kind of truth psychoanalysis represents is bound to the question: what form of knowledge is commensurate to the human mind? Do we need a special discipline of our own? For the Ancient Greeks, the relationship between man, nature and forces beyond both remained open to investigation. This investigation bridged imaginative and empirical approaches. As Lacan pursues something unique, and uniquely problematic, about human psychology, Ancient Greece and Rome provide more valuable precedents than both the rigid cosmological schema of Judeo-Christianity and a complacent, post-Darwinian consensus according to which humans are just one animal amongst many.

The second argument informing this study concerns the benefit of approaching Lacan's work through its literary and philosophical references rather than by seeking a fixed theory, leading, as it does, to an appreciation of the richness and complexity of the seminars themselves. We know Lacan's teaching chiefly through transcripts of live events, excerpts of a conversation that extended across three decades of public seminar courses. Behind the forbidding, almost inhuman books published under his name are occasions involving discussion, jokes, puns, improvisation and an evolving intellectual milieu. Antiquity is not an archive for Lacan but an active battleground on which he takes his place alongside thinkers he admires and whose own investigations he feeds off (and who are often in his audience). Lacan's readings of Plato emerge from the groundbreaking seminars of intellectual historians Alexandre Koyré and Alexandre Kojève. Discussion of Parmenides and Heraclitus allows for confrontation with Heidegger and Sartre. Ovid's myths provide common ground with the erotic philosophy of Pierre

Klossowski. Lacan's classical references serve as his own *points de capitons*, quilting points that connect ideas amongst these thinkers as well as concepts within his own ever-evolving theory. In a competitive and performative intellectual environment they are part of the seminar's drama, a challenge to the growing crowd he attracts, and one that places intellectual history (and psychoanalysis's unique contribution to it) in the foreground.

In attempting to read Lacan's texts closely, to situate them in their intellectual context and trace the development of his ideas, this book is part of a comforting tradition: the university's answer to the problem of what one is to 'do' with psychoanalysis. While less common as an approach to Lacan, precedents abound in the thriving field of 'Freud Studies'. Interest in Freud's classicism has extended well beyond those directly involved in psychoanalysis itself. Scholars return to Freud's classical references (Oedipus, Narcissus, Empedocles, Rome, Egypt) to discover how an apparently new mode of thought could enter existence and become epoch defining. Ernest Jones's reverential three-volume *The Life and Work of Sigmund Freud* (1953) helped mythologize Freud's intellectual journey, which in turn attracted and gave material to more acute readings such as Henri Ellenberger's *The Discovery of the Unconscious* (1970) and Frank Sulloway's *Freud: Biologist of the Mind* (1979). In all these, Freud's classical education plays a starring role, allowing him to pursue questions of sexuality and psychology beyond the confines of neurons and cell biology. Freud enters uncharted intellectual territory by drawing upon a combination of well-established disciplines bound to a distinctly nineteenth-century, Central European worldview or *Weltanschauung*.

Freud's recourse to myth and poetry, naturally, provides ample material for those seeking to discredit the intellectual credentials of psychoanalysis (see the work of Frederick Crews, 1995, or Richard Webster, 1996). Recently, they have inspired more nuanced studies in an intellectual environment less concerned with establishing the truth value of psychoanalysis than with tracing networks of association in Freud's thought, understanding the processes of reading, writing and memory that underlie his quest. Superior examples include Graham Frankland's *Freud's Literary Culture* (2000) and Richard Armstrong's *A Compulsion for Antiquity: Freud and the Ancient World* (2005). These historicize Freud's work, pursue ideas as they develop over his career, and explore the function that particular figures and texts serve for him. Freud's classicism becomes entwined with questions of nationhood, Judaism, Freud's childhood, his friendships and his unique intellectual ambitions.

'Lacan Studies', to the extent that such a thing exists, is a different beast. This certainly reflects the difference between Freud and Lacan on a general level – Freud's artful, narratively rich essays versus Lacan's defensive, unapologetically difficult seminars – but also more specific factors. The distinct academic field that has grown around Freud's writing has thrived on the solidity and universality of the official texts. Freud arrives in the form of a standardized complete works, dense with scholarly apparatus and with that crowning signifier of a stable text, a six-volume concordance to match those for Shakespeare and the Bible. This is not to mention the readily available information on Freud's childhood (eight hours a week studying Latin, six hours a week learning Greek), his fully catalogued library at Maresfield Gardens and, of course, the preserved consulting room itself with its collection of antiquities: a crossroads for Freud's life, theory and clinical practice.[1]

The history of publishing Lacan's teaching, far from clarifying his development, has added to the complications. *Écrits*, the first book published in his name, comprising a compilation of papers spanning 30 years, eventually appeared in 1966 when Lacan was 63. None of the annual seminars into which he had put the vast majority of his thought and work appeared until Lacan was persuaded to allow *Seminar XI* to be transcribed in 1973. Two years later, his first seminar of 1953 appeared, alongside the twentieth one. To date, 14 of the 27 seminars have been officially published in French. The situation is even patchier in English: the *Écrits* received a complete English translation only in 2006. Now, 30 years after Lacan's death, English translations of the majority of the Lacanian seminars still remain unavailable other than as bootlegs, whether from a specialist bookshop or online. What's more, under the dutiful supervision of his son-in-law Jacques-Alain Miller, the officially published texts have the un-annotated rawness of bootlegs, kept purposefully free of any significant introduction, annotation or notes (this will be explored further in Chapter 1).

The situation is similarly unsettled with regards to biographical sources. Lacan's classicism, like Freud's, can be traced to a particularly thorough schooling.[2] And, as with Freud, his acquaintance with Greek and Roman authors was clearly a point of pride in adulthood; the seminars reveal Lacan's knowledge of Greek and Latin, for example his close engagement with Aristotle's Greek (Lacan, 1998, p. 52) and with the Latin poetry of Lucretius (1991, p. 227). But it is not possible to study the actual texts Lacan worked with due to the absence of archives and the selling-off of his estate, including his library. Roudinesco discusses the missing library in her recent book *Lacan: In Spite of Everything* (2014), the impossibility of knowing exactly which books Lacan read, which passages he marked, how he gathered his references for the seminars. She sees this as part of a larger suppression of supplementary material, connected to the conscious decision to publish Lacan's oral oeuvre without biographical notes or contextual references.

Repression manifests itself in activity. The repression of sources, according to Roudinesco, has encouraged 'an escalation of interpretation which becomes excessive' (p. 122). This interpretation, significantly, is still carried out by a generation that knew Lacan in person, often individuals who were trained and treated by him, who have their own first-hand knowledge of the social and intellectual contexts in which Lacan worked, and who fought over his legacy in the immediate aftermath of his death. One of these fights involved Roudinesco herself in conflict with Jacques-Alain Miller. Roudinesco's monumental biography *Jacques Lacan* (1997) contains a wealth of clues as to the sources and significance of Lacan's classicism, but it is a resource that few practicing Lacanians draw upon in print, partly for reasons of academic tone but partly because of professional alliances (Roudinesco is scathing of Miller's involvement as Lacan's editor). So a division appears: Lacan's biography on one side, still founded on rumour, anecdotes and general notoriety, and Lacanian scholarship on the other, producing dense texts for the initiated, rich with neologisms and topology.

The difference between Freud studies and Lacan studies has had clear consequences. In Lacan's case, the fragmentary publication, minimal annotation and concentrated exegesis have exacerbated the effects of his notoriously difficult style, widening the gap between those already initiated into it and those outside. As a result, the use of Lacanian concepts in scholarship can seem either clumsy or provocative or both. In the words of one academic, while Roland Barthes proves 'an ever-graceful option' and Foucault 'an acceptable turn', Lacan remains 'a prospective breach of etiquette' (Flaxman, 2003). This partly reflects how he is used when people do turn to his ideas, often raided for concepts with which to forward arguments regarding a book, film or art work; applied rather than studied.

As well as making Lacan more human, a more overarching study throws light on the texts we use. By way of example, *Seminar XI: The Four Fundamental Concepts of Psychoanalysis* (1977) presents itself, for readers of English, as an apparently stand-alone introduction rather than a compilation of ten years' thought recharged and repackaged for a new audience of elite philosophy students at the École Normale Supérieure; *Seminar VII*'s (2008) consideration of tragedy and *Seminar VIII*'s reading of Plato's *Symposium*, published in

English for the first time in 2015, are read independently for their respective treatments of ethics and transference but rarely for ideas regarding beauty and mortality that bridge the seminars and evolve between them (these will be touched on in Chapter 4); *Seminar XX* (1998) appeared in English initially as fragments in an anthology concerning feminine sexuality while, read as a whole, the seminar is as much concerned with Aristotle and Parmenides (see Mitchell and Rose, 1985). Roaming across the decades, the distance across which themes, characters and texts recur is striking. The seminar of 1969 sees the return of the slave in Plato's *Meno*, central to discussions in *Seminar II* (1991) in 1955. In the second seminar, Lacan recommends reading *Parmenides*, a dialogue he gets around to discussing 18 years later in *Seminar XX*. Each instance carries traces of the earlier discussion while reflecting significant developments in Lacan's thinking. Within the winding, 30-year performance of his teaching, Lacan is always subtler, more complex and more self-conscious than a singular exegesis of his theory could convey. Any individual expression of an idea is a palimpsest of its previous incarnations, a hub of echoes and allusions as well as revision. This applies to none more than to apparently basic sounding ones such as 'subject', 'other', 'real' or 'unconscious'.

This study is a series of explorations rather than a comprehensive survey, discreet but interlinked essays that reflect the loops and intersections of their subjects. I concentrate mainly on the philosophers of Ancient Greece rather than Rome, although the Roman poet Ovid plays a large role in the final two chapters. The first two chapters centre on Plato, but in significantly different ways. Chapter 1, '"Surprised by Truth": Socrates, Plato and the Lacanian Seminar', continues this introduction's consideration of the seminar project itself. Plato (and the elusive Socrates) gives Lacan a means of thinking through the meaning of teaching. The fact that a clinical analyst is likely also to be a teacher of psychoanalysis and, finally, a writer of psychoanalytic literature is sometimes taken for granted, yet these activities – therapeutic, pedagogic and literary – each have their own relationship with authority and so operate their own processes of transference. This becomes important as Lacan's own fame spreads while, within his theory, knowledge is becoming an ever more suspect concept. With the help of Plato's dialogues, the seminar itself becomes a means of exploring pedagogical anxieties.

Chapter 2, 'The Myth of Sexual Reproduction', concerns a different anxiety, anxiety over the role of Greek myth in psychoanalytic theory. What implication does the centrality of figures such as Oedipus and

Narcissus have for the scientific aspirations of psychoanalysis? The question involves a deeper and more complicated one: can human sexuality be understood 'scientifically' or does its wayward nature demand a new method of analysis entirely? I consider the role that Aristophanes' myth of Eros (from Plato's *Symposium*) plays for both Freud and Lacan. For Freud, it arises at moments of theoretical struggle. Lacan returns to Freud's impasses, but by employing a closer reading of Plato in conjunction with the new insights of Claude Lévi-Strauss, he can turn the category of myth to his advantage, making it a tool to probe the limits of what we can conceive.

In 'Creation and Castration: Making Something out of Nothing', I extend this consideration of myth to cosmology and creation myths in psychoanalysis. I ask why Lacan comes out repeatedly on the side of 'creationism' over evolutionism. This relates to a problem at the heart of Freud's elaboration of psychoanalysis: the difficulty of situating an initial, primal event at the origins of a trauma, when trauma itself depends upon the relation between an event and a previous incident. As Lacan recognizes, it is a problem akin to philosophy's struggle to account for prime movers. Lacan's return to Aristotle's exploration of cause in the *Physics*, in particular the concept of *tuche* ('luck' or 'chance'), bridges this chapter with the next, 'Exploiting Tragedy: Psychoanalysis, Fate and Free Will'. Freud's appropriation of Greek tragedy – and, with it, tragic fatalism – has led to criticism of psychoanalysis. For Lacan, tragedy and fate form part of a larger exploration of interpretation and point of view. This is something that Aristotle and the tragic dramatists themselves recognized, and it reflects the value tragedy retains for psychoanalysis.

The final chapter, 'Unknown Pleasures: Orgasms and Epistemology', explores a tradition of mythologizing the female orgasm. It centres on the figure of Tiresias and his claim that women experience greater pleasure in sex than men. Lacan declares that the transgendered Tiresias should be 'the patron saint of psychoanalysis'. This provocative assertion pertains to the controversies of *jouissance* and psychoanalysis's theories of feminine sexuality more broadly, but also to the wider, intractable questions on which the discipline is founded. When is knowledge about other people's pleasure really just a fantasy? And when might we want to maintain this: our fantasies of others and others' fantasies of ourselves? This includes the fantasy of knowledge, our desire to know and for others to attempt to know us. Lacan is unafraid to challenge the very presumptions on which psychoanalysis is founded, asking what it is we want when we seek an answer to the riddle of ourselves.

Notes

1 For more on Freud's education, see Winter (1999); for more on his antiquities, see Barker (1996), Gamwell and Wells (1989), and Scully (1997).
2 On Lacan's very traditional education at the Jesuit Collège Stanislas, run by the Marianist Fathers, see Roudinesco (1997), who records Lacan helping his brother with Latin at the age of 14.

References

Armstrong, R. (2005) *A Compulsion for Antiquity: Freud and the Ancient World*, Ithaca, Cornell University Press.
Barker, S. (1996) *Excavations and Their Objects: Freud's Collection of Antiquity*, Albany, SUNY Press.
Crews, F. (1995) *The Memory Wars: Freud's Legacy in Dispute*, New York, New York Review of Books.
Ellenberger, H. (1970) *The Discovery of the Unconscious*, New York, Basic Books.
Flaxman, G. (2003) 'Past imperfect, future unknown: The discourse of theory', *Journal of Cultural and Religious Theory*, vol. 4, no. 2 [online]. Available at www.jcrt.org/archives/04.2/flaxman.shtml (accessed 3/4/2015)
Frankland, G. (2000) *Freud's Literary Culture*, Cambridge, Cambridge University Press.
Gamwell, L., and Wells, R. (1989) *Sigmund Freud and His Art: His Personal Collection of Antiquities*, Albany, SUNY Press.
Jones, E. (1953) *The Life and Work of Sigmund Freud*, New York, Basic Books.
Lacan, J. (1977) *Seminar XI: The Four Fundamental Concepts of Psychoanalysis* (ed. J.-A. Miller, trans. A. Sheridan), London, Penguin.
Lacan, J. (1991) *Seminar II: The Ego in Freud's Theory and in the Technique of Psychoanalysis* (ed. J.-A. Miller, trans. J. Forrester), New York, Norton.
Lacan, J. (1998) *Seminar XX: Encore – On Feminine Sexuality: The Limits of Love and Knowledge* (ed. J.-A. Miller, trans. B. Fink), New York, Norton.
Lacan, J. (2007) *Écrits: The First Complete Edition in English* (trans. B. Fink), New York, Norton.
Lacan, J. (2008) *Seminar VII: The Ethics of Psychoanalysis* (ed. J.-A. Miller, trans. D. Porter), Oxford, Routledge.
Mitchell, J., and Rose, J. (1985) *Feminine Sexuality: Jacques Lacan and the École Freudienne*, London, Norton.
Roudinesco, E. (1997) *Jacques Lacan* (trans. B. Bray), New York, Columbia University Press.
Roudinesco, E. (2014) *Lacan: In Spite of Everything* (trans. G. Elliot), London, Verso.
Scully, S. (1997) 'Freud's antiquities: A view from the couch', *Arion*, vol. 5, no. 2, pp. 222–233.
Sulloway, F. (1979) *Freud: Biologist of the Mind*, Cambridge, Harvard University Press.
Webster, R. (1996) *Why Freud Was Wrong: Sin, Science and Psychoanalysis*, New York, Basic Books.
Winter, S. (1999) *Freud and the Institution of Psychoanalytic Knowledge*, Stanford, Stanford University Press.

1

'SURPRISED BY TRUTH'

Socrates, Plato and the Lacanian seminar

> You know that the schools of antiquity were gradually deserted. They were schools to which students came to hear people speak. They were what Lacan, when he founded his own school, called 'a refuge from civilization and its discontents.' He viewed his own school on the model of the schools of antiquity: a place of refuge from civilization and its discontents. When we read Plato, it is clear that there was passion around the schools – people wanted to know if the playboys of the time would come to hear Socrates or not. It was trendy. It was big news.
>
> *Jacques-Alain Miller (1996, p. 218)*

> We can't discourage curiosity enough – these aren't lectures for the fashion-conscious. If they come in order to believe that we are going to turn psychoanalysis into an extension of the Platonic dialogue, they are wrong. They should get better informed.
>
> *Jacques Lacan (1991a, p. 20)*

Introduction

There are myriad Platos, as there are myriad faces of psychoanalysis. From one angle, both are engaged with society, establishing universal principles to help men and women find happiness, suggesting how we might improve ourselves and the communities we live in. From another angle, they present such profoundly alternative models of truth that they must resist easy assimilation if their challenge to the status quo is to remain meaningful; they seek to unsettle complacency with new ways of thinking – ways already shaped by society's resistance – and therefore remain aloof from the crowd.

The aloof Plato is the defiant figure devoted to the rebel Socrates. His Academy is situated beyond the city that sentenced his master to death. Psychoanalysis is born of a less violent social rejection, but Freud's confrontation with hostility to his ideas is evident throughout his writings. And it is often a point of pride: in the words of one psychoanalytic dictionary: 'It is true of any scientific discovery that it takes shape not by following the dictates of common sense but by flying in the face of it' (Laplanche and Pontalis, 1974, p. vii). Public resistance to previous paradigm shifts looms large in Freud's thoughts. Men such as Copernicus and Darwin introduced ideas that were not just new but potentially indigestible. As such, psychoanalysis must be prepared to do the same. Indeed, this is a particular challenge for a discipline concerned with our own minds, about which we might understandably feel we know best, and concerning which a timeless, instinctive 'folk psychology' abounds. Psychoanalysis must be wary of the very recognition it craves if it is to avoid lapsing into easy over-familiarity (read as 'an extension of the Platonic dialogue', for example). And its quest for truth may prove no help or comfort at all. Lacan (2007) depicts Freud sailing towards New York Harbor, commenting that 'They do not know we are bringing them the plague' (p. 336).[1] This is the dark Freud of *Civilization and its Discontents*, of the inexorable death drive, the interminable analysis, one from whom even his own disciples must part company if they are to present themselves as men of medicine.

An ambiguous place in society obviously has implications for the institutions by which these schools of thought are passed on. Jacques-Alain Miller, comparing Lacan's founding of the École Freudienne de Paris to Plato's Academy, has in mind Lacan's own comment in *Seminar VIII*: 'The Academy was a city, a refuge reserved for the best and brightest' (Lacan, 2015, p. 84). Both Lacan and Miller touch on a complex implication, however: sanctuary can become a form of snobbery. To complete the paradox, the snobbery then seduces the very crowd it had sought to avoid. Hence the ambivalence that can be heard in Miller's description: was the passion that came to surround the Academy a *threat* to its status as refuge? Was it the reason it eventually emptied? Having escaped civilization, civilization flocked to it. And, if this is the case for Plato's Academy, what does it say about Lacan's use of the Academy as a model? Lacan, in his own quote about Plato, is dismissive of the 'fashion-conscious'. Yet it is no secret whose seminars became the trendiest, the biggest news.[2]

Lacan's ongoing engagement with Plato centres on this question of how knowledge relates to the society around it, a question explored in the content (and manifest in the form) of both Plato's dialogues and Lacan's seminars. Should truth feel familiar or unfamiliar? The apparent complexity and dogmatism of Lacanian theory has struck many as elitist. He is beset by accusations of fraud, described as 'an amusing and perfectly self-conscious charlatan' (Goldwag, 2007, p. 101; see also Webster, 2002[3]), his theory 'an incoherent system of pseudo-scientific gibberish' and his writings revealing 'a narcissistic enjoyment of mystification as a form of omnipotent power' (Minsky, 1996, pp. 175–176). This chapter is born of working with the Lacanian texts and realizing that if they are, indeed, infamously mystifying and seductively powerful, it is for two reasons: their origins in live presentations and a deep, abiding suspicion about 'knowledge', the experience of imparting and acquiring it.[4] The two factors are, of course, entwined. It is the live seminar, via his engagement with Socrates and Plato, that provides Lacan with a means of teaching sceptically, provocatively, as a defence against 'knowledge' itself.

What kind of knowledge is psychoanalysis?

While Plato set up his academy in the leafy northwest suburb of Athens, Lacan's seminar moved through the Paris of the 1950s and 1960s on a journey that tells its own story of resistance. Changes of venue came about as a result of splits and controversies, but were enabled by successive institutions promising a fitter home, a new audience, a safe refuge. Much of this chapter centres on Lacan's second seminar (1953), which followed his forced resignation from the Société Psychanalytique de Paris when controversy over his analytic and training methods came to a head. The seminar marks his entry into the new Société Française de Psychanalyse (SFP). As such, it is no surprise that questions of truth, knowledge and pedagogy arise.

This is the context for Lacan's outburst in the quotation at the head of this chapter: 'We can't discourage curiosity enough – these aren't lectures for the fashion-conscious'. Why should a parallel between psychoanalysis and Platonic dialogue cause Lacan anger? I'd like to explore this question via the context of the seminar as a whole. *Seminar II* presents an occasion for Lacan to get things straight. Following directly from his forced resignation, it is a traumatic moment but also an opportunity. Entry into the SFP has allowed Lacan to shape a new teaching routine. It will take place at Saint Anne Hospital, the capital's main mental hospital. Lacan is 52 years old and his own theory is at an advanced stage of development. He is conscious of the baggage students will bring, conscious of what he has elaborated and how he must take pains to define his theory in opposition to the endless, easier ideas about Freud circulating. The relationship between psychoanalysis and Plato is a good place to start.

When Lacan rebukes those attending his seminars who believe that psychoanalytic treatment might resemble a Platonic dialogue, Freud and his disciples must shoulder some of the responsibility. Parallels between Freud and Plato had long been asserted: Oskar Pfister (1921) and Max Nachmansohn (1915), students of Freud, had linked Freud with Plato in papers that received Freud's approval. Nachmansohn writes: 'Of all thinkers of the western world Plato was the first to observe our subject deeply and to describe it plainly' (p. 76). Freud isn't averse to the association. In his 1920 preface to the *Three Essays on Sexuality*, Freud (1905) writes: 'Anyone who looks down with contempt upon psychoanalysis from a superior vantage-point should remember how closely the enlarged sexuality of psychoanalysis coincides with the Eros of the divine Plato' (p. 42).[5]

Plato is distinct amongst Freud's classical references. Sophocles, with Oedipus, gives body to a universal truth; Empedocles lends Freud the cosmological opposition of Philia and Neikos (unity and strife) to draw upon metaphorically. But neither Sophocles nor Empedocles could be seen as being on an equivalent intellectual quest as Freud.[6] A comparison with Plato is natural enough if psychoanalysis pursues the same questions as the philosopher – how do we become whole and content? – even more so if it places the erotic life at the centre of its 'philosophy' alongside self-knowledge and the balancing of appetites. Finally, there is the link between the Socratic dialogue and an analytic session, both dissipating false opinions through conversation alone – a connection possibly supported by Freud's 1879 translation of an extended essay by John Stuart Mill in which he comments at length on the functioning and effects of Socratic questioning.[7]

Lacan's concern will be to demonstrate what is fundamentally different about psychoanalysis. His outburst regarding Plato and the 'fashion conscious' in the midst of *Seminar II* occurs during a debate prompted by a paper delivered the previous evening by philosopher and celebrated historian of science, Alexandre Koyré, entitled 'Problems of the Platonic dialogue'. Koyré is an iconic figure when it comes to Lacan's thoughts about teaching. Alongside his friend, colleague and fellow émigré Alexandre Kojève, he was responsible for the influential seminars on Hegel that shaped an intellectual generation including Jean-Paul Sartre, Raymond Queneau, Georges Bataille, Maurice Merleau-Ponty and André Breton (see Drury, 1994). It is in these seminars at the École Pratique des Hautes Études that Lacan, in a telling phrase, describes himself as being 'initiated into Hegelian philosophy' (2009, p. 42). What Koyré is doing here is partaking in an educational experiment of Lacan's, one that alludes to both Plato's Academy and Freud's projected college of psychoanalytical education.[8] Alongside the weekly seminars, the new teaching routine Lacan established at Saint-Anne initiated a series of lectures by other philosophers and intellectuals including Jean Hyppolite, Maurice Merleau-Ponty and Claude Lévi-Strauss, who often then took their place in the audience for Lacan the following day.[9] The plan is to facilitate a cross-fertilization of ideas, and the reader gathers that Koyré's paper achieved this, inspiring a lively debate regarding the relationship between analytic technique and Socrates' technique of *maieutics*, whereby he draws out latent knowledge from his interlocutor through subtle questioning (*maieutics* literally refers to midwifery).

Discussion had apparently spilled beyond the confines of Koyré's seminar into the night, the training analyst Octave Mannoni particularly concerned about how this comparison echoes commonplaces about psychoanalysis adopted by the 'general public'. At Lacan's instigation, he reiterates his comments about *maieutics* and analysis:

> I would like to challenge this all too easy assimilation by drawing attention to the fact that for Plato, there is a forgotten truth, and maieutics consists in bringing it to light, in such a way that the dialogue is a mixture of truth and error, and dialectic is a kind of sieve for truth. In analysis, it isn't the same kind of truth, it is a historical truth, whereas the first kind appears, from one point of view, as a truth of natural science.
>
> (Lacan, 1991a, p. 15)

Mannoni highlights a category of truth that is not absolute and universal but specific to a patient and a context. Lacan wants to follow this further, seizing on the opportunity to bridge his theory and Koyré's lecture. Koyré's comments on Plato's dialogue, the *Meno*, he argues, 'can, without any undue contrivance, be inserted into the framework of the teaching being developed here'. And he asserts that the function of the Tuesday lectures is to help 'crystallise the questioning left dangling at the outer edges of the domain we are investigating in the seminar' (Lacan, 1991a, p. 4). Distinguishing between the use of psychoanalysis to recover the truth of an individual psyche and Socratic dialogue to bring out universal philosophical truths is important and introduces a question that will shape the year's seminar: what exactly is psychoanalytic knowledge? What are the seminar's attendees (mostly in training) gathered to learn? And, when the training is complete, exactly what form of expertise will someone on the couch be paying for? Indeed, Lacan's first response to Mannoni's concerns over the eagerness of the 'general public' to 'tag psychoanalysis on to Platonism' shares his disdain:

> There are two sorts of public, the one here, which at least has a chance of finding out what's what, and the other, which drops in from all kinds of places, to sniff out a little of what's happening, which thinks this is funny, a subject for passing comments on, for dinner-table conversation, and which understandably gets a bit lost. If they want to find out which way is up, all they need to do is to be a bit more assiduous.
> (Lacan, 1991a, pp. 19–20)

Lacan's response is significant for more than its peevishness. It defines the seminars as an exclusive intellectual space, or even process, but, with the demand for attentiveness and rigour, they are by no means arbitrarily so. Part-timers seek a reflection of what they already believe (i.e. psychoanalysis as Socratic dialogue) and do not realize the intellectual upheaval demanded of them.

The *Meno* is a valuable starting point for Lacan's seminar because it explores the definition of knowledge and its place in society. It opens with a question from Meno himself, a wealthy political figure: 'Can you tell me Socrates, is virtue something that can be taught?' The question is forced upon Plato by the success of the Sophists, freelance professors who travelled through Greece providing an education concerned with citizenship and political leadership of a kind neglected by the established schools (Meno had been a student of the Sophist *Gorgias*). This practical education was particularly sought after in Athens, with its fledgling democracy, where the Sophists thrived by providing a curriculum focused on rhetoric and debate. Plato refers to the Sophists collectively as 'the teachers of *areté*', most often translated as 'virtue'. Protagoras, credited as having invented the role of professional Sophist, captures the pragmatic, outward-looking nature of this 'virtue' when he defines it as 'the proper care of one's personal affairs, so as best to manage one's own household, and also of the State's affairs, so as to become a real power in the city' (Plato, *Protagoras*, 318e–319a); Meno, more succinctly, states: 'Virtue is the desire of things honourable and the power of attaining them.' To most Sophists, the attempts of previous philosophers to understand 'the nature of things' were a waste of time. It was practical life that mattered, not truths about the origins of the universe and its functioning.

The difference between the Sophists and Socrates was that while Socrates also came to regard questions of cosmology as a waste of time (having begun his studies with them), education and philosophy were, for him, a quest for knowledge, not forms of *training*. The Sophists challenge this line of criticism at its core; for them, the experience of knowledge is itself illusory. The *Meno* presents the Sophistic argument that one can never find out anything new: either one knows it already, in which case there is no need to find it out, or one does not, and in that case there is no means of recognizing it when found. It is as a way out of this dilemma that Socrates propounds a theory of knowledge as recollection: *anamnesis*. Learning is not a matter of discovering something new, but rather of recollecting eternal truths that the soul knew before birth but has since forgotten (Plato, *Meno*, 81b).

To demonstrate this, Socrates calls upon one of Meno's slave boys. The slave is led to realize, through dialogue alone, that he already contains mathematical knowledge.[10] This gives the dialogue a special place in intellectual history, Lacan claims. The Socrates of the *Meno* is 'the one who within human subjectivity inaugurates that style from which the notion of knowledge as tied to certain requirements of coherence has arisen, knowledge which is the prerequisite for any future progress of science' (Lacan, 1991a, p. 5). This is science defined by abstract truths – truths themselves evidenced by their internal logic and so independent of the subject who possesses them.

But the question that initiates Plato's dialogue does not concern mathematics or science. Rather, as we've seen, it is a question about virtue (*areté*) and whether it can be taught, and Socrates himself is never certain that it can. It is the inadequacy of this radical new science/*episteme* that interests Lacan as he seeks to define the nature of psychoanalytic knowledge: 'The aim and paradox of the *Meno* is to show us that the *episteme*, knowledge bounded by a formal coherence, does not cover the whole of the field of human experience' (Lacan, 1991a, p. 15–16).

> At the very moment when Socrates inaugurates this new being-in-the-world ... he realizes that science will not be able to transmit the means to achieve the most precious thing, the *areté*, the excellence of the human being. Here already there is a decentring – it is by starting off

with this virtue that a domain is opened up to knowledge, but this very virtue, with respect to its transmission, its tradition, its formation, remains outside of the domain.

(Lacan, 1991a, p. 5)

This is a problem, one that 'puts into question one of the fundamental premises of classical thought', Lacan (1991a) claims. 'We are told that man is the measure of all things. But where is his own measure? Is it to be found in himself?' (p. 67). Plato's investigation of the relationship between knowledge and uniquely human assets such as virtue leads the philosopher to analyse a third term: *doxa*. Its meaning lies somewhere between received wisdom, general opinion and convention. In the *Meno* (its first appearance in Plato's writing), it is associated with *orthe doxa*: socially correct views. Clearly, then, when Socrates pursues a form of knowledge *beyond* 'virtue' the enterprise carries a specific social threat. As Mannoni notes, thinking back to the previous night, Koyré has identified *orthe doxa* with 'the customs which people live by', which means anyone who lives by these customs – and, perhaps, does well by them – 'feels himself threatened in the face of epistemological investigation' (Lacan, 1991a, p. 15). A clear example of this defensiveness in the *Meno* is supplied by the figure of Anytos, a prominent Athenian who appears towards the end of the dialogue. He certainly feels threatened by all this newfangled philosophizing, with the new forms of authority it implies (Plato, *Meno*, 90b). He suggests that any Athenian gentleman is qualified to pass knowledge of virtue on to the next generation (93a), but Socrates, pointing out how many Athenian gentlemen have had dissolute sons, explains that *doxa*, right opinion, is something you have to take on trust. Truth is situated beyond the received wisdom of civilized Athens. Hence his scepticism regarding the bridging of virtue and *episteme*: virtue belongs to the crowd, or in Lacan's (1991a) words, Socrates 'by dint of *episteme* … misses out on *orthe doxa*' (p. 21). It is a distinction the hard-nosed Sophists acknowledge but see as unproblematic.[11] But Socrates makes it a problem, encouraging the questioning ever further and so becoming a threat to power. Anytos leaves the *Meno* in a rage. The historical Anytos will be an accuser of Socrates at the trial that leads to the philosopher's death. As ever, for Plato, abstract questions of truth and authority carry the bitter taste of a very real injustice.

So where does psychoanalysis belong in this new classification of truths: *episteme, areté, doxa*? Lacan turns to these categories to communicate the novelty of psychoanalysis and to demonstrate it in a characteristically counter-intuitive way. Psychoanalysis *does* deal with *orthe doxa*, Lacan (1991a) asserts:

> the *orthe doxa* which Socrates leaves behind him, but in which he feels completely enveloped – since after all, that's also where he starts out from ... we ourselves place it, once again, at the centre. That's what analysis is.
>
> (p. 20)

This *orthe doxa* is equivalent to what Lacan names the symbolic order – at various times in his teaching signifying language, culture, the network of symbols into which we are born and out of which we are formed. The symbolic order represents everything that will set Lacan's theory apart from previous thinking, unsettling the very idea of selfhood that persists from Plato to Lacan's contemporaries. This is why it is important, in Seminar II, to emphasize it. The symbolic order that corresponds to Plato's *orthe doxa* is everything 'that has constituted [the subject]: his parents, his neighbors, the whole structure of the community, and not only constituted him as symbol, but constituted him in his being' (Lacan, 1991a, p. 20). Psychoanalysis does not transcend it, does not make it evaporate, but shines a light on it as the substance of which we're made. We cannot exist as an individual, an 'I', with a name and identity, without the symbolic order. It splits us from the rest of existence and undermines the integrity of our selfhood, if by that we mean an illusory, coherent 'I' independent of this process. If there is a forgotten/repressed component of our existence that it is the task of psychoanalysis to draw into the light, it is this.

So psychoanalysis places *orthe doxa* at the centre. But here we arrive at the distinct challenge it has created for itself. Is psychoanalysis *itself* a form of *orthe doxa*? For Freud, it is clear, the theoretical quest is bound to the idea and ideals of science (i.e. *episteme*), the legacy of his training in medicine and neuropathology under pioneering physiologists such as Ernst Brücke. Yet, as much as psychoanalysis may aspire to the status of rational 'science', it is science that must be practised, and this clinical practice is nothing more or less than talking. The paradoxical status of psychoanalytic theory is reflected in Lacan's tortuous attempt to situate it:

> Everything which takes effect in the field of analytic action precedes the constitution of knowledge, which doesn't change the fact that in

> operating in this field we have constituted a knowledge, and one which has even proved itself to be exceptionally efficacious.
>
> (Lacan, 1991a, p. 19)

Analysis, to be effective, must slip in before knowledge constitutes itself – before the patient grasps onto a particular explanation, settles into a new fantasy. But psychoanalytic theory itself is a form of knowledge, and an efficacious one. The fact that there are two epistemological scenes here – the clinic and the seminar – complicates things. Language is central to both the construction and communication of psychoanalytic theory (it is language in which it arises) and its practice in the clinic. But, Lacan suggests, the theory should make us generally wary of the constitution of knowledge by language, because this 'constitution', akin to our own constitution from *doxa*, is at the root of any problems we may wish to solve.

Lacan's epistemological sensitivity is overarching: it is not just psychoanalysis, but all 'knowledges' that suppress the very process by which they have come into being. The error is to think that the discovery of a truth is akin to coming across something static, eternal, pre-existing the quest itself. This fundamental error

> exists in all knowledge, in as much as it is only a crystallization of the symbolic activity, and once constituted, it forgets it. In all knowledge once constituted there is a dimension of error, which is the forgetting of the creative function of truth in its nascent form.
>
> (Lacan, 1991a, p. 19)

Knowledge obliterates its own creation, presenting itself as apparently timeless, and this is reason enough to treat it cautiously. 'The knowledge to which truth comes to be knotted must actually be endowed with its own inertia' (Lacan, 1991a, p. 4). All this is announced before an audience of trainee analysts, present for education and instruction. Their chosen area of expertise is not only prey to this phenomenon, Lacan asserts, but one of the most vulnerable: 'Nowhere is this degradation more obvious than in psychoanalysis.' And the more we know, the greater the risks. 'All of you are taught in a more or less pre-digested form in the so-called institutes of psychoanalysis – sadistic, anal stages etc.', Lacan notes disparagingly:

> It would be stupid for a psychoanalyst systematically to neglect them, but he must be aware of the fact that that isn't the dimension in which

he operates. He must fashion himself, come to be at ease in a domain other than the one where what in his experience is slowly constituted out of knowledge is deposited, laid down.

(Lacan, 1991a, p. 4)

A dull process of accretion – 'constituted … deposited, laid down' – is opposed to the dynamic 'operates.' This leads directly, a moment later, to Lacan's comment on the 'two sorts of public', those who follow his seminars and those outside who are defined by an already constituted set of beliefs. But what is this *other* domain in which the analyst must come to be 'at ease', must 'fashion himself', with a sense of aristocratic *areté*?

With regards to the position of psychoanalysis – how it *operates* – Lacan reaches, finally, for a comparison to something beyond both the philosopher and the unruly crowd. Surprisingly, perhaps, Lacan compares the analyst to two political leaders of antiquity: Themistocles and Pericles. 'In the end, for Socrates, though not necessarily for Plato, if Themistocles and Pericles were great men, it was because they were good psychoanalysts' (Lacan, 1991a, p. 4). The reason Lacan gives is that their interpretations had an effect. They made truth their own to serve a specific purpose in a specific circumstance:

To give the reply that one has to in response to an event in so far as it is significant, in so far as it is a function of symbolic exchange between human beings – it could be the order given to the fleet to leave Piraeus – is to give the right interpretation. And to give the right interpretation at the right moment, that's to be a good analyst.

(Lacan, 1991a, p. 20)

Themistocles was offered an oracle suggesting that Athens should build a wooden wall and interpreted it as the need to build up a navy.[12] This was central to their military success. Interpretation here is not a demonstration of objective knowledge *or* convention, it is a tool with which to break through to something new, to change the situation. Pericles, famous as a statesman and great political leader, also bluffed his way through a critical historical moment, using supposed astronomical knowledge to calm the crew of 100 Athenian ships when faced with an eclipse, before leading them to plunder the coasts of the Peloponnese (Plutarch, *Pericles*, XXXV).[13]

This brings us back to the issue of elitism. Mannoni speaks up again, arguing that Pericles and Themistocles intervened successfully due to their high social status, because 'they were so well-integrated into their social milieu' (Lacan, 1991a, p. 20) and questioning the implications. Lacan's response is ambiguous and perhaps a little self-conscious: 'It is obvious that at that time it was only the masters who made history …. It is precisely because only gentlemen [English in original] have something to say in this story that they find the right words' (pp. 20–21). Mastery as a position to be exploited will inform Lacan's thinking on both practicing and teaching analysis over the next decades. But, as the context here shows, it is an odd mastery, defined by bluff, opposition to convention and, more even than that, by not having, by definition, any fixed place amongst the authorities of society. Socrates 'misses out on *orthe doxa*' by dint of episteme, Lacan notes, then adds cryptically, 'Maybe he wasn't altogether there at the time?' This is elucidated in *Seminar VIII* when Lacan (2015, p. 10) explores the concept of Socrates' *atopia*.

> Wasn't his behaviour truly insane and scandalous, despite the praiseworthy light his disciples devotedly cast on it by emphasizing its heroic facets? It is clear that they could not but record a major characteristic of Socrates that Plato himself qualified with a term that has remained famous to those who have taken up the problem of Socrates: his *atopia* within the order of the city.
>
> (p. 10)

It is in Book VI of the *Republic* that Plato argues that philosophers only ever emerge on the basis of *atopic* conditions, from the Greek *atopos* meaning 'out of place'. These 'eccentric' or delocalizing conditions include exile; being born in a small city; being in a precarious state of health; possessing a divine sign (see Badiou, 2006). The anti-civic threat of Socrates' *atopia* is brought back into discussion by Hegel (1974). He sees Socrates' *atopic* passion for truth as a pivotal intellectual moment, one that moves philosophy's focus from the ethical life of the community to the inner life of the individual. Hence Hegel's description of Socrates as 'the ruin of Athens.' Socrates ruins Athens by placing the key to universal truth within each man, instituting a rift with merely conventional morality, demanding we search for a truth beyond the truths we're given.

An inevitable division opens up between this radical Socrates and a Plato who does build institutions, does write, does concern himself with the politics of society. For Nietzsche, Socratism – the protests of the barefoot rebel – becomes a splinter of slave morality haunting a Plato who 'was really too noble' for such a thing, a master rather than a cowardly moralist (on Plato's argument that immorality equates simply to an error of understanding, Nietzsche comments: 'This way of reasoning smells of the *mob*').[14] For Lacan, it is the outreaching Plato who can often smell of the mob. And this division within Plato, between the crowd-pleasing icon and the subversive iconoclast, will prove valuable to Lacan as he seeks to rescue Freud's theories from Freud himself.[15]

Teaching beyond the pleasure principle

Psychoanalysis against nature

> Please read Freud. You are going to have three weeks. And while worshipping the Golden Calf, keep a small book of the law in your hand, read *Beyond the Pleasure Principle*.
>
> *Jacques Lacan (1991a, p. 60)*

It would not be much of an exaggeration to say that Lacan's return to Freud is a return to *Beyond the Pleasure Principle*. The only qualification would be that Lacan in fact reads the essay's message throughout the entirety of Freud's output, recasting Freudian theory through its prism. The pleasure principle had asserted that humans pursue what they consider pleasurable. In *Beyond the Pleasure Principle*, Freud considers an aspect of human psychology apparently at odds with this tendency. Why do we repeat unpleasant things? Freud's investigation is prompted by patients' obsessive revisiting of traumatic incidents (the effects of war trauma in particular), but also such phenomena as masochism, anxiety dreams, the failure of patients to progress while in analysis, as well as a more general impulse to repeat, seen as much in self-defeating life-patterns as in infantile games. What sort of logic could account for an instinct such as this? The question leads Freud to formulate what he terms the 'death drive', a force opposed to *eros*, the pleasure-seeking life instinct, one that seeks to return to a stasis; that betrays a logic 'beyond the Pleasure Principle'.

The essay serves as a talisman for Lacan. If Freud himself is the 'golden calf', then *Beyond the Pleasure Principle* becomes the true God, the Law that marks obedience and intellectual discipline, eschewing the easy pleasures of idolatry. At a time when *Beyond the Pleasure Principle* was frequently seen as an embarrassing, speculative excursion, one that could be left out of orthodox psychoanalytic theory, Lacan (2007) declares that it is the 'touchstone of mediocrity of analysts, whether they reject it or disfigure it'

(p. 285). In 'Subversion of the subject', Lacan states that 'to evade the death instinct in [Freud's] doctrine is not to know his doctrine at all' (p. 679). Lacan's fidelity will set him apart, a fidelity to its obscurity and complexity. He declares, 'It is always best to begin to tackle questions at their most difficult point …. That's why I wanted to begin with *Beyond the Pleasure Principle*' (1991a, p. 21).

Freud's essay, with its formulation of the death drive, allows Lacan to separate man, and therefore his ego, from any logic of self-preservation and fulfilment. Why should mankind, displaying the most developed sense of self of all animals, have such an uncertain grip on *self-interest*? Patterns of behaviour and forms of desire that don't reflect a logic that can be extrapolated from nature demand an alternative logic to explain them, one Lacan will identify with structures of language and association found uniquely within the human unconscious. This is what makes Freud's essay important, not in spite of the challenge it presents ('No other text so profoundly questions the very meaning of life') but because of it (Lacan, 1991a, p. 24).

These concerns lie behind a very different use of Plato in *Seminar II*. The Plato Lacan needs here is one who represents the origin of a mistake: the instinctive appeal of what is good. For, while the Socrates of the *Meno* is valuable for bringing epistemological concerns to light, the system of his disciple teaches an order of values according to which mankind can find its correct bearings. Lacan's turn away from Plato in the second seminar is worth quoting at length because it exposes the interconnected ideas with which he is working – starting, of course, with the vexed issue of teaching:

> Pedagogical procedures belong to a completely alien register to that of analytic experience. I'm not saying that they are without value, or that they might not be made to play an essential role in the Republic – we need only refer to Plato.
>
> One may want to fit man in to a harmonious, natural mode of functioning, one may want to get him to connect the stages of his development, allow him the free blossoming of what in his organism, reaches, in its own time, maturity, and to give to each of these stages its time for play, then its time for adaptation, time for stabilization …. An entire anthropology can be ordered around this. But is that the anthropology that justifies psychoanalyses, that is to say, sticking them on a couch so that they can tell us a lot of bloody nonsense? What's the relation between that and gymnastics, music? Would Plato have

understood what psychoanalysis was about? No, he wouldn't have understood it, despite appearances, because at this point there's an abyss, a fault, and this is what we are in the process of looking for, with *Beyond the Pleasure Principle*.

(Lacan, 1991a, p. 85)

Beyond the Pleasure Principle divides Plato from psychoanalysis. The natural – 'harmonious', 'stages', 'blossoming', 'adaptation' – is set against language ('nonsense'), the medium which makes humans human. To think otherwise is to fundamentally misunderstand the nature and implications of the unconscious, its relation to language and the abyss this places between man and any concept of the natural.

There is a context to Lacan's defiant adherence to *Beyond the Pleasure Principle*. In his 'Seminar on the purloined letter' (1966), even though many analysts 'do not hesitate to reject' *Beyond the Pleasure Principle* as 'superfluous and even risky speculation',

> It is nevertheless difficult to consider this text – which serves as a prelude to the new topography represented by the terms 'ego', 'id', and 'superego', which have become as prevalent in the work of theorists as in the popular mind – to be an excursion, much less a *faux pas*, in Freudian doctrine.
>
> (Lacan, 2007, p. 33)[16]

The theorists associated here with the popular mind in their use of 'ego', 'id' and 'superego' are those in the school of Ego Psychology, a reading of Freud's late theory (e.g. *The Ego and the Id*, 1923) that Lacan is at pains to distance himself from. The émigré ego psychologists of New York, such as Heinz Hartmann and Rudolf Loewenstein, posited two main forces in human life: a hedonistic pleasure principle and a reality principle that challenged it, representing the difficulties and obstacles a subject faces in trying to have their way (see Hartmann, 1958). Psychoanalysis, for these practitioners, must strengthen the subject to endure this clash, balancing psychological demands and synthesizing response. This is where 'adaptation' comes in. Hartmann's *Ego Psychology and the Problem of Adaptation* was published in 1939. All stress the importance of a unified, conflict-free ego.

It is this specific definition of 'the ego' that *Seminar II* seeks to undermine, and *Beyond the Pleasure Principle* will be Lacan's weapon. This is why, although the official title of *Seminar II* is 'The Ego in Freud's Theory and in the Technique of Psychoanalysis', *Beyond the Pleasure Principle* is the text Lacan returns to most often.[17] The fact that Freud writes *The Ego and the Id* and *Beyond the Pleasure Principle* at a similar moment in his career provides Lacan with evidence that he was pursuing anything but a simple, self-interested ego.

> What Freud introduced from 1920 on are additional notions, which were at that time necessary to maintain the principle of the decentring of the subject. But far from being understood as it should have been, there was a general rush, exactly like the kids getting out of school – *Ah! Our nice little ego is back again! It all makes sense now! We're now back on the well-beaten paths of general psychology* …
>
> Mr. Hartmann, psychoanalysis's cherub, announces the great news to us, so that we can sleep soundly – the existence of the *autonomous ego*.
> (Lacan, 1991a, p. 11)

'Decentring' is the word Lacan uses to describe the effect of Socrates' division of truth and knowledge five pages earlier in the seminar ('Here already there is a decentring', p. 5). 'Decentring' is opposed to an easy understanding that leads to sleep – a vision of the autonomous ego that is easy to grasp because it seems to chime with so many schools of thought. Here, the 'well-beaten paths of general psychology' include all the fields that would try to understand man according to natural instinct and biological need. The work of one leading proponent of ego psychology, David Rapaport (1960), provided a means to apparently connect this analytic approach back to a basis in biology. Ethology, the scientific study of animal behaviour (its name derived from *ethos*, meaning character), also looms large in the second seminar.[18] But the well-beaten paths lead back to Plato and Aristotle.

Plato is important here for establishing ego psychology as a bigger conceptual mistake than a mere schism within psychoanalysis might suggest: one with deep roots and broad implications. Modern science (often via Plato's disciple Aristotle) smuggles Platonic assumptions of the good, the right, the harmonious back into common belief. Psychologists of the behaviourist school, for example, are concerned with nothing less than 'how one in effect fixes the level, the low-water mark, by which to measure the perfection, or *areté* of [the] species' (Lacan, 1991a, p. 8). Where Plato introduced an artisan god to underwrite design and goodness in the world, Aristotle grounded form (and formal virtue) in function. But a faith in there being a rational logic to human behaviour persists, and with it the potential of locating *correct* behaviour. In the twentieth century, this mingles with post-Darwinian thought undetected (see Barnes, 1995). This is why, when Lacan wants to demonstrate the novelty of his approach, he traces the deep, commonplace misunderstandings he is countering back to Plato himself.

Human desire cannot be tweaked until it recovers a natural harmony comparable to music (as a figure like Erixymachus in the *Symposium* would like).[19] Against 'an entire anthropology' that seeks common, harmonious forms underlying music and mankind is the simple phenomenon of repetition – repetitive desire – presented by *Beyond the Pleasure Principle*. This demands further caution with regards to any identification between psychoanalysis and Platonic *maieutics*, for repetition must not be confused with any meaningful return such as the reminiscence of eternal truths on which Socrates will found his epistemology.

Speech – 'sticking them on a couch so that they can tell us a lot of bloody nonsense' – may be the medium of analysis, but it does not grant us access to a truth buried deep within us. Instead, in the 'depths' we discover external structures of language and history. Rather than leading us to the hidden heart of a unified subject, it shatters the very concept. Repetition 'vacillates beyond all the biological mechanisms of equilibration, of harmonization and of agreement. It is only introduced by the register of language, by the function of the symbol' (Lacan, 1991a, p. 90). The importance of Plato's role in establishing the distinctive implications of repetition is felt again nine years later. Now at the École des Hautes Études, and having been told by the IPA that he was to be struck off their list of training analysts, Lacan is still using the comparison to emphasize what is distinct about psychoanalysis: recollection is not Platonic reminiscence, 'it is not the return of a form, an imprint, a *eidos* of beauty and good, a supreme truth, coming to us from the beyond. It is something that comes to us from the structural necessities … at the level of the structure of the signifier' (Lacan, 1977, p. 47).[20]

As heard here, it is not just the function of memory that is qualified by the signifier but the place of truth itself:

> It isn't an accident that Plato places reminiscence at the centre of his entire theory of knowledge. That natural object, the harmonic correspondent of the living being, is recognizable because its outline has already been sketched. And for it to have been sketched, it must already have been within the object, which is going to join itself to it. That is the relation of the dyad. Plato's entire theory of knowledge is dyadic.
>
> *(Lacan, 1991a, p. 87)*

Lacan (1991a, 2007) refers to this 'dyadic' account of Plato's on several occasions to distinguish an alternative model. Truth, for Plato, is a product of harmonious reciprocity. Lacan presents this as a 'myth' according to which we might be united with the world beyond us; a deeply ingrained fantasy of truth as correspondence. This comforting vision is felt even more keenly in the Neo-Platonic depiction of knowledge as union or return to the One (see Koyré, 1943, 1950). This fantasy of knowledge survives until the time of Descartes (according to a narrative of intellectual history that Lacan derives from Koyré). Descartes' *cogito* exposes the true situation in which we find ourselves: the reduction of knowledge to a pure point of consciousness jettisons any hope of intuitive access to wider truths. It is in *Seminar XI* that Lacan (1977) develops its implications at greatest length: 'the cogito marks ... the break with every assurance conditioned by intuition' (p. 261).[21] Two consequences of this perspective will be crucial for Lacan's investigations: one is the way it shifts focus onto how longingly we *desire* truth (and the unity of self and world it implies). The other is the need, if we are to imagine we know something, for there to be an authority who can guarantee this knowledge: a third party, whether this is a scientific system or God, underwriting it. Descartes is forced to reintroduce the presence of a benign God to authenticate knowledge. Lacan describes the function of this third party as the big Other, a repository of truth and authority. This is the position that the patient views the analyst as occupying. Lacanian theory, therefore, must work hard to preserve a sense of the desired unity as a fantasy. Yet desire itself, the desire for *episteme* that placed Socrates so at odds with the world, is essential if we are to be led beyond the familiar. The question is: where does that leave the idea of teaching?

Science, surprise, seduction

Many of Lacan's thoughts on desire generally have their origin in his thoughts on teaching and the seduction and desire it involves. Socrates helps crystallize these ideas. This concern is central to *Seminar VIII*'s analysis of the *Symposium* in relation to transference, but its concerns clearly emerge from Lacan's consideration of the *Meno* six years earlier. Lacan pays particular attention to an episode at the end of the *Symposium* when the drunken young statesman Alcibiades bursts in and praises the enigmatic Socrates for the knowledge he has contained within him, like offerings (*agalma*) hidden inside the hollow statue of a god. For Lacan, Alcibiades demonstrates that the effect of Socrates is founded on wisdom he is believed to contain, more than the explicit content of his teachings. From this mysterious, projected object of longing, Lacan will devise his theory of the *objet petit a*, the object cause of desire, but it emerges from a situation of teacher and disciple, and a desire for knowledge.[22] Likewise, in *Seminar X*, when Lacan famously remarks that love involves giving something you do not have, it is in the context of looking back at the *Symposium* and this desire for Socrates and the wisdom he is purported to contain. Via Socrates, Lacan moves the analyst's role from that of possessor of truth (whether this truth is *episteme* or *doxa*) to the one who is able to exploit and manipulate a position of presumed knowledge. This applies to a teacher as well, if not more so.

But how to effect this transference? By creating a sense of a quest, of longing; by remaining devoted to a truth that is out there, in spite of reservations Lacan may have when it appears to have arrived. Socrates himself 'aims only at truth' (Lacan, 2015, p. 82). Socrates is driven to *atopia* by love, love of wisdom; 'he is a "philo-sopher" in the etymological sense of the word' (Hadot, 1995, p. 57). It is this that necessitates psychoanalysis remain aligned with science after all, with the troublesome love of *episteme*.

> This is what any investigation does which, at the outset of the philosophical approach, tends to articulate itself as science, and Plato teaches us, rightly or wrongly, faithfully or unfaithfully, that this was what Socrates was doing. Socrates demanded that we not be content with that to which we have this innocent relation known as *doxa*, and which is – why not, for God's sake? – sometimes right, but rather that we ask why, that we be satisfied only by the assured truth which he calls *episteme*: science, knowledge that provides its reasons. This, Plato tells us, was the point of Socrates' *philosophein*.
>
> (Lacan, 2015, p. 44)

The rigor of science is seductive: 'What might surprise us is the seductive power of such a severe discourse, which is attested to us here and there in one or another of the dialogues' (pp. 82–83). And the idea of a seduction into wisdom via mystery would not have seemed so odd in Ancient Greece. In the slave boy episode of the *Meno*, the classicist W. K. C. Guthrie (1968) hears a Plato heavily under the influence of mystical cult leader Pythagoras, the tone of the fictional Socrates becoming more solemn as he introduces the doctrine of 'certain priests and priestesses and many of the inspired poets' (p. 17). This is an initiation into the mysteries that will be explored further in the *Phaedo* and *Phaedrus*; Lacan (2015) himself notes in *Seminar*

VIII that Pythagorism holds an 'essential role and function' in any attempt at understanding Platonic thought' (p. 68).

Teaching should create and maintain wonder, like the mystery cults. Science can be defined by wonder. This is why Lacan, contrary to what we might expect, seeks to preserve the tenor of scientific quest in Freud's own researches, compared to those who would rather psychoanalysis relinquish its claims to scientific status and align itself with philosophy, literature or even myth. Lacan's employment of structuralism, mathematization and topology all serve a similar purpose, communicating thoroughness and exactitude, positing an object of knowledge behind the teaching that is at once profound and precise. Lacan (2007) presents psychoanalysis's concern with the symbolic function as the approach that 'situates us at the heart of the movement that is establishing a new order of the sciences'. And he seeks out the approval of Plato again: 'This new order simply signifies a return to a notion of true science whose credentials are already inscribed in a tradition that begins with Plato's *Theaetetus*' (p. 235; see also 1977, p. 47).

This is one of several occasions that Lacan identifies the rigour of structuralism with Plato's dialogue *Theaetetus*. The *Theaetetus* is the only Platonic dialogue devoted to the question of what knowledge actually is. But the three definitions Plato explores are each shown to be unsatisfactory. As such, it is *aporetic*, it ends in an *impasse* (210c; cf. 183a5, 187a1). The emphasis, as before, is wonder (*thaumezein*). This, Plato explains in the *Theaetetus*, is the only true beginning of philosophy (155d). It is the chief attribute of the philosopher.

Lacan repeatedly emphasizes the need to preserve a sense of wonder. 'The truth is always new', he states in his 'Presentation on psychical causality', inspired by a passing reference to Plato's *Parmenides*: 'For neither Socrates nor Descartes, nor Marx, nor Freud, can be "gone beyond", insofar as they carried out their research with the passion to unveil that has an object: truth' (2007, p. 157). To achieve this it is necessary to rid oneself of predetermined ideas. This is the task: to unsettle preconceptions even among those who think they already know, whether these regard Platonic parallels or anything else. Dull 'understanding' – the static knowledge we've seen criticized above – is best defended against by preserving curiosity. This is certainly important for the analyst when confronted by a patient. Lacan (1991a) identifies 'two dangers in anything related to the understanding of our clinical domain'.

> The first is not to be sufficiently curious. Children are taught that curiosity is a terrible fault, and on the whole, it's true, we aren't curious, and it isn't easy to generate this feeling in an automatic way.

The second is to understand. We always understand too much, especially in analysis. Most of the time, we're fooling ourselves.

(p. 103)

This clearly extends beyond the clinic to a general distaste for 'knowledge' as something monolithic and unselfconscious, 'democratic' perhaps yet intellectually and ideologically supine. If Lacan's Socrates ('my inconvenient Socrates') is anti-civic, that is because the civic and the ethical are not one and the same. Socrates' fatal mistake, Lacan (2015) notes, was to swim against the tide of the masses: 'Everyone knows that one has to wait for the masses before making the slightest wave on the shore of justice, for they will necessarily arrive there tomorrow. This is how astonishment works – things get chalked up to wrongdoing [*faute*]' (p. 11). In the eyes of the masses, what is astonishing appears as a fault.

Lacan continues: given that,

> in the social bond, opinions have no place if they are not borne out by all that ensures the city's equilibrium, and thus Socrates not only did not have his place – he was no place …. what is so surprising about the fact that it resulted in a death sentence?
>
> *(p. 10)*

Then, in a typically audacious act of association, he bridges Socrates' death sentence with the intellectual quest that led Freud to formulate the death drive: 'As for Freud, on the other hand, wasn't it in strict accordance with the rigour of his path that he discovered the death drive? It too was quite scandalous, albeit less costly to Freud himself' (p. 10). And Lacan returns us to *thaumasios* – wonder, astonishment – linking their techniques.

> 'Are we dealing with the death drive or dialectic?' My answer is 'Yes.' Yes, if the one brings the other with it and astonishes you.
>
> I am willing to admit that I'm getting off track, that I need not take you through all the most far-reaching paradoxes, and that by doing so at the outset, I am making sure you are astonished – if you weren't already – by Freud if not by Socrates.
>
> If you are unwilling to be astonished by anything, these paradoxes will undoubtedly prove simple to resolve.
>
> *(p. 11)*

An atopic Socrates, finally, is needed for an atopic Freud. A position counter to social equilibrium dramatizes a teaching intended to startle. Cherish the impasses, Lacan suggests. Beware answers. This, of course, is difficult when teaching relates to a body of knowledge like psychoanalysis, with institutions, examinations, qualifications, dictionaries, conferences, associations. This is where the style of the seminar comes in: always promising, never handing over anything predigested.

There is a general reason for this. As Lacan (2007) puts it: 'A truth, if it must be said, is not easy to recognize once it has become received' (p. 340). Lacan's students are already immersed in both psychoanalytic and philosophical learning, but the effect is to insulate them from his teaching: 'Of their philosophy [classes] most have retained but a grab-bag of phrases – a catechism gone haywire – which anaesthetizes them from being surprised by truth' (p. 709).

Yet, Lacan asserts, a psychoanalyst addressing psychoanalysts must be especially alert to the dangers of premature understanding. In 'Position of the Unconscious', as he considers the effect of language on the subject, a subject spoken by language and 'sealed' into it so that he or she remains oblivious to its determining effect, Lacan proposes the necessity for psychoanalysis to be extra cautious: Any discourse 'is within its rights to consider itself not responsible for this effect' – that is, 'any discourse except that of the teacher when he addresses psychoanalysts' (2007, p. 709). 'I have always considered myself accountable for such an effect,' he continues, 'and, while unequal to the task of guarding against it, it was the secret prowess of each of my "seminars".' Then he adds: 'For the people who come to hear me are not the first communicants Plato exposed to Socrates' questioning' (p. 709).

The importance of the seminar itself is clear. In *Seminar XX*, one of Lacan's most extended considerations of the play of knowledge and ignorance, Lacan (1998) concludes that 'there is no contradiction between my position as an analyst and what I do here' (p. 2). Roudinesco (2014) argues that the equation between therapy and seminar was acknowledged, 'to the extent that for his analysands attendance at the seminar was equivalent to a session' (p. 95).

The disorientating form of the seminars responds to a general theoretical concern about knowledge and authority, but this is also a personal issue bound to the stage Lacan's career has reached. The fact that so many of Lacan's ideas were already circulating in more or less misunderstood form as he was teaching is a constant unspoken influence on his style. While it is possible, and some have tried, to distinguish early, middle and late seminars there is a real sense in which they are all 'late'. Lacan presented his first report on the 'mirror phase' at the Congress of the International Psychoanalytical Association in 1936. The seminar series began in private in 1952 and became public in 1953, 17 years later, after the fame of the mirror stage has spread. When the 'first' seminar occurs, Lacan is 51, and the mirror stage has appeared in Simone de Beauvoir's *The Second Sex* (1949) and Franz Fanon's *Black Skin, White Masks* (1952) alongside references to the 'Other'.[23] In the second seminar, Lacan (1991a) expresses his concern to Lefèbvre-Pontalis: 'The mirror stage isn't a magic word. It's already a bit dated. Since I put it out in 1936, it's about twenty years old. It's beginning to be in need of a bit of renovation' (p. 102). Soon Lacan would have a new generation arriving at his psychoanalytic work via the Marxist-Psychoanalytic synthesis of Louis Althusser. It is no surprise, then, if Lacan's immediate concern is reclarifying his theory and the demands it makes of its audience.

The interactive, confrontational drama of the seminar provides a solution of sorts. There is one instance when Lacan is happy to draw a parallel with the open, questioning process of *maieutics*. It is no longer psychoanalytic treatment that is being compared, however, but his seminar: 'I know it was our first meeting, and that it is always hard to knit something into a dialogue. It really is an art, a *maieutics* …. The important thing is that it is still with us, alive and open' (Lacan, 1991a, p. 14). The seminars provided Lacan with a space in which to teach in an 'alive and open' way. It allowed him both to tantalize his audience with the promise of new revelations while drawing attention back to their own desire. It was a special occasion for special people, a form of its own. In a telling moment of *Seminar VIII*, Lacan (2015) picks up on an exchange in the *Symposium*: Agathon, the great tragedian, 'announces some hesitation, fear, and intimidation too' at speaking before the men gathered for the symposium. Socrates compares this to Agathon's recent triumph on the tragic stage and suggests that the difference is because on the tragic stage he is addressing 'a crowd, a throng' and that here it is a question of something else. 'Here, by goodness, we don't know very well what we're getting into' (p. 111).

The question concerns how one communicates in an elite (intellectually open) space, with the demands on the teacher – and effects on the audience – involved. This ideal of the seminar as an exclusive event had been preserved for Lacan through the example of Kojève's seminars on Hegel. There are several similarities between Lacan's seminar and Kojève's that are worth noting. Both grew through word of mouth and were initially confined to a relatively small circle (Macey, 1988). In both, foreign texts played a significant part in the overall purpose and seductive effect of the seminar. Kojève's lectures at the École Pratique des Hautes Études between 1933 and 1939 marked the beginning of Hegelian studies in France.[24] It was only in 1939 and 1941 that two volumes of Jean Hyppolite's translation of *The Phenomenology of Spirit* appeared. In the 1950s, one of the factors that enhanced Lacan's status was the poverty of the existing French translation of Freud's work (see Webster, 2002). Lacan's use of Freud's German, his insistence on the return, not just to Freud, but to the sacred text of the *Gessamelte Werke*, is a key part of his intellectual armory.[25]

Both Kojève and Lacan resisted publishing their ideas. We have seen the ways in which Lacan's seminars were self-consciously constructed to keep ideas 'alive and open', and the figure of Socrates cements the association of this quality with speech rather than writing. But it is a Socrates we only know through texts. Ultimately, of course, Plato's overarching project is manifest not just in the Academy, but also the written dialogues that preserve his mentor. That these are literary artifacts unlike any others suggests the complexity of this transition, its dangers but also creative opportunities. Inevitably, it is a precedent on Lacan's mind as he finally accepts the transformation of his seminars into their own unique printed form.

Snobs, mobs and *poubellication*: writing resistance

> On the cover of a collection I brought out ... I found nothing better to write than the word *Écrits*.
>
> It is rather well known that those *Écrits* cannot be read easily. I can make a little autobiographical admission – that is exactly what I thought. I thought perhaps it goes that far, I thought they were not meant to be read.
>
> *Jacques Lacan (1998, p. 26)*

Socrates never writes. He tells the story of the ancient Egyptian god Theuth, inventor of the alphabet, and what the god and king Ammon (Thamus in Greek) said to Theuth about his invention: It will encourage forgetfulness, excess trust in external, written characters, in what is merely the semblance of truth. 'They will be hearers of many things and will have learned nothing; they will appear to be omniscient and will generally know nothing; they will be tiresome company, having the show of wisdom without the reality' (Plato, *Phaedrus*, 274b–276a). But we read this in a text. It survives, thanks to Plato, and survives in a remarkable form.

In the following section I explore the extent of Lacan's conflict over publication. It is a conflict because Lacan senses opportunity as well as danger. In the quotation above, concerning the *Écrits*, 'cannot be read easily' is identified with 'not meant to be read', but the two are not identical. It is inevitable that Plato-Socrates will become involved in Lacan's conflicted feelings about writing, as well as teaching more broadly. Plato's exceptionally slippery literary creations provide Lacan with another stimulating precedent in relation to how we might respond to an impasse.

Superficially, Lacan's comments on publishing display a disdain for the whole thing. Lacan revives a snobbery about 'publication' that was prevalent at the dawn of printing, expressed by those aristocrats who preferred to circulate work by manuscript and saw the printing of a text with one's name on, sent out into the world to be read by anyone who laid hands on it, as vulgar.[26] Lacan (1991b) is clearly well aware of this tradition when he comments on the anonymous contributions to his journal, *Sciliciet*,

> It is very curious that the non-signed should appear paradoxical, whereas of course over the centuries all the honest men there have been have always at least acted as if someone had torn their manuscript from their hands, as if someone had played a dirty trick on them. No one expected to be sent a note of congratulations on publication.
>
> (p. 191)

Of course, central to anxieties about publication was the way the act of publishing moved material from an elite circle to the masses. A note of snobbery arises regularly in Lacan's thoughts on the relationship between psychoanalytic theory and society beyond. He describes Freud's *Three Essays on the Theory of Sexuality* as 'covered over for the masses by so many pseudo-biological glosses' (the more elite 'Lacanian' Freud, of course, is defined by a less pseudo-biological theory) (2007, pp. 431–432). The degradation of Freud's theory of the ego, id and superego, the fact that 'the current use of these terms is bastardized and even ass-backwards', is evident 'in the fact that the theorist and the man on the street use them identically' (p. 33). He dismisses rival theories concerning feminine sexuality as signifying 'nothing preferable to what the hoi polloi give us' (p. 613).

Lacan (1998) makes his feelings felt in Joycean somersaults of *linguisterie* that themselves force attention to the limitations of print:

> That is why … when I forget myself (*m'oublie*) to the point of publishing (*p'oublier*), in other words, of forgetting everything (*tout-blier*) – the

whole (*tout*) has something to do with it – I deserve to have to put up with people talking about me and not at all about my book.

(p. 61)

Being talked about: if there is a fate worse than the academy it is this. To become a fashionable name contributing to the chatter. The context for this complaint is a distinction he is drawing between truth ('the whole' and therefore impossible, inexpressible) and language, the 'other' pleasure granted us in its place. But he cannot keep an autobiographical note from creeping in. The translator, Bruce Fink, noting echoes lost in the conversion from oral seminar to published text, writes that *p'oublier*, as well as evoking forgetting (*oublier*) and publishing (*publier*) echoes rubbish bin (*poubelle*).

If there is genuine anger here, it is bound to a situation in which Lacan might be gulped down by anyone interested in psychoanalysis at the very moment when he is being excluded from all official institutions of psychoanalysis.

> In my own case, what wound up being written – that is, typed up on the basis of the stenography – concerning what I had said about ethics seemed more than utilizable by the people who were, nevertheless, simultaneously engaged in pointing me out to the attention of the *Internationale de psychoanalyse* with the result that is well known. They would have liked to see preserved, all the same, my reflections on what psychoanalysis brings with it by way of ethics. It would have been sheer profit [for them] – I would have sunk to the bottom while *The Ethics of Psychoanalysis* would have stayed afloat .... I stopped my *Ethics* from being published. I refused to allow it to come out because I'm not going to try to convince people who want nothing to do with me. One must not convince.
>
> *(Lacan, 1998, pp. 52–53)*[27]

Why not? Hubris, certainly. Perhaps because convincing encourages conviction, a closed-mindedness Lacan seeks to avoid. There is a similar danger, a phenomenon Lacan terms 'university discourse'. Here, again, Kojève, and Kojève's own disdain for publication, is on his mind. In 1972's defiantly complex paper *L'étourdit*, Lacan (2009) includes a footnote in which a distinction becomes clear between teaching (as intervention) and knowledge, belonging to institutions:

> Kojève whom I hold to be my master for having initiated me into Hegel ... only philosophized under the title of the university discourse

into which he had settled provisionally, but knowing well that knowledge only functioned there as a semblance and treating it as such: he showed this in all sorts of ways, handing over his notes to whoever could profit from them and posthumously showing his derision for the whole adventure.

(p. 42)[28]

'University discourse' constitutes one of the four discourses parsed in *Seminar XVII*, alongside the discourse of the master, the hysteric and the analyst. These are presented as four equations by which we might understand four different relationships between authority, knowledge and desire. University discourse describes the use of supposedly 'objective', 'neutral' knowledge to acquire a position of power: power that is more often than not in the unacknowledged service of some greater ideology. But while it is fully elaborated in 1969, we have seen how the roles of Plato and Socrates allow Lacan to explore equivalent themes early in the seminar series.

So, finally, the act of writing and publishing transforms an initiating 'master' (Kojève) into an academic. In *Seminar XVII*, Lacan (1991b) considers the difficulty of translating his own theories into academic language and presents the medium not merely as a threat but as a fundamental alteration of his message:

From a strictly academic motive, I say, flows the fact that the person who has translated me [into a thesis – Anika Lemaire], by virtue of having a background in the style, in the form of imposition of the university discourse, cannot do anything other, whether he believes he is commenting on me or not, than reverse my formula, that is, give it a significance that, it has to be said, is strictly contrary to the truth, without even any homology at all with what I claim.

(p. 41)

Not only miss, but reverse. What in his theory is profoundly altered? Lemaire synthesizes and clarifies Lacan's thought – but loses the style. The question becomes how one might publish without becoming university discourse.

Publication, for both Kojève and Lacan, was the work of a disciple. Raymond Queneau published Kojève's *Leçons d'introduction à la lecture de Hegel* (1947) from notes taken in the seminars taught before the war. Into the place of tension between Lacan and publication came Jacques-Alain

Miller, a student of Althusser at the ENS and, when Lacan transferred his seminar to the university in 1964, a star contributor. If the fragment of Miller on Plato's Academy that heads this chapter sounds eerily like Lacan himself – strident, allusive, elliptical – it may make us wonder exactly whose voice it is we hear in the seminars printed under Lacan's name. Elizabeth Roudinesco's (1997) exploration of this relationship and its controversies played a significant role in severing Lacanian biography from Lacanian theoretical work (led by Miller himself).[29] David Macey (1988) has written on the complex status of the *Écrits* and the seminars: 'The resultant text is as much Miller's as it is Lacan's. Chapter titles, headings and punctuation are all Miller's; he is a joint signatory of the publisher's contract and has the legal status of a co-author' (p. 7).

Speaking to the press after winning a court case against the review *Littoral*, which had printed several sessions of the eighth seminar, Miller (1985) appears to cast himself as Plato in his simultaneous act of codifying and ventriloquism:

> I observe that people don't really catch onto a seminar until I have established it .... Until this work, which consists partly of editing but mostly of logicization, has been done, a seminar isn't understood, apart from a grain gleaned here or there .... Counting for nothing means putting myself in a position where I can write 'I' and that 'I' is Lacan's, an 'I' that continues the author and prolongs him beyond his death.
> (*Libération*, 14–15/12/85, quoted in Macey, 1988, p. 7)

There is clearly a tension here, a supposed reduction of self to the point where one may appropriate another's intellectual identity altogether, not as theft but a possession of sorts, allowing for the correct establishing of ideas within the original lectures. Yet an account that presented Lacan as purely hostile to publication, his seminars preserved only by Miller's intervention, would be inaccurate. Lacan's performed resistance to print needs to be qualified.

The seminars are astonishingly crafted, both as weekly sessions and as a sequence of talks over several months. Lacan's pride in his performance is evident throughout. Of the crisis that led to *Seminar II*, he writes in a letter to his former analyst, Rudolph Loewenstein: 'I've only been able to survive [these months] by keeping going ... my seminar of texts and supervision, without having once missed one, nor, I believe, without its inspiration or quality having in any way wavered.' When his seminar of 1963 is cancelled following a further schism, with the SFP this time, which had allowed Lacan's name to be struck from the list of training analysts, he laments to those who have shown up for the first session that until the previous night he had thought 'that I would be giving you this year what I have been dispensing for ten years now. My seminar for today was prepared with the same care as I have always devoted to it, every week, for the last ten years.' The seminars are clearly stages on which he can perform the drama of his ongoing martyrdom, but the care he puts into them is unambiguous. In the second session of 1960 Lacan describes his audience 'tasting. They are asking themselves: will it be a good year?' (2015, p. 247). An aside in the second seminar reveals he has already planned the theme for the following year's course.

This is not care over an entirely transient phenomenon. Clément (1983) describes the seminars as Lacan's 'major work' (p. 18). And a description of the scenario involved qualifies any sense that they might be experienced as spontaneous, transitory events, or indeed as entirely 'oral' (this is a description of the seminar of 1964):

> There were tape recorders and the room bristled with wires in which we happily tangled our feet. Near Lacan, his secretary, admirably impassive, stood watch, and a stenographer recorded the lectures on a stenographic machine as Lacan spoke. As if all this apparatus were not enough, people also took notes: some occasionally, others determined not to miss a thing, noting down every word, leaning over toward their neighbors if by chance a word or syllable escaped them.
>
> *(pp. 12–13)*

This allows for a feedback loop in which Lacan participates. A few weeks into *Seminar XX* he states:

> Thanks to someone who is willing to polish up what I tell you here, four or five days ago I received the nicely scrubbed truffle in my elocutions this year [and declares that] rereading the first transcription of this Seminar, I found that it wasn't so bad.
>
> (Lacan, 2007, p. 137).

It is in this same seminar that he refers to Miller writing up *Seminar XI*: 'I was able to get the sense … that what I put forward that year was not as stupid as all that' (1998, p. 27).

As the process gathers pace, and a quantity of published work comes to seem inevitable, a new interest in Plato's literary style emerges, in particular his creation of texts that defend themselves. For Lacan, the question of how Plato preserves in written form any sense of Socratic *aporia* is more than theoretical. The strangeness of the dialogues, their distancing effects, their layers of fiction and context are all of active interest. 'What in fact is this text?' Lacan (2015) asks when he turns to the *Symposium*. 'Is it a fiction or a fabrication, as many of his dialogues clearly are …? Why this genre? Why this law of the dialogue?' (p. 27). These are questions familiar to classicists. They, like Lacan, have probed what this unprecedented form reveals. Martha Nussbaum (1986) describes Plato's dialogues as displaying 'an acute self-consciousness about the relationship between the choice of a style and the content of a philosophical conception' (p. 122). Plato's work 'is a new kind of writing'. It is 'the deliberate structuring of a new literary genre'. Even Aristotle was at a loss about how to respond to it (see *Poetics*, 1447 b7). Crucially, the openness of the dialogues forces a relationship with the reader 'who is invited to enter critically and actively into the give-and-take, much as a spectator of tragedy is invited to reflect (often along with the chorus) on the meaning of the events for his own system of values' (p. 126). By writing philosophy as drama, 'Plato calls on every reader to engage actively in the search for truth' (p. 134). As Guthrie (1968) describes:

> Most of the value of a Platonic dialogue, especially from the early or middle period, lies in the direct impression which it makes on a reader. It cannot be analysed and presented as a collection of neatly tied and labeled parcels of philosophical doctrine. At least, to do so would be to travesty Plato, who made it clear that he did not believe philosophy could be retailed in that way. It could only be a product of living contact between mind and mind …. [Dialogues] at least avoid the defects (in his view) of continuous treatises which try to expound philosophy 'like any other subject of instruction'.
>
> *(pp. 9–10)*

In this account, 'Lacan's seminar' could be substituted for 'Platonic dialogue' and 'psychoanalysis' for 'philosophy' without undue contortions. Both men are defined by a sense of the exceptionalism of their modes of enquiry, the exceptional self-consciousness demanded of both teacher and audience when considering psychoanalysis or philosophy if they are to maintain the necessary vigilance regarding their own positions.

This is one explanation of the difficulty of Lacan's published work, but, of course, it doesn't escape accusations of elitism. Koyré (1945) himself was greatly interested in the dramatic nature of Plato's early dialogues, the positioning of a reader-spectator for whom the drama is played out (Alenka, 1987), and he saw the complexity of these dramas as suited to an elitist ideology. He explains, approvingly, that Plato 'never asserts that science and, of course, philosophy, are accessible to all, or that everyone is capable of dealing with these subjects. He always taught the contrary' (p. 7). The dialogues are difficult because Plato wanted to make them difficult. 'It constitutes a test and allows for the differentiation between those who understand and those, doubtless the majority, who do not' (p. 7). Koyré, in his Columbia lectures published in 1945 as *Discovering Plato*, is intensely interested in this aspect of the dialogues: in particular, he is drawn to an aristocratic outlook in Plato that identifies knowledge with virtue and sees philosophy as bound to governance (Alenka, 1987).

Lacan's 'elite' is intellectual rather than political but, with his comments on the less 'assiduous' attendees, it is easy to see an equivalent, defensive separation of those inside from those outside. Lacan's 'essays' in *Écrits* are largely gathered from the transcripts of semi-improvised conference papers and guest lectures, 'refined on paper to a fever pitch of compression, manifold reference and syntactical complexity and obliquity', in the words of one commentator (Forrester, 1990, p. 106). But not for the sake of it. Lacan describes his style as a barrier to 'aberrant interpretations', texts organized to prevent skim reading (Macey, 1988, p. 8). They demand work. As with Plato, Bruce Fink locates the resistant style as emerging at a distinct point in Lacan's career, beginning with 'The Freudian thing' (1955/6) and explicitly theorized in 'Instance of the letter' (1957). Lacan's papers in this later period, Fink (1995) writes, 'seem to be written for a yet-to-be-determined public; perhaps they are written for posterity, or perhaps they are designed to (or at least written in such a way as to) create a new audience, an audience of analyst/philosopher/ literary critics' (p. 7). Here, for Fink, we can see Lacan having understood that he'd moved beyond any sort of pre-existing university discourse into what he would formulate as the analyst's discourse, one that turns our attention towards our own desire in a way that is familiar from the seminars and similar to analytical sessions themselves.

As Lacan's wariness over his own role grows, a very different Plato appears, one who is more cunning about his communications, sometimes a quite startling, provocatively reimagined figure. In *Seminar VIII*, Lacan (2015) says:

> I think there are good reasons to read Plato's texts from the perspective of what I call his dandyism, and to see his writings as the outer trappings. I would go so far as to say that he tosses us, we dogs, little good and bad scraps of an often rather infernal sense of humor.
>
> (p. 84)

Humour is now seen as a critical ingredient of the Platonic dialogue, identified with a self-reflexive irony and an aloofness. At its extreme this new Plato is an outright satirist, never more so than when his work addresses society at large such as in *The Republic*:

> What Plato saw on the horizon was a communitarian city, as thoroughly revolting to his way of thinking as it is to ours. A well-organised studfarm [*haras*] for everyone, that is what he promises us in a pamphlet, which has always been the bad dream for all those who cannot get over the greater discord between society and their sense of the good. It is called *The Republic*, and everyone has taken it seriously, believing that it was what Plato truly wanted.
>
> (p. 83)

The *Symposium* provides the clearest example of this equivocation, hedged within an elaborate system of frame narratives (Plato describes Apollodorus giving an account of the symposium based on information he has from Aristodemus, who was present when it occurred several years before). While there are some uses of frame narratives in the *Phaedo*, *Parmenides* and the *Republic*, nowhere else does Plato take such trouble to distance himself from the content of a dialogue as in the *Symposium* (see Johnson, 1998). The appeal of this new, challengingly enigmatic form for Lacan is enhanced by its association with the man who first drew his attention to it, the challengingly enigmatic Kojève. Lacan (2015) has approached Kojève for his thoughts on the *Symposium* in preparation for *Seminar VIII*:

> I was encouraged by many things he told me about ... aspects of Plato's work, namely, about the following, which is quite obvious – that Plato hides from us what he thinks just as much as he reveals it to us. It is thus only as a function of each individual's abilities – in other words, up to a certain limit which assuredly cannot be gone beyond – that we can glimpse it. You shouldn't hold it against me, therefore, if

> I don't give you the last word on Plato, because Plato has clearly decided not to give it to us.
>
> (p. 61)

Dialogues avoid the pitfalls of attempting to state the whole truth, and the same truth to all. They are multifaceted, an effect born of their dramatic nature. This allows us to read between the lines, and to probe the silences:

> As I was saying goodbye to Kojève, I remarked to him, 'We didn't get around to speaking about the *Symposium* very much.' And as Kojève is a very superior kind of guy, in other words, a snob, he replied, 'In any case, you will never be able to interpret the *Symposium* if you do not know why Aristophanes had the hiccoughs.'
>
> (p. 61)

The answer that Lacan arrives at, after much pondering, is that 'if Aristophanes has the hiccoughs, it's because throughout Pausanius' discourse he's been splitting his sides laughing – and Plato has been doing the same' (p. 62).

This ambiguous, potentially comic nature of the dialogues allows Lacan to divide a Socratic Plato from the Plato who tries to teach more straightforwardly, who reveals an unwavering, superior realm of higher values. When, in *Seminar XI*, Lacan (1977) mentions Socrates himself as associated with the idea of the *good*, it is hurriedly qualified by venturing into the question of whose voice the dialogues present:

> The Socratic discussion introduced the following theme – that the recognition of the conditions for the good in itself would have something irresistible for man. This is the paradox of the teaching, if not of Socrates himself – what do we know about him other than through the Platonic comedy? I will not even say Plato's comedy – for Plato develops in the terrain of the comic dialogue and leaves all questions open – but of a certain exploitation of Platonism, which may be said to perpetuate itself in general derision. For, as we all know, the most perfect recognition of the conditions of the good will never prevent anyone from dashing into its opposite.
>
> (p. 234)

Socrates is hidden within Plato, undermining any straightforwardly pedagogical aspirations regarding man and what is good for him – and

Plato himself is hidden with his dialogues. Humour is the index of critical self-awareness. Alain Badiou (2008) claims that Lacan was the 'first to recognize the properly comic genius that sparkles in Plato's dialogues' (p. 231).[30] Plato is so valuable to Lacan as he pursues his own self-deconstruction because he represents a way of communicating that lies *diagonal* to the four discourses: in Badiou's account, Plato's dialogues lie between the master's injunction, the hysteric's disruption, the reasoning of the university, and the ominous silence of the analyst. It is in this sense that Badiou sees them founding philosophy itself, not with a set of questions and categories of enquiry but 'via the free play they establish, under the shelter of literary form, between these disparate regimes of discourse'. They do not need to resolve the questions they raise and, as such, 'philosophy's plasticity ... enables it to instruct through the example of deadlock. Platonic *aporia* is attended by the *atopia* of his discourses' (Badiou, 2008, p. 239).

The dialogues, as literary works, allow instruction through impossibility, liberating the reader and ennobling the otherwise sullied act of publication. But Lacan's retrieval from them of a radically *atopic* Socrates has not been without criticism. Miriam Leonard (2005), in her study of the relationship between Ancient Greece and post-structuralist thought, alights on the meeting of Lacan, Nietzsche and Socrates as a particularly unhealthy crossroads of influence. She describes a 'Lacanian Socrates' propping up Lacan's 'radically *atopic* ethics of psychoanalysis. An *atopia* which, as we have seen, not only masks a reactionary gender politics but is also profoundly anti-civic' (p. 168). And if Lacan's reading owes a debt to Nietzsche, it only allows him 'to reassert Nietzsche's distaste for democracy' (p. 189). There is plenty to this, but I hope I have suggested at least two aspects of Lacan's return to Greek philosophy that may be used in his defence. One is the extent to which Lacan's career-long engagement with Socrates reflects his own uneasy thoughts about assuming the role of teacher and leader. The other is his careful awareness of, and fascination with, the literary qualities of the dialogues and the *multiple* Platos and Socrates they reveal, alternately aloof, aristocratic, plebeian, mystical, self-critical. Like many over the centuries, he returns to Plato because Plato represents the start of something fundamental he seeks to correct, but also because Socrates represents an ideal, if an impossible one. The dialogues, and the seminars they inspire, allow Lacan to be both a Socrates and a Plato and to position psychoanalysis as a discipline defined by its self-consciousness with regards to the constitution of knowledge.

Coda: the atopic academy

> One day somebody who is perhaps here, and will no doubt not make herself known, accosted me in the street just as I was getting into a taxi. She pulled over on her scooter and said to me, 'Are you Dr. Lacan?'
>
> 'Yes, I am', I said to her. 'Why?'
>
> 'Are you holding your seminar again?'
>
> 'Yes, of course, soon.'
>
> 'Where?'
>
> And then, no doubt I had my reasons for this, and I ask her to take my word for it, I answered, 'You'll see.'
>
> Jacques Lacan (1991b, p. 12)

In this telling anecdote delivered near the start of the seventeenth seminar, Lacan encounters a fan on the street. It is telling that she recognizes him, telling that it has become a game tracking the seminar down, but equally telling is the fact that Lacan cannot see if she made it in the end. The year is 1969, in a Paris still agitated with revolutionary ideas, but one institution is apparently thriving: Lacan's seminar has grown from the thirty or so attendees at Saint-Anne Hospital, mostly fellow analysts and trainees, and the four to five hundred analysts and students who would crowd the École Normale Supérieure to an amphitheatre at the Faculté de Droit packed with up to a thousand people.[31]

A contemporary reader is met by uniform pages, from the first seminar to the twentieth. As we learn more about the changing context in which they were delivered, how should it affect our reception of the texts? Clearly the context affects Lacan himself. On several occasions in later seminars, he regrets the overcrowding. In the sixth session of *Seminar XX*, he admits his hope that the crowd might diminish so that he can, again, 'walk around among you' as he teaches. In *Seminar XVII*, he is relieved to make out attendees he recognizes in the crowded auditorium.

> There are many familiar faces here, but I am delighted by this, as I am also delighted with the relative decrease in numbers I can observe – last time, it was a bit like a crowded Metro in here.
>
> A fair few of you were already part of that very old audience before following me to that place from which I had to emigrate.
>
> (Lacan, 1991b, p. 25)

A few moments later he reintroduces an old reference: the slave in Plato's *Meno*. In this context, it might be construed as a message for those who recognize it, proof of a continuum over the years, but also of Lacan's willingness to move with the times. In *Seminar XVII*, Meno's slave belongs to the exploited proletariat, a victim of philosophy's appropriation of knowledge, of what was once the slave's own: 'To see this it is enough to read Plato's dialogues from time to time, and, as God only knows, for the past sixteen years I have been making an effort to get those who listen to me to do it' (p. 21).

Are there some in the audience who remember the slave's first outing 15 years earlier? Is this knowing recognition the reward for their loyalty during Lacan's wandering exile? They, at least, can see that Lacan was ahead of the revolutionaries. His comment comes in a moment of nostalgic reflection on teaching, utopias and his unique seminar, provoked by a visit to the experimental university set up by the May revolutionaries at Vincennes. Lacan's presentation there provoked an eruption of protest, heckles preserved in the appendix of *Seminar XVII* in which the moment is transcribed.[32] Out on the streets, authorities and institutions are in question, activism spills into the seminar itself but, Lacan suggests, this is nothing new for him. 'What I said by, for, and in your presence is at each of these moments, if we define them by their geographical locations, always already interrupted' (pp. 16–17). With characteristic boldness he is comparing *les événements* to his seminar, to the interference he has faced from within and without institutions throughout his career. His seminar does not need to fear protests because it has always been a small protest of its own: 'it's no recent thing that, because of its composition, my audience gives rise to – what? This is precisely what I am wondering about – a certain discomfort' (p. 26). In a neat piece of symbolism, Lacan recalls students at the ENS smoking during his seminars to the extent that the smoke went through the ceiling so that students in the library space above could no longer breathe. 'These are extraordinary things that can obviously only occur because of the audience that you are. It is the importance of this that I am showing you.' Amidst the ruptures, the seminar is the point of continuity, an atopic academy. 'We shall therefore continue what I am doing here, where "here" is always at the same time, whether here or somewhere else, Wednesday at half-past twelve for the last seventeen years' (p. 30).

Within nostalgia, of course, is disappointment and resignation. Publication, for Lacan, arises alongside the growth of his fame, but also as the flipside of a failure, entwined with his frustration with the seminar experience as it grows and his hopes of *dialogue* are disappointed. Early seminars are more participatory. The new teaching routine at Saint-Anne is a fantasy of both escape and communication. There is clearly a side to Lacan that craved dialogue and response: 'Yesterday evening's meeting marked a definite step forward in comparison with the first session, since we maintained the dialogue better and for longer' (1991a, p. 27). In this seminar, he actively encourages participation and laments the lack of contributions, advising his audience not to try to be clever, to express themselves openly. Looking back on those years, he describes the predominant tenor of his memories as 'having fun'. All this, perhaps, dissipates as the fame and the audience grows. Roudinesco (1997) quotes one attendee who was witness to Lacan's post-performance anxiety, an outburst that reveals the less appealing side of being recorded rather than responded to: 'What do they come for?' Lacan asked. 'What do they think? Their eyes are so blank. And all those tape recorders are like guns trained on me! They don't understand; I'm absolutely convinced they don't understand anything!' (p. 302).

Inevitably, Plato accompanies him into nostalgia and cynicism, a Plato who reflects on his own failed ideals as a teacher. In *Seminar II*, the *Republic*, with its 'pedagogical procedures', is a moralistic foil for psychoanalysis (1991a, p. 85). But by the seminar of 1960, the *Republic* is a bitter vision. Plato has Critias compare the perfect society of the Republic to that of Atlantis (*Timaeus*). But Atlantis is lost, and this is the significance Lacan finds in the comparison: the myth of Atlantis 'seems to me rather to echo the failure of Plato's political dreams' and 'it is not unrelated to the venture of the Academy' (2015, pp. 83–4). The Academy may have been 'a sort of Utopia of which [Plato] thought he could be the leader', but clearly this is Utopia in its literal sense as 'no place', a fantasy (p. 84). This is the bittersweet context for his description of the Academy as 'a city, a refuge reserved for the best and brightest' (p. 84).

Studying Lacan in the context of his evolving seminar, the extent to which his theory is about communication, its promises and failures, assumes a new significance. Famously, the overture to the *Écrits* opens with Lacan (2007) modifying the saying 'The style is the man himself' to 'the style is the man one addresses' (p. 3). The impact that the experience of the seminars had on Lacan's theorizing – on his theories of intersubjectivity, knowledge, desire, the very meaning of psychoanalysis – cannot be overestimated. Miller (2001), who was in a privileged position of insight, provides the penultimate word on this:

> The Seminar of Lacan was not a method. We can develop this point further. This seminar, as I see it, was done by someone who sought to

justify himself. It was ministered by someone who perhaps wanted to be pardoned for the practice of psychoanalysis. Sometimes, this is lost in the post-analytic experience of analysts, but for Lacan there was a certain sin in practicing psychoanalysis: the attempt of the professional to master a real which does not lend itself to being mastered. It is in this way that psychoanalysis is like an imposter, as Lacan asserted toward the end of his life. This is what energized him such that he presented himself every week in front of the audience, in front of the big Other, to defend his cause.

Lacan performed authority but also doubt, struggles with impasses, and it is the latter that opened up new depths in Freudian theory.

> A theory including a lack that must be rediscovered at every level, be inscribed here in indetermination, there in certitude, and form the knot of the uninterpretable, I am employed there certainly not without experiencing an *atopia* without precedent. Here is the question: who am I to dare such an elaboration? The answer is simple: a psychoanalyst.
>
> (Lacan, 1991a, p. 20)

Notes

1 The anecdote, in a thought-provoking chain of communication, is supposedly told to Lacan by Jung. It has emerged, however, that Jung denies this, casting doubt over whether Freud himself ever said such a thing. According to Roudinesco (2014), 'I have been able to establish that Freud never uttered this sentence and that Jung had never spoken to anyone of this story about a plague. Freud actually said: "They will be surprised when they know what we have to say"' (p. 105).
2 When Lacan forms his breakaway École Freudienne de Paris, he chooses the word *school* rather than *society* or *association*, 'drawing inspiration from the Greek model' (Roudinesco, 2014, p. 71).
3 Webster's essay was originally written in 1994 and formed part of the manuscript of *Why Freud Was Wrong: Sin, Science and Psychoanalysis* (1996); it was omitted from the published version of the book.
4 See Bailly (2009) on the significance of oral teaching as the basis of Lacan's canon.
5 This will be considered at greater length in the following chapter. Interest in these parallels endures; more recent examples of a Platonic psychoanalysis include Gerasimos (1988) and Kofman (1999).
6 See reference to Empedocles in *Analysis Terminable and Interminable* (Freud, 1937, p. 245).
7 This refers to Mill's long review of George Grote's three-volume *Plato, and the Other Companions of Socrates* (1865). Burgoyne (2001) argues that it may have had a considerable influence on Freud as he developed the idea of psychoanalysis. Grote and Mill 'took the radicalising of the individual's relation to the world as their central

theme' (p. 161). The dialectical technique had a therapeutic intention. The idea was to 'dissipate' false opinions and 'unconsciously imbibed sentiment' inherited from previous generations. The idea of psychoanalysis's proximity to Plato's thought survives Freud: a book by Patrice Georgiades is deliberately titled *De Freud à Platon* (1934). Georgiades is one of the first to discuss Plato's three parts of the soul in relation to Freud's concepts of ego, id and superego. On the subject of dialogue and dialectic, see Simon (1973).
8. Plato himself sets out the first recorded curriculum in Book VII of the *Republic*. Freud (1926) had proposed a broad program for training analysts. As Lacan (2007) describes, alongside psychiatry and sexology, we find 'the history of civilization, mythology, the psychology of religions, literary history, and literary criticism' (p. 238). But Lacan is keen to note, 'Nothing in any of the Institutes affiliated with his name has ever been sketched out in this direction' (pp. 395–396). Lacan's projected curriculum provides a valuable snapshot of his own ambitions as a teacher, even if it needs to be taken with a pinch of salt: 'For my part, I would be inclined to add: rhetoric, dialectic (in the technical sense this term takes on in Aristotle's *Topics*), grammar, and poetics – the supreme pinnacle of the aesthetics of language – which would include the neglected technique of witticisms' (p. 238).
9. It also instituted one area of Lacanian teaching remarkably passed over: patient presentations. See Lacan's recollection in *Seminar XIX* (1972/3), 4/11/71, I p. 47. Also Plastow (2011).
10. Socrates draws a square with sides of two feet and asks the boy to calculate how long the side of a square would be if it had twice the area. Socrates leads him, with questions alone, into recognizing that the larger square would have sides equal to the diagonal of the smaller square (Plato, *Meno*, 84c–85d).
11. In the *Gorgias*, they even propose that rhetoric creates truth itself, a pragmatic truth moulded from *doxa*, or the opinions of the people, through the process of debate.
12. Socrates uses this example in the lost dialogue by Aeschines, *Alcibiades*.
13. Plato uses this as an example of oratory in Gorgias, 455d and is critical in 515e.
14. Nietzsche (2003), V.190.
15. Guy Le Gaufey (1991) has examined how Lacanian psychoanalysis and Socratic philosophy vie for the prize of *atopia* in *Seminar VIII* (see Leonard, 2005). For a criticism of Lacan – and the influence of all this on his own 'anti-civic' mentality – see Leonard (2005). Nietzsche's Socrates can also be found in *The Birth of Tragedy; Human, All-Too-Human; Untimely Meditations*.
16. Freud (1937) admits *Beyond the Pleasure Principle* 'found little sympathy' (p. 244) and was not really accepted even by psychoanalysts.
17. The other two main texts under consideration, *Group Psychology and the Analysis of the Ego* (1921) and *The Ego and the Id* (1923), barely get ten mentions between them.
18. Lacan is, at times, happy to draw on ethology: it is from ethology that he draws the primacy of the 'image' as sexual trigger (e.g. 1988).
19. 'Just as medicine creates agreement in one area, music creates it in another, by implanting love and concord between the elements involved … you should gratify and promote the love of well-ordered people' (Plato, *Symposium*, 187c/d).
20. Again, Plato allows Lacan (2007) to distinguish repetition from reminiscence: 'And this is also why psychoanalysis allows us to differentiate in memory the function of remembering. The latter, rooted in the signifier, resolves the Platonic *aporias* of reminiscence through the ascendancy of history in man. One need but read *Three Essays on the Theory of Sexuality* – which is covered over for the masses by so many pseudo-biological glosses – to note that Freud has all accession to the object derive from a dialectic of return' (pp. 431–432).

21 Regarding the influence of Koyré, see Nobus (1999) and Koyré (1957): 'It is not Galileo, in any case, nor Bruno, but Descartes who clearly and distinctly formulated the principles of the new science' (p. 99). It is Gaston Bachelard who coins the idea of an epistemological break.
22 Guy Le Gaufey (1991) argues that when Lacan wrote his commentary on the *Symposium*, the *objet petit a* was still in its embryonic phase: Up to at least 1959, the concept unambiguously referred to 'the lower case other, the other of the imaginary.' But from the seminar on the *Transference* onwards, 'the *objet a* will begin to find the elaboration which we recognize in his later texts' (p. 168).
23 See Macey (1988, p. 277, n. 220). Darian Leader (2003) writes on Lacan's attempts to counter the apparent 'easiness' of the early mirror stage: reformulations of the mirror stage after the 1930s 'testify to his effort to undermine quick assimilations of his concepts' (p. 36).
24 Lacan (1991b) describes Kojève as solely responsible for introducing him to Hegel.
25 See Lacan's (2007) criticism of the *Standard Edition*'s 'instinct' for *Trieb* or, for example, his return to Freud's putative slogan, '*Wo Es war, soll Ich werden*' (discussed in chapter 4).
26 See, for example, Woudhuysen (1996) or, conversely, Marini (1992). Marini points to multiple evidence of concern, care and elaboration in preparing the papers for publication. She connects Lacan's desire to put things down in writing with a period of reflection (see 'The Freudian thing', 'Instance of the letter', 'Signification of the phallus').
27 Lacan also distorts the name of *Association psychanalytique internationnale* – from which he was essentially forced out in 1963 – to evoke the Communist Internationale.
28 Of relevance to our concerns here is Lacan's helping to set up the review. The Latin adverbial *Scilicet* (*scire licet*) means 'it goes without saying'; Lacan translated it, as he stated in the first issue of the review, as 'You are permitted to know.' Texts published in *Scilicet* were to be unsigned, 'at least by anybody who would publish as a psychoanalyst'. The no-signature rule appeared to Lacan (2001) as 'a radical solution … the right one to disentangle the contortions by which in psychoanalysis experience is forced to reject anything that might change it' (pp. 283–292). See Sedat, 2005.
29 Lacan originally felt Miller should be listed as co-author. For the facts of publishing and biographical disputes, see Weslati (2013) and Forrester (1990).
30 Again, with a helping hand from Nietzsche (2003), who wrote that he had questioned 'Plato's concealment and Sphinx nature' as a result of the tradition that reported the finding of 'nothing Egyptian, Pythagorean or Platonic' but a volume of the comic playwright Aristophanes under Plato's pillow at his death (VI.2.43).
31 In 1925, the number of students attending Lacan's seminars was 25; in 1963 there were 500 attendees; by the mid-1970s, nearing 1,000 (see Forrester, 1990).
32 Lacanian-trained analysts set up a department of psychoanalysis at the University of Vincennes. Lacan became its scientific director in 1974.

References

Alenka, Y. (1987) 'Alexandre Koyré: Between the history of ideas and sociology of knowledge', *History and Technology*, vol. 4, pp. 115–148.
Aristotle, *Poetics*, trans. Malcolm Heath (1996), St Ives, Penguin.
Badiou, A. (2006) 'Lacan and the Pre-Socratics', in Žižek, S. (ed.) *Lacan: The Silent Partners*, London, Verso, pp. 7–16.

Badiou, A. (2008) *Conditions*, New York, Continuum.
Bailly, L. (2009) *Lacan: A Beginner's Guide*, Oxford, Oneworld.
Barnes, J. (1995) *Cambridge Companion to Aristotle*, Cambridge, Cambridge University Press.
Burgoyne, B. (2001) 'Freud's Socrates', *European Journal of Psychotherapy*, vol. 4, no. 1, pp.159–165
Clément, C. (1983) *The Lives and Legends of Jacques Lacan* (trans. A. Goldhammer), New York, Columbia University Press.
de Beauvoir, S. (1949) *Le Deuxième Sexe*, Paris, Gallimard.
Drury, S. B. (1994) *Alexandre Kojève: The Roots of Postmodern Politics*, New York, St Martin's Press.
Fanon, F. (1952) *Black Skin, White Masks*, Paris, Éditions du Seuil.
Fink, B. (1995) 'Science and psychoanalysis', in Fink, B., Feldstein, R. and Jaanus, M. (eds) *Reading Seminar XI: Lacan's Four Fundamental Concepts of Psychoanalysis*, Albany, SUNY Press, pp. 55–64.
Forrester, J. (1990) *The Seductions of Psychoanalysis: Freud, Lacan and Derrida*, Cambridge, Cambridge University Press.
Freud, S. (1905) *Three Essays on the Theory of Sexuality*, in Strachey, J. (ed.) *The Standard Edition of the Complete Psychological Works of Sigmund Freud*, vol. 7, London, Hogarth Press, pp. 125–323.
Freud, S. (1921) *Group Psychology and the Analysis of the Ego*, in Strachey, J. (ed.) *The Standard Edition of the Complete Psychological Works of Sigmund Freud*, vol. 18, London, Hogarth Press, pp. 65–143.
Freud, S. (1923) *The Ego and the Id*, in Strachey, J. (ed.) *The Standard Edition of the Complete Psychological Works of Sigmund Freud*, vol. 19, London, Hogarth Press, pp. 3–67.
Freud, S. (1926) *The Question of Lay Analysis*, in Strachey, J. (ed.) *The Standard Edition of the Complete Psychological Works of Sigmund Freud*, vol. 20, London, Hogarth Press, pp. 179–258.
Freud, S. (1937) *Analysis Terminable and Interminable*, in Strachey, J. (ed.) *The Standard Edition of the Complete Psychological Works of Sigmund Freud*, vol. 23, London, Hogarth Press, pp. 209–254
Georgiades, P. (1934) *De Freud à Platon*, Paris, Fasquelle.
Gerasimos, S. (1988) *Plato Freud: Two Theories of Love*, London, Wiley-Blackwell.
Goldwag, A. (2007) *'Isms & 'Ologies: All the Movements, Ideologies and Doctrines That Have Shaped Our World*, New York, Vintage.
Guthrie, W. K. C. (1968) *The Greek Philosophers: From Thales to Aristotle*, London, Routledge.
Hadot, P. (1995) *Philosophy as a Way of Life: Spiritual Exercises from Socrates to Foucault*, London, Wiley-Blackwell.
Hartmann, H. (1958) *Ego Psychology and the Problem of Adaptation* (trans. D. Rapport), New York, International Universities Press.
Hegel, G. W. F. (1974) *Lectures on the History of Philosophy, I* (trans. E. S. Haldane and F. H. Simpson), London, Routledge & Kegan Paul.
Johnson, W. A. (1998) 'Dramatic frame and philosophical idea in Plato', *American Journal of Philology*, vol. 119, no. 4, pp. 577–598.
Kofman, S. (1999) 'Mirror and oneiric mirages: Plato, precursor of Freud', *Harvard Review of Philosophy*, vol. 7, no 1, pp. 4–14.
Koyré, A. (1943) 'Galileo and Plato', *Journal of the History of Ideas*, vol. 4, no. 4, pp. 400–428.
Koyré, A. (1945) *Discovering Plato*, New York, Columbia University Press.
Koyré, A. (1950) *The Significance of the Newtonian Synthesis*, Chicago, University of Chicago Press.

Koyré, A. (1957), *From the Closed World to the Infinite Universe*, Baltimore, John Hopkins University Press.
Lacan, J. (1973) 'L'étourdit', *Scilicet*, vol. 4, pp. 5–52.
Lacan, J. (1977) *Seminar XI: The Four Fundamental Concepts of Psychoanalysis* (ed. J.-A. Miller, trans. A. Sheridan), London, Penguin.
Lacan, J. (1988) *Seminar I: Freud's Papers on Technique (1953–1954)* (ed. J.-A. Miller, trans. J. Forrester), Cambridge, Cambridge University Press.
Lacan, J. (1991a) *Seminar II: The Ego in Freud's Theory and in the Technique of Psychoanalysis* (ed. J.-A. Miller, trans. J. Forrester), New York, Norton.
Lacan, J. (1991b) *Seminar XVII: The Other Side of Psychoanalysis* (ed. J.-A. Miller, trans. R. Grigg), New York, Norton.
Lacan, J. (1998) *Seminar XX: Encore – On Feminine Sexuality: The Limits of Love and Knowledge* (ed. J.-A. Miller, trans. B. Fink), New York, Norton.
Lacan, J. (2001) *Autres Écrits*, Paris, Seuil.
Lacan, J. (2007) *Écrits: The First Complete Edition in English* (trans. B. Fink), New York, Norton.
Lacan, J. (2009) 'L'étourdit: A bilingual presentation of the first turn' (trans. *Cormac Gallagher)*, The Letter: Irish Journal for Lacanian Psychoanalys, vol. 41, pp. 31–80.
Lacan, J. (2015) *Seminar VIII: Transference* (ed. J.-A. Miller, trans. Bruce Fink), London, Polity Press.
Lacan, J., *Seminar XIX: The Knowledge of the Psychoanalyst* (unpublished) [online]. Available at www.valas.fr/IMG/pdf/THE-SEMINAR-OF-JACQUES-LACAN-XIXa_le_savoir_du_P.pdf (accessed 29/08/2015).
Laplanche, J. and Pontalis, J.-B. (1974) *The Language of Psycho-Analysis* (trans. D. Nicholson-Smith), New York, Norton.
Leader, D. (2003) 'Lacan's myths', in Rabaté, J.-M. (ed.) *The Cambridge Companion to Lacan*, Cambridge, Cambridge University Press, pp. 35–49.
Le Gaufey, G. (1991) *L'incomplétude du symbolique*, Paris, EPEL.
Leonard, M. (2005) *Athens in Paris: Ancient Greece and the Political in Post-War French Thought*, Oxford, Oxford University Press.
Macey, D. (1988) *Lacan in Contexts*, London, Verso.
Marini, M. (1992) *Jacques Lacan: The French Context* (trans. A. Tomiche), Piscataway, Rutgers University Press.
Miller, J.-A. (1985) *Libération*, December 14–15.
Miller, J.-A. (1996) *Reading Seminars I and II*, Albany, SUNY Press.
Miller, J.-A. (2001) 'Lacan's nightingale' (trans. Gary Marshall), *International Lacanian Review* [online]. Available at www.lacan.com/jamnigh.htm (accessed 27/08/2015).
Minsky, R. (1996) *Psychoanalysis and Gender: An Introductory Reader*, London, Routledge.
Nachmansohn, M. (1915) 'Freuds Libidotheorie verglichen mit der Eroslehre Platos', *Internationale Zeitschrift für Psychoanalyse*, vol. 3, pp. 65–83.
Nietzsche, Friedrich (2003) *Beyond Good and Evil* (trans. R. J. Hollingdale), London, Penguin.
Nobus, D. (1999) *Key Concepts of Lacanian Psychoanalysis*, New York, Other Press.
Nussbaum, M. C. (1986) *The Fragility of Goodness: Luck and Ethics in Greek Tragedy and Philosophy*, Cambridge, Cambridge University Press.
Pfister, O. (1921) 'Plato: A fore-runner of psycho-analysis', *International Journal of Psychoanalysis*, vol. 3, pp. 169–174.
Plastow, M. (2011) 'The presentation of patients and the question of structure' [online]. Available at www.fsom.org.au/images/Ecritique%20PDFs%202011/Michael%20Plastow%20Presentation%20of%20Patients%20TWFinal.pdf (accessed 17/8/2015).
Plato, *Euthyphro, Apology, Crito, Phaedo, Phaedrus*, trans. H. N. Fowler (1999), Cambridge, MA, Harvard University Press.

Plato, *Laches, Protagoras, Meno*, trans. W. R. M. Lamb (1989), Cambridge, MA, Harvard University Press.

Plato, *Lysias, Symposium, Gorgias*, trans. W. R. M. Lamb (1989), Cambridge, MA, Harvard University Press.

Plato, *Theaetetus, Sophist*, trans. H. N. Fowler (1921), Cambridge, MA, Harvard University Press.

Plutarch, *Greek Lives*, trans. R. Waterfield (2008) Oxford, Oxford World Classics.

Rapaport, D. (1960) *The Structure of Psychoanalytic Theory: A Systematic Attempt*, New York, International Universities Press.

Roudinesco, E. (1997) *Jacques Lacan* (trans. B. Bray), New York, Columbia University Press.

Roudinesco, E. (2014) *Lacan: In Spite of Everything* (trans. G. Elliot), London, Verso.

Sedat, J. (2005) 'Scilicet', in Alain de Mijolla (ed.) *International Dictionary of Psychoanalysis*, New York, Macmillan.

Simon, B. (1973) 'Plato and Freud: The mind in conflict and the mind in dialogue', *Psychoanalytic Quarterly*, vol. 42, pp. 91–122

Webster, R. (2002) 'The cult of Lacan: Freud, Lacan and the mirror stage' [online]. Available at www.richardwebster.net/thecultoflacan.html (accessed 25/08/2015).

Weslati, H. (2013) 'Héritage Lacan: Le jour ou Jacques Alain Miller a déclaré la guerre' [online]. Available at http://criticallegalthinking.com/2013/05/06/the-lacanian-trials/ (accessed 03/07/2014).

Woudhuysen, H. R. (1996) *Sir Philip Sidney and the Circulation of Manuscripts*, Oxford, Oxford University Press.

2
THE MYTH OF SEXUAL REPRODUCTION

> In quite a different region, it is true, we *do* meet with such a hypothesis; but it is of so fantastic a kind – a myth rather than a scientific explanation – that I should not venture to produce it here, were it not that it fulfils precisely the one condition whose fulfilment we desire ....
>   What I have in mind is, of course, the theory which Plato puts into the mouth of Aristophanes in the *Symposium*.
> *Sigmund Freud (1920, p. 57)*

> I will take the liberty of setting a myth before you ... It is to be what is put into the mouth of Aristophanes .... This fable is a defiance to the centuries, for it traverses them without anyone trying to do better. I shall try ....
> *Jacques Lacan (1977, p. 197)*

Introduction

What does it mean to use a myth as a 'hypothesis?' Or, more broadly, how can a story that is, by definition, untrue contain 'truths' that demand it be retold over the centuries? Aristophanes is one of the six characters in Plato's *Symposium* invited to speak on love. He recounts a myth about love's origin, and Freud and Lacan are not alone in turning to it to convey lessons about human attachment. Freud (1920) gives an economical précis of this myth, according to which love is bound to the original nature of our ancestors:

> Everything about these primeval men was double: they had four hands and four feet, two faces, two privy parts, and so on. Eventually Zeus

decided to cut these men in two, 'like a sorb-apple which is halved for pickling.' After the division had been made, 'the two parts of man, each desiring his other half, came together, and threw their arms about one another eager to grow into one.'

(pp. 57–58)

Such is the origin of love, according to Aristophanes. The myth surfaces at several significant moments in the work of both Freud and Lacan. Its first appearance in psychoanalytic literature is in the *Three Essays*, but Freud returns to it in *Beyond the Pleasure Principle*. The changes in his use of the myth between these two works reflect his struggle to provide a new logic for sexual desire once his notion of an abstract libido has uncoupled sexuality from assumptions about natural harmony or growth. The truth value of psychoanalysis itself is at stake, hence the categories of 'science' and 'myth' have personal and professional significance. Lacan returns to the role that Aristophanes' myth plays in Freud's work, but also to the role it plays in the source text: Plato's *Symposium*. Plato provides Lacan with a means of approaching the philosophical questions underlying Freud's struggle. These concern not just the value of myth, but a disturbing uncertainty regarding sexual reproduction itself.

This is the uncertainty alluded to in this chapter's title. To ask how natural sex is may seem bizarre, but it is a question at the heart of Freud's exertions. In addition to the complications introduced by a libido that can attach to anyone or anything, sexual reproduction – the notion of being created by two parents – originally proves a greater challenge to the imagination than more straightforward ideas of autochthony, emerging self-formed from nature; Freud's theories of infantile development place the mystery of where babies come from at the foundation of our epistemic impulse (see Freud, 1905). And if *asexual* reproduction is a more intuitive, comfortable idea, this may be for a further reason, for as Freud, Lacan and Plato all seek to demonstrate in their own ways, it is sexual reproduction that brings with it mortality. These are the relationships – of individuals and ideas – that this chapter explores.

Freud's use of Aristophanes' myth

The problem with sex

To understand the meaning that Aristophanes' myth held for Freud and its significance as a conclusion to *Beyond the Pleasure Principle*, it is necessary to trace its presence from the start of his career. It arises at moments when Freud is concerned about the nature of the forces psychoanalysis is dealing with, conscious of the implications they have for the intellectual status of his theory. The first published reference to the myth in Freud's work occurs in the landmark *Three Essays on the Theory of Sexuality* (1905). In these essays, Freud sets out, for the first time, the concept of libido and the development of the sexual instinct in human beings from infancy to maturity. Libido is Freud's attempt to place psychoanalysis on a scientific footing.[1] It is an abstract force, present in us from birth, the displacement of which by various events can provide us with an explanation of our eventual sexuality and our psychological make up more broadly. In his striving for scientific rigor, Freud unshackles human sexuality from any supposedly 'natural' logic. He accepts this happily. 'Popular opinion has quite definite ideas about the nature and characteristics of this sexual instinct', the *Three Essays* continues. It is supposed to be absent in childhood, and its aim, when it arises, is sexual union.

> The *popular* view of the sexual instinct is beautifully reflected in the poetic fable which tells how the original human beings were cut up into two halves – man and woman – and how these are always striving to unite again in love.
>
> (p. 46)

Here, Aristophanes' 'poetic fable' is to be a foil for the brand new ideas of psychoanalysis. It reflects the 'popular' view, reminiscent of folk psychology, set against a *science* of the libido.

Freud presents it as an anonymous 'fable' (*poetische Fabel*). The 'love' it mythologizes is emphatically heterosexual, allowing Freud to continue: 'It comes as a great surprise therefore to learn that there are men whose sexual object is a man and not a woman, and women whose sexual object is a woman and not a man' (p. 46). How is this possible? A theory of polymorphous libido will explain, providing a rationale for distinguishing between the biological '*aims*' of sexuality and the strange 'objects' we choose (Freud reminds us that even kissing, for example, is not logically connected to sex but arises from the pleasurable stimulation of mucous membranes associated originally with eating). Libido can be displaced, repressed and dammed up. Crucially, these processes can then be analysed. The comforting Aristophanic 'fable' is a straw man. Like Lacan in the previous chapter, Freud is willing, even eager, to frame psychoanalysis as counterintuitive.

Yet this popular view of the myth does not reflect Plato so much as a tradition of *misreading* Plato. In the version of the myth written by Plato himself, the original, double-bodied humans come in three *different* combinations: male–male, male–female, and female–female (*Symposium*, 189d). The sexual inclinations of these creatures, post-split, reflect their original pairing, placing the 'heterosexual' pairing in a minority.

If it is a foundation myth, then it records the foundation of homosexuality: Aristophanes himself draws attention to the fact that the myth explains the occurrence of same-sex desire.[2] And, of course, the *Symposium* has a special place in the history of defences of homosexuality (and of criticisms of homosexuality) (Gill, 1999, p. xxi).[3] So why does Freud, as we've seen, at the opening of the *Three Essays*, pick an argument with Aristophanes' myth? A reference in Henri Ellenberger's (1981) monumental account of Freud's intellectual background provides a clue.

Ellenberger, in seeking to understand the tensions between Freud's scientific ambitions and his cultural background, emphasizes the significance of *Naturphilosophie*, a blending of Romantic philosophy and science that was dominant in Germany through the first half of the nineteenth century. Though its roots lie in the writings of Goethe, it was first formulated as a system by Friedrich Wilhelm von Schelling. *Naturphilosophie* contended that nature and spirit both sprang from one source, the *Weltseele* or world-soul (tellingly, Schelling's philosophy of nature emerges from his studies of Plato, in particular the *Timaeus*; see Grant, 2006; Sallis, 1999). Ellenberger (1981) notes two features of *Naturphilosophie* that will resurface in Freudian psychoanalysis: a vision of nature as the conflict of a positive and a negative force, and the significance of 'primordial phenomena', the original forms from which later life has metamorphosed. Of these, he gives two examples: the *Urpflanze*, a model for all plants, and the myth of the Androgyne:

> In his *Symposium*, Plato had told in a figurative sense that the primordial human being possessed both sexes, which had later become separated from each other by Zeus and that, ever since, man and woman were searching for each other in an effort to reunite. This myth, taken over by Boehme, Baader, and others was well suited to express the Romantic idea of the fundamental bisexuality of the human being, and it was elaborated in many ways by the Romantics.
>
> *(pp. 202–203)*

Ellenberger also neglects the same-sex pairs found in the original version. The presence of German theologian Franz von Baader and the Christian mystic who greatly influenced him, Jakob Boehme, suggests we have moved on from Plato's pagan and homoerotic symposium. Baader is in fact the conduit through which the works of Boehme became known to Schelling and other Romantic philosophers. He also believed he had discovered the foundation of love, but where Freud looked to infancy, Baader sited it in God. So this is a 'fundamental bisexuality' that unambiguously underpins heterosexuality, a distinctly Christian Neoplatonism associated with romantic, heterosexual union. (Interestingly, while the *Three Essays* contains Freud's first *published* allusion to Aristophanes' myth, there is another in a love letter from Freud to his betrothed illustrating the intensity of his longing for union with her; Jones, 1953.)[4]

In the nineteenth century, a Romantic desire for synthesis, alongside a renewal of interest in Boehme and the philosopher Paracelsus, drew attention back to the figure of the Androgyne. Raymond Furness (1965) traces androgyny as a symbol of perfection and harmony from the Presocratics and Pythagoreans, through German mysticism to three Austrian writers very much in Freud's milieu: Robert Musil, Georg Trakl and Rainer Maria Rilke. But Freud is set against an all-encompassing synthesis achieved at the expense of analytical thinking (i.e. classification and examination). Freud associates *Naturphilosophie* as much with a style of pseudo-investigation as with any particular content. Jones (1953) captures this in his own description:

> *Naturphilosophie* is the name of the pantheistic monism, close to mysticism ... [which] was eagerly accepted by the average educated man and literary lady. The Universe, Nature, is one vast organism .... What characterized the German *Naturphilosophie* is the aspiration expressed in the name 'speculative physics' (which Schelling himself gave to his endeavors) and the unbalanced megalomaniac emotionalism of the phantasy and style of these writers. An English philosopher puts it thus: 'They exhibit tendencies that seem foreign to the course of European thought; they recall the vague spaciousness of the East and its reflection in the semi-oriental Alexandria.'
>
> *(p. 47)*

The damning description, 'eagerly accepted by the average educated man and literary lady', is reminiscent of those who swallowed the 'popular fables' in Freud's account, finding them familiar and pleasing. 'Monism', 'mysticism' and the 'East' are all rocks Freud will spend his career trying to avoid. The concept of libido is intended to align psychoanalysis with the counter-tradition symbolized by the Institute of Physiology in Vienna in which Freud began his medical career as a neurologist (1876–82) under the iconic figures of Ernst Brücke and Emil Du Bois-Reymond. In the words of Du Bois-Reymond:

> Brücke and I pledged a solemn oath to put into effect this truth: No other forces than the common physical and chemical ones are active within the organism. In those cases which cannot at the time be explained by these forces one has either to find the specific way or form of their action by means of the physical-mathematical method or to assume new forces equal in dignity to the chemical-physical forces inherent in matter, reducible to the force of attraction and repulsion.
>
> *(Jones, 1953, p. 45)*

Freud's values reflect the areas of research in which pioneering discoveries were being made, often of physical forces that came to replace the speculative forces of Romantic philosophy. The mid-nineteenth century saw the introduction of a general concept of 'energy' itself, a term not previously used in physics, taking over concepts such as the seventeenth-century *vis viva* ('living force').[5] Other advances included Michael Faraday's research into electromagnetism in the 1820s, and Du Bois-Reymond himself pioneered research into the electrical properties of biological cells and tissues. So it is natural that when Freud first attempts to formulate psychoanalysis, he uses purely neurological terms. This is the early work preserved in the unpublished *Project for a Scientific Psychology* (1895). In this, he introduces 'Q' as the physical–mathematical term for a general nerve-force. It is, according to Freud,

> a quantity – although we possess no means of measuring it – a something which is capable of increase, decrease, displacement and discharge …. We can apply this hypothesis in the same sense as the physicist employs the concept of a fluid electric current.
>
> *(1894, p. 60)*

The editors of the *Standard Edition* reject any literal interpretation, however, claiming that Freud 'repeatedly emphasizes the fact that the nature of "neuronal motion" is unknown to us' (1895, p. 393). We are already between science and speculation.

The libido of the *Three Essays* allows Freud to preserve his desire to ground his theory in a physical force, but Freud has now embarked on a new type of investigation and a new direction of study, looking historically back to infancy in his quest to understand our psychology. The libido's fragile intellectual position, involved in explanations that are at once biological and historical, explains the importance of distancing it from the popular 'fable' of the Androgyne: to re-emphasize its *abstract* element. No attraction will now be seen as innate; there is no mythical logic to sexuality (i.e. the propagation of life; harmony of the sexes). Yet this libido, as a singular force with which to explain all, brings with it its own threat to the scientism of psychoanalysis. Monism and mysticism threaten to return by the back door. Aristophanes' tale of Eros, which seemed quaint alongside the abstract libido, will be pressed into very different service as Freud struggles to avoid letting his theory collapse back into notions of the world spirit. It is this struggle that will culminate in *Beyond the Pleasure Principle*.

The dangers of Eros

Association with a Platonic conception of Eros initially appeals to Freud. He mentions it in a combative 1920 preface to the *Three Essays*, citing an essay by his pupil Max Nachmansohn, noting the failure of popular opinion to embrace psychoanalytic theory as a whole, particularly 'that part of the theory … which lies *on the frontiers of biology* (i.e. the libido).' In his defence, Freud (1905) claims the intellectual precedent of Schopenhauer and then Plato: 'Anyone who looks down with contempt upon psychoanalysis from a superior vantage-point should remember how closely the enlarged sexuality of psychoanalysis coincides with the Eros of the divine Plato (cf. Nachmansohn, 1915)' (p. 42).[6] This is the first time Freud himself makes an explicit comparison between his own theories and those of Plato. Subsequently, in *Group Psychology and the Analysis of the Ego*, Freud (1921) writes: 'Yet [psychoanalysis] has done nothing original in taking love in this "wider" sense. In its origin, function and relation to sexual love, the "Eros" of the philosopher Plato coincides exactly with the love-force, the libido of psychoanalysis' (p. 91). At this stage, Freud is still placing Eros in quotation marks. He resists incorporating it thoughtlessly, unscientifically: 'one gives way first in words, and then little by little in substance too' (p. 91). But it will prove his undoing nonetheless.

Graham Frankland (2006) traces the transformation of Eros in Freud's work, from being no more than a classical prop to a vastly expanded role: a concept that, by the mid-1920s, threatens to overwhelm his sexual theory entirely. The problem is that Eros can seem a cool, bland thing compared to the libido. It is this asexual element that is most threatening. A clue to dangers ahead can be heard in Freud's first use of the term, in his study of Leonardo da Vinci (1910). Here, Eros is 'the preserver of all living things', and Freud wonders that it was not 'worthy material for [daVinci] in his pursuit of knowledge' (pp. 69–70). Already, in 'preserver of all living things', there is an element of stasis and harmony that will not sit easily with the libido as *drive*.[7] But it is the conjunction of a self-preserving Eros with another classical reference, Narcissus, that makes the problem critical.

Narcissus also has a widening domain in Freud's work. Mentioned in passing in *Leonardo da Vinci* (as Freud equates homosexuality and auto-erotism), by the 1915 addition to the *Three Essays* narcissism has come to define the original state of the ego itself: narcissistic or ego-libido is 'the great reservoir from which the object-cathexes are sent out and into which they are withdrawn once more'; this self-enclosed libidinous ego 'is the original state of things' (1905 [2015 edn], pp. 139–140). Self-love precedes attraction to objects. Perhaps sensing that this inherent narcissism is a problematic model of man – divorcing him from healthy, outreaching sexuality altogether – Freud turns to ideas of self-preservation again: 'Narcissism in this sense would not be a perversion, but the libidinal complement to the egoism of the instinct of self-preservation, a measure of which may justifiably be attributed to every living creature' (1914, p. 73–74). And, as evidence, Freud describes 'the efforts of Eros to combine organic substances into ever larger unities' (i.e. building life) (pp. 42–43); 'Eros, which holds together everything in the world', as he puts it a year later (1921, p. 92). This conception now combines Plato's Eros with the evolutionary theories of Herbert Spencer (1820–1903), who applied the principles at a cosmic level, seeing all structures in the universe developing from states of simple, undifferentiated homogeneity towards complex, differentiated heterogeneity.[8]

But, as a result of all this, a supplementary question has begun to trouble Freud: why do creatures use sexual reproduction at all? Or, to put the question in relation to human psychology as he is formulating it, why does the mental apparatus, which 'above all [is] a device for mastering excitations' (1895, p. 42), abandon the safe realms of narcissism and begin attaching sexual desire to external objects (see Kochhar-Lindgren, 1993)? Freud draws his response from an idea he had explored in the early *Project*, suggesting that 'damned-up' libido causes pain, and that pain must be relieved by a redistribution of the sexualized energy. Desire is an overflow of this energy.

And by 1910 he has introduced the concept of the Oedipus complex to account for the process by which libido gets directed outwards. Ideal development involves the dispersion of initially narcissistic libido via the Oedipal triangle (see Freud, 1914; Kochhar-Lindgren, 1993).

Narcissus is implicitly opposed to Oedipus in Ovid's original telling of the myth. He appears within Ovid's account of Thebes in the *Metamorphoses*, precisely where we might expect to find Oedipus himself (Oedipus is mysteriously absent). Several artfully constructed parallels between the two figures indicate that this is not a coincidence, although Ovid's motivation remains unclear. Yet there is something more than arbitrary about this substitution, and Ovid's thought-provoking sleight of hand haunts Freud two thousand years later. They represent two opposed instincts, one towards the same, one towards what is different. And it is not just in relation to sexual theory that Narcissus's regressive nature poses a threat: the two figures present different models of thought as well. Freud associates narcissism with forms of primitive magical thinking by which our beliefs subsume reality rather than take full account of it: 'the now established omnipotence of thought among primitive races [is] a proof of their narcissism' (1913, p. 75).[9] Freud compares 'the evolutionary stages of man's conception of the universe with stages of the libidinous evolution of the individual' (p. 76). As such, 'the scientific stage has its full counterpart in the individual's stage of maturity where … he seeks his object in the outer world'. In the former category, the 'primitive', Freud places *Naturphilosophie* itself, due to its belief in souls – in common with primitive animism.

So the distinct, sexual nature of the libido is key to the integrity of psychoanalysis for multiple reasons. But a question arises:

> If the self-preservative instincts too are of a libidinal nature, are there perhaps no other instincts whatever but the libidinal ones? At all events there are none other visible. But in that case we shall after all be driven to agree with the critics who suspected from the first that psycho-analysis explains *everything* by sexuality, or with innovators like Jung who, making a hasty judgment, have used the word 'libido' to mean instinctual force in general.
>
> (Freud, 1920, p. 52)

For Freud, the dangers of *Naturphilosophie* were bound to his concerns about Jung's innovations. This is the final ingredient in the knot of anxieties out of which *Beyond the Pleasure Principle* emerges, a knot involving the universal Eros and the intellectual status of psychoanalysis itself. The theoretical crisis that leads to Freud's essay is precipitated by the appearance of Jung's *Transformations and Symbols of the Libido* (1912–13). In this work, Jung expands the libido concept until it fills the universe itself, calling upon ancient myths in defence of his theory:

> I would remind the reader of the cosmogenic significance of Eros in Hesiod, and also of the Orphic figure of Phanes, the Shining One, the First-Created, the 'Father of Eros.' Orphically, too, he has the significance of Priapus; he is bisexual and equated with the Theban Dionysus Lysius. The Orphic significance of Phanes is akin to that of the Indian Kama, the god of love, who is likewise a cosmogenic principle.
>
> (Jung, 1991, pp. 137–138)

Eros is not just a cosmic force here, but an origin – an original harmony incorporating the sexual harmony of the Androgyne – and also, muddily, a principle of love and activity.[10] The legacy of *Naturphilosophie* is unambiguous. Like his early nineteenth-century predecessors, Jung presents an unapologetically Romantic synthesis, steeped in Eastern mysticism. It is founded on anthropology rather than science. Final evidence that it is these associations, as much as any theoretical issues, that underlies Freud's deep anxieties over a monistic libido, his insistence that sex equals science, is provided by Jung himself in his autobiography:

> I can still recall vividly how Freud said to me, 'My dear Jung, promise me never to abandon the sexual theory. That is the most essential thing of all. You see, we must make a dogma of it, an unshakeable bulwark.' He said that to me with great emotion, in the tone of a father saying, 'And promise me this one thing, my dear son: that you will go to church every Sunday.' In some astonishment I asked him, 'A bulwark – against what?' To which he replied, 'Against the black tide of mud' – and here he hesitated for a moment, then added, 'of occultism.'
>
> (Sulloway, 1992, p. 362)

Beyond the Pleasure Principle: Freud's mythic-molecular vision

> I take a walk in the evening at 6:30, my hands stained from the white and red blood of the sea animals, and in front of my eyes the glimmering debris

of cells, which still disturb me in my dreams, and in my mind nothing but the big problems connected with the names of testicles and ovaries – universally significant names.

Letter from Freud to Eduard Silberstein, April 5, 1876
(Boehlich, 1989, p. 158)

Beyond the Pleasure Principle (1920) is Freud's final attempt at maintaining a treasured *dualism* of forces within human life as opposed to the single, universal spirit described by Jung and his Romantic predecessors. It is here that Eros is set against an opposed but equally fundamental 'death drive'.[11] On one hand, the essay is Freud's most self-consciously speculative work, but it is also his deepest delving into the realms of molecular and evolutionary biology, a return to the researches of his youth, referred to in the letter to his friend Eduard Silberstein above.

In 1874, a young Freud had been sent to Trieste by his teacher, the zoologist Carl Claus, to dissect marine life: his mission – to discover whether eels are sexed, whether they reproduce sexually or asexually (Reidel-Schrewe, 1994). It is a question dating back to what R. J. Hankinson (1995) describes as 'perhaps Aristotle's most influential mistake' when, in his *History of Animals*, he claims that some creatures do not reproduce themselves at all but are rather perpetuated when fortuitous material circumstances occur – and gave as an example eels arising from mud. Uncertainty over the eel persisted into the nineteenth century. Freud's research, which will become 'Observations on the configuration and finer structure of the lobed organs in eels described as testes' (his first publication) in the Proceedings of the Imperial Academy of Sciences in Vienna (1877), constitutes a significant contribution to the debate. Providing evidence that the eel was bisexual, it would have been very much in line with another theory of androgyny, one more likely to appeal to Freud: Darwin's own idea of the 'descent of man' from hermaphroditic or androgynous origins.

Reidel-Schrewe (1994) observes that most scholarship on Freud's intellectual background emphasizes the neurological component of his pre-psychoanalytic days, research completed after his medical degree was obtained in 1881, rather than the early zoological studies. But Freud recalled his six years working under Brücke as the most rewarding of his early life. And the questions to which he was seeking answers on a biological level linger well into the next century. *Beyond the Pleasure Principle* (1920) is notorious for its tangents, convolutions, collisions and its premise. I suggest this is, in part, because there are at least two different levels of questioning at work in the essay. The question most immediately provoking Freud's speculations is, as we've seen in the chapter above: why do we repeat unpleasant things? Freud posits a *repetition* compulsion beyond the pleasure principle. He then extends this force until it concerns not just repetition but a more general, anti-libidinous instinct to *return*. It is in this way that a new dualism arises: the outreaching life drive versus a backwards-reaching death drive. The stated challenge of *Beyond the Pleasure Principle* is to see whether this apparently paradoxical and distinctly mythopoeic impulse back towards the inanimate – towards death – can be rendered scientific. But lingering beneath this is the old conundrum of sexual reproduction and its opposition to a more intuitive vision of autochthony.

One recent discovery in this area is of particular fascination to Freud: meiosis. Meiosis is the type of cell division by which eggs and sperm are produced. Here, of course, we are drawing close to an actual origin, that of sexual reproduction. And, in so far as death is a property of sexed creatures, to an origin of death itself. This is a valuable context with which to understand *Beyond the Pleasure Principle* and its use of Aristophanes' myth: the biology of Freud's time and advances in Germany in particular. It was in the second half of the nineteenth century that the mechanisms of cell division began to be understood. Eduard Strasburger, Walther Flemming, Heinrich von Waldeyer and the Belgian Edouard Van Beneden laid the basis for cytology (the study of cells) and for cytogenetics, the branch of genetics concerned with the cell. Strasburger coined the terms 'nucleus' and 'cytoplasm'. Van Beneden discovered how chromosomes combined during the production of gametes, those cells that fuse with another cell during fertilization. Meiosis was discovered and described for the first time in 1876 and described at the level of chromosomes by Van Beneden in 1883. But it wasn't until 1890 that the significance of meiosis for reproduction and inheritance was explained by the German evolutionary biologist, August Weismann (1834–1914). It is the figure of Weismann who looms large in *Beyond the Pleasure Principle*, seeming to point a way through the darkness.

Freud begins chapter 6 of *Beyond the Pleasure Principle* with a summary of Weismann's work on the immortality of germ plasm:

> The greatest interest attaches from our point of view ... to the writings of Weismann. It was he who introduced the division of living substance into mortal and immortal parts. The mortal part is the body in the narrower sense – the 'soma' – which alone is subject to natural death. The germ-cells, on the other hand, are potentially immortal, in

so far as they are able ... to develop into a new individual, or, in other words, to surround themselves with a new soma.

(1920, pp. 45–46)

The germ plasm theory Freud describes was Weismann's greatest contribution to biology. It states that inheritance of characteristics only takes place by means of the germ cells (gametes such as egg cells and sperm cells). Other cells of the body, somatic cells, play no part in heredity. The implication of this is termed the 'Weismann barrier': there can be no inheritance of characteristics acquired during a parent's life. Nothing 'learned' in the body is passed on, contrary to the theory that had been proposed by Jean-Baptiste Lamarck (1815–1822) (Lamarck also believed that organisms progressed up an evolutionary 'ladder', the simplest organisms arising via spontaneous generation). This is, of course, a crucial step towards the modern study of genetics. The aspect of the theory that interests Freud, however, involves the splitting of the self into mortal and immortal parts. Weismann's lecture, 'The duration of life', delivered in 1881, argued that unicellular organisms that reproduced by splitting in two could not be said to die.

> I am well aware that the life of the individual is generally believed to come to an end with the division that gives rise to two new individuals, as if death and reproduction were the same thing. But this process cannot be truly called death. Where is the dead body? What is it that dies? Nothing dies; the body of the animal only divides into two similar parts.
>
> *(1889, p. 25)*

The implication, as Weismann noted in 1889, is that among unicellular organisms that reproduced by splitting 'death and reproduction were the same thing' (Small and Tate, 2003, p. 129).[12] In *Beyond the Pleasure Principle*, Freud first seems to agree with Weismann, but this doesn't quite fit Freud's argument for a fundamental death drive. Indeed, in the context of evolutionary history, it implies that death is a relatively recent invention, not inherent at all. Freud turns to Protozoa for evidence of a fundamental death drive, one that might precede sexual reproduction. He uses the definition of death supplied by German biologist Max Hartmann, death as the 'definitive end of individual development':

> In this sense protozoa are also subject to death; with them death invariably coincides with propagation, but it is, so to speak, disguised

by the latter, for the whole substance of the parent organism may be absorbed directly into the new individuals.

(1920, p. 47)

Death and reproduction are one. As a result of this, the dualism needs to be recast once again, no longer opposing life and death but the mortal and the immortal. Science has its own realm of the immortal: autochthonous, self-reproducing life. This can be found within us as well as beyond us. In his analysis of narcissism six years earlier, Freud has used to Weismann to argue that, while 'the individual himself regards sexuality as one of his own ends ... from another point of view he is an appendage to his germ-plasm .... He is the mortal vehicle of a (possibly) immortal substance' (1914, p. 78).

This is the context for a curious tangent in *Beyond the Pleasure Principle*, as Freud wonders whether mortality itself is necessary. We are accustomed to think so, he notes, 'strengthened in our thoughts by the writings of our poets', but this belief in the necessity of dying may be 'another of those illusions which we have created'. He turns to biology to test the validity of the belief but warns, 'we may be astonished to find how little agreement there is among biologists on the subject of natural death and in fact that the whole concept of death melts away under their hands' (1920, p. 45).

Death can only happen to individuals. Individuality only arises in the context of finite, sexually reproducing creatures (not when we turn to the cellular mutations of asexual life forms). Now the question 'why sexed reproduction' is shadowed by sexual reproduction's implication in mortality. Accounting for its origin becomes even more pressing. Freud gropes for a conclusion by looking for a beginning: we need more information on the origin of sexual reproduction and of the sexual instincts in general. He speculates that the origin of reproduction by sexually differentiated germ cells might be pictured 'along sober Darwinian lines' as due to its genetic advantage, an advantage that 'was arrived at on some occasion by the chance conjugation of two protista, [and] was retained and further exploited in later development' (p. 56). It is not clear why this explanation is insufficient. Yet Freud continues: 'apart from this, science has so little to tell us ... that we can liken the problem to a darkness into which not so much as a ray of hypothesis has penetrated'. This sentence, marking the beginning of Freud's return to Plato, is an echo of Darwin himself (of lines that clearly preoccupied Freud). In his paper, 'On the two forms, or dimorphic condition, in the species of primula', Darwin (1861) writes:

> We do not even in the least know the final cause of sexuality; why new beings should be produced by the union of the two sexual elements, instead of by a process of parthenogenesis .... The whole subject is hidden in darkness.
>
> *(p. 94)*

Darwin leaves off here. Freud cannot resist casting his net wider, drawing on resources beyond science. He refers to Aristophanes' myth, according to which primeval man was split in half, love being the desire of the two halves to rejoin, and swiftly converts it to a mythic-molecular vision:

> Shall we follow the hint given us by the poet-philosopher and venture upon the hypothesis that living substance at the time of its coming to life was torn into small particles, which have ever since endeavored to reunite through the sexual instincts? ... That these splintered fragments of living substance in this way attained a multicellular condition and finally transferred the instinct for reuniting, in the most highly concentrated form, to the germ cells?
>
> *(1920, p. 59)*

Where, in the *Three Essays*, Aristophanes' account of Eros was a 'fable', it is now simultaneously 'myth' and 'hypothesis'. Its ambiguous status within Plato's dialogue is acknowledged ('put into the mouth of Aristophanes'), but the myth is still identified with the 'poet-philosopher' Plato himself. Where, before, myth was opposed to science, now it patches over a gap where science runs out. The myth might point towards an underlying universal logic, an instinct residing in the germ cells but which matches our intuitive psychological beliefs about attraction. And it appears to resolve Freud's conflicting theoretical intuitions, for the myth pictures a desire at once turned upon ourselves *and* seeking an external object, the longed-for resolution of Eros, Narcissus and Oedipus. Narcissus longed to be split so that he could rejoin with himself: 'How I wish I could separate myself from my body!' Narcissus cried (Ovid, *Metamorphoses*, III 588). Aristophanes' tale of Eros presents a fulfilment of that wish. It is both narcissistic and founded on a primal rupture. And in its tale of severance it discovers a *source* for sexual attraction in the instinct to return.

Finally, while maintaining the benefits of its mythic status, Aristophanes' myth promises to tie together the disparate strands of Freud's essay. It is the closest Freud will come to synthesizing classicism, zoology and evolutionary biology. But only a sentence later he confesses: 'I am not convinced myself and … I do not seek to persuade other people to believe.' The tone of humility is Freud's final gesture of intellectual rigour. He is still waiting for science to shine its light, for the discovery of something new to break the repetitive cycle that has come to mark both sexual and epistemological desire.

Lacan's use of Aristophanes' myth

The lamella: immortal desire

The week he introduces Aristophanes' myth into *Seminar XI* (1977), Lacan has been trying to communicate his own interpretation of libidinal energy, under the heading of the 'drive'. The drive is not so much a force connecting someone to their chosen object of desire, however, but an incessant pulsation, a loop, returning to the subject around a space where its object is supposed to be. Where desire thinks it has found its object, drive describes the force we're confronted with when desire fails to stop. It is relentless. But Lacan isn't content to leave the force in metaphorical limbo, avoiding questions as to its origins or its physical nature; he wants to think further about this drive he has conjured up, as a way of thinking about psychoanalysis more broadly.

It is at this point that he announces he will 'take the liberty of setting a myth before you'. It is to be what is 'put into the mouth of Aristophanes on the subject of love in Plato's *Symposium*' (p. 197). But unlike Freud, who turns to Plato's myth to find a precedent, Lacan seeks to compete with it. He describes himself as 'defying, perhaps for the first time in history, a myth that acquires so much prestige', and offers a myth of his own 'under the same heading'. In fact, what Lacan gives us seems initially to have little connection at all. Lacan keeps 'the heading' but, where Aristophanes describes the splitting of primal people, Lacan describes the splitting of an egg's membranes: 'Whenever the membranes of the egg in which the fetus emerges on its way to becoming a new-born are broken, imagine for a moment that something flies off' (p. 197). It is this extra 'something' he names 'the lamella'.

The lamella becomes an almost infinitely expandable concept in Lacan's theory. At certain points it is a force akin to the drive or the libido; at other times it relates to the immortal life force that threatens the individual from within – because it is itself immortal. It connects to Lacan's exploration of both myth and biology, and to Freud's wrestling with sex and death.

> The lamella is something extra-flat, which moves like the amoeba. It is just a little more complicated. But it goes everywhere. And it is something – I will tell you shortly why – that is related to what the sexed being loses in sexuality, it is, like the amoeba in relation to sexed beings, immortal – because it survives any division.
>
> (p. 197)

If the lamella defies easy understanding, this is no accident. It is an extraordinary example of how Lacan merges ideas accumulated over several years of seminars into a single concept, providing a solution that draws on all of them and challenges us not to settle into it too easily. It is closer to a (unsolvable) crossword clue than to a coherent concept, thick with Lacan's reading of Freud, and Freud's impasses in particular, but also with the philosophy of Plato, the prism through which the myth enters Western culture.

For this reason, in exploring the lamella, Lacan's reading of the *Symposium* in *Seminar VIII* (2015) is a helpful place to start. While it is the figure of Socrates for whom he turns to the dialogue, Lacan enjoys a close relationship with the text as a whole. He argues that it is dominated by one theme throughout, our own fundamental lack. This, naturally enough, is the light in which he views Aristophanes' myth. In contrast to Freud, Lacan does not focus on the implicit romantic promise, but draws out a deep streak of pessimism, overlooked by many of those who have turned to the myth over the centuries. It is shot through with violence and impossibility, Lacan reminds us.

> It is clear that in the first behaviour which follows the birth of these beings which are born from such a division in two, what Aristophanes shows us at first and what is the underpinning of what immediately comes here in a light which for us is so romantic, is this kind of panicky fatality which is going to make each one of these beings seek above all his half, and then, clinging to it with a tenacity, which one might say has no way out, effectively makes them perish side by side because of their incapacity to rejoin one another.
>
> (1977, p. 197)

Already there is a very particular emphasis, a sense of failure in Aristophanes' account that Lacan sees defining the *Symposium*'s message as a whole. To describe this sense of an inherent split within the subject, one which we can never fully repair, Lacan uses the concept of castration. In Freud's theory, castration anxiety is bound to fear of the father's authority, the law, and the law of gender in particular. Lacan retains plenty of this but, as his reading of the myth suggests, the concept of castration in Lacanian theory relates to a law of simply *being* – being individual and therefore mortal. This informs his pursuit of the motive force of sexuality. Four weeks before the eleventh seminar begins, Lacan delivers a paper, 'On Freud's "Trieb"', in which he cites the *Symposium* as an exceptional dialogue in foregrounding the issue of castration, 'the altogether new mainspring Freud introduced into desire' (2007, p. 723). He argues that Socrates, throughout the *Symposium*, is equally concerned with 'the function of lack' (2015, p. 113). By way of example, Lacan points to the speech of Agathon. Agathon delivers a flowery and romantic eulogy befitting his role as poet, but, as a eulogy on a fantasy, Lacan sees it characterized by its *Nichtigkeit*, its vacuousness. It is hollow in itself, and masks the hollowness around which desire forms.

> Everything Agathon says, for example, about the beautiful – that it belongs to love and that it is one of love's attributes – succumbs to Socrates' questioning: 'Is the love about which you spoke love of something? Does loving and desiring something mean having it or not having it? Can one desire what one already has?'
>
> *(2015, p. 113)*

Eros is founded on absence not presence, nothing not something. This is central to Plato's overarching strategy in the *Symposium*. As Lacan recognizes, over the course of the dialogue, Plato moves the focus of his enquiry towards a desire without physical end. The question becomes that of Eros's goals: *can* desire be satisfied? Aristophanes' myth plays its part in the overall scheme. Freud, in overlooking this fact (like most who return to the myth), tangles himself in a theoretical knot. Lacan's reading of the myth as pessimistic may seem idiosyncratic but it is true to its source, and a closer look at the *Symposium* reveals why.

An excess of longing is present in the myth from the very start, and explicitly bound to mortality. Desire exists before the circle-people are split (indeed, this is the source of their trouble): it is a desire to compete with the gods (see Ludwig, 2002).[13] Plato writes that, unlike the immortal gods, humans in the *Symposium* are not naturally happy *being mortal beings*, so they seek to climb to the gods. Zeus's decision to split them is a response to this original overreaching desire to conquer the realms of the immortal. If the myth concerns love, then already it is a side effect of an exile from the immortal. After a great deal of thought, Zeus informs the other gods: 'I have an idea by which human beings could still exist but be too weak to carry on their wild behaviour' (190c). In this context, the judicial violence of his solution is palpable:

> Zeus cut the [humans] into two, as people cut sorb-apples in half before they preserve them or as they cut hard-boiled eggs with hairs. As he cut each one, he told Apollo to turn the face and the half-neck attached to it towards the gash, so that humans would see their own wound and be more orderly.
>
> *(190e)*

The original 'circle-people' are split, not as part of any divine plan, but as a cautionary punishment imposed by Zeus to check their power. (This is elided in Freud's conventionally bland account: 'Eventually Zeus decided to cut these men in two, "like a sorb-apple which is halved for pickling"'). The navel is left as a cautionary reminder (191a), along with a continued threat: 'If we think they're still acting outrageously, and they won't settle down, I'll cut them in half again so that they move around hopping on one leg' (190d). What's more, Plato emphasizes that the split severs the people from the immortal gods as well as within themselves. The humans' original roundness was derived from their heavenly origin: from the sun, earth and moon, for male, female and mixed pairs respectively (190b) (see Ludwig, 2002). All this is lost. The moral delivered at the end of the myth draws attention away from love and back to fearful veneration: to avoid further punishment, 'everyone should encourage others to show due reverence towards the gods' (193b). We live under threat of Zeus's knife.

Crucially, for both Plato's theory of love and Lacan's theory of desire, in Aristophanes' account reproduction is an afterthought, introduced as a *solution* to the problem of desire. At first, the newly divided humans, clinging to their other halves 'died from hunger and from general inactivity, because they didn't want to do anything apart from each other' (191a–b). It is because of this that Zeus moves the genitals around to the front, allowing sexed reproduction (rather than reproduction with the earth, as had been the way) (191b). As Paul Ludwig (2002) notes, Eros is not to be simply identified with sex. Indeed, Zeus devises sex as an anodyne for Eros because the goal of permanent bodily reunion or fusion is impossible.

All this is noted by Lacan. What is really of significance in the *Symposium*, Lacan (2015) asserts, is the idea that attraction is born of the violence described above; on loss and subsequent lack:

> These beings, split in two like pear halves, die, at a time x that is not specified since it is a mythical time, in a futile attempt to fuse anew. They are doomed to vain efforts to procreate in the earth, and I will skip the whole mythical discussion as it would take us too far afield. How is their problem to be resolved? Aristophanes speaks to us like little Hans does: their genitalia – which are in the wrong place, because they are where they were when the beings were round, that is, they are on the outside – are unscrewed and screwed back onto the stomach, just like the faucet in Hans' dream, as reported in Freud's case history.
>
> (p. 93–4)

'Little Hans' was a five-year-old boy whose father corresponded with Freud about his son's constellation of anxieties and obsessions, including the fantasy of a detachable penis that would screw into his belly. Freud located a fear of castration at the centre of Little Hans's phobias, and it is as such that the case here serves not only to emphasize the absurdity of the divided people's hopes, but as a useful bridge between Aristophanes' myth and Freud's theory, even if Freud himself failed to see it.

It is the mystical seer Diotima who finally pops the bubble of fantasy, exposing Aristophanes' myth as infantile. Socrates gives voice to her teaching in a famously odd act of ventriloquism.[14]

> 'The idea has been put forward,' she said, 'that lovers are people who are looking for their own other halves. But my view is that love is directed neither at their half nor their whole unless, my friend, that turns out to be good. After all, people are even prepared to have their own feet or hands amputated if they think that those parts of themselves are diseased.'
>
> (Plato, *Symposium*, 205e)

With this vivid, medical literalism, combined with subtle philosophical distinction, Diotima moves the entire debate towards a consideration of what underlies desire: why we seek pleasure in the first place.

In a revealing aside at the opening of *Beyond the Pleasure Principle*, Freud (1920) expresses his longing for 'any philosophical or psychological theory which was able to inform us of the *meaning* of the feelings of pleasure and unpleasure' (p. 7). It is a rare admission that he finds himself and psychoanalysis on the edge of metaphysics. Freud finds nothing to his purpose. But Plato is more comfortable moving beyond the immediate goals and objects of desire to the *purpose* of pleasure itself. The lover loves what is good, Diotima demonstrates, and desires that it become their *own*. They desire this because it brings happiness. What is this sensation for? For Plato, happiness is a clue to what might be sought beyond the material and mortal, beyond the transient and therefore illusory. Better than the good itself is to have the good *forever*. With this ingenious refinement, a dimension beyond the material and transient is established. At this point, the speech of Socrates-Diotima becomes increasingly mystical; the language remains tied to biology but a new realm beyond the material opens up:

> the object of love is not beauty, as you suppose … [it is] Reproduction and birth in beauty …. And why is reproduction the object of love? Because reproduction is the closest mortals can come to being permanently alive and immortal. If what we agreed earlier is right, that the object of love is to have the good *always*, it follows that we must desire immortality along with the good. It follows from this argument that the object of love must be immortality as well.
> (Plato, Symposium, 206e–207a)

According to Diotima's teaching, by using the power of mind we can move from the love of one body to love of beauty itself, to the good, and then to the reproduction of the good as virtue. This is one way to ground a logic for desire, even if it depends on a metaphysical realm of values. But curiously, as with Freud, an interest in *physical* immortality haunts the dialogue. An impulse towards immortality can be seen in all nature, Plato writes: 'mortal nature does all it can to live forever and to be immortal. It can only do this by reproduction: it always leaves behind another, new generation to replace the old' (207d). Like Freud, Plato presents an image of the individual as subordinate to the immortal life of its species. And, again, this force is at work inside us as well as beyond us, an immortal 'life force' threatening to subsume the mortal individual from within. Plato points out that, even while alive and supposedly consistent, an individual is degenerating and being rebuilt in fragments, 'for instance, his hair, skin, bone, blood and his whole body' (207d). The attention Socrates-Diotima pays to a *physical* immortality distinguishes this from other Platonic dialogues, which concentrate on the immortal soul (e.g. *Phaedo*, *Republic*). This is the way that every mortal thing is maintained in existence, Diotima argues, not by being completely the same, as divine things are, but because everything that grows old and goes away leaves behind another new thing of the same type. 'This is the way, Socrates, that mortal things have a share in immortality, physically and in all other ways' (208a–b).

Diotima exposes Aristophanes' account of Eros as insufficient. Yet it is his myth that gets retold through the millennia. More often than not, it eclipses its original context; Freud is not the first or last to confuse his view with Plato's own (see Hatfield and Walster, 1978). Against Socrates-Diotima's vision of human life, in which individuality is obliterated, part of the seductive power of Aristophanes' myth lies in its presentation of love as specific to each man and woman. The singularity of our chosen object underpins our own uniqueness. Martha Nussbaum (1979) finds in Aristophanes' myth an unprecedented expression of this idea: that love is a response to a person's unique individuality.[15] And, of course, that individuality is a reflection of our *own* individuality. Aristophanes' myth is, above all, a myth of the singularity of our desires: the fantasy of finding 'the one' is concomitant with the fantasy of our own uniqueness.

It would seem straightforward that desire emerges precisely from this greedy egotism, from an (over)abundance of selfhood. Yet, as Plato shows us, we desire what we feel is lacking. This is what Lacan (1977) wants to salvage from the *Symposium*:

> Aristophanes' myth pictures the pursuit of the complement for us in a moving and misleading way, by articulating that it is the other, one's sexual other half, that the living being seeks in love. To this mythical representation of the mystery of love, analytic experience substitutes the search by the subject, not of the sexual complement, but of the part of himself, lost forever, that is constituted by the fact that he is only a sexed living being, and that he is no longer immortal.
>
> (p. 199)

This primal loss becomes an increasing focus in Lacan's work from *Seminar XI* onwards – a primal loss of immortality, as in Aristophanes' myth, moving psychoanalysis away from previous developmental narratives. The lamella is a particularly useful concept to introduce in this eleventh seminar – a seminar in which Lacan has a new audience, comprising of philosophy students at the École Normale Supérieure – because he is seeking to present psychoanalysis as a theory concerned with philosophical questions of being and nothingness as well as narratives of infancy.

This is one function of the lamella – almost as a satire of psychoanalytic schools that privilege the primal loss of the breast, of the mother. Lacan even asserts that the lamella is 'an organ' (p. 141), evoking Melanie Klein (1967) and the object-relations school. Klein theorized the 'part-objects' (breast, faeces, penis, etc.) with which we begin to negotiate the inner and outer, ourselves and others. This school of thought receives Lacan's explicit criticism in both 'Position of the unconscious' and *Seminar XI*, where the lamella is hedged in with warnings not to focus analytically on the 'breast', and the dangers of thinking our attachment might be an attachment to something as organic as weaning (2007, p. 719). This is a continuation of the previous year's concerns. Much of the imagery relating to pregnancy and the placenta can be traced to the 1963 seminar on anxiety in which Lacan presents an initial 'separation' comparable to the lamella myth, exploiting the imagery of birth and motherhood to distinguish himself from the familiar psychoanalytic accounts: 'The characteristic separation at the beginning ... is not the separation from the mother', he asserts (2014, pp. 166–167).

Lacan's refusal of biological literalism is partly responsible for leaving the influence of his own medical training underexplored. But it lends him an array of imagery and emboldens his own incorporation of Freud's scientific references.[16] When Lacan returns to *Beyond the Pleasure Principle*, it is to both the speculative and scientific strands of the essay. His speculative inheritance concerns the death drive. Insofar as the lamella represents 'drive', Lacan borrows many of its connotations from the 'death drive' itself, rather than the libido. Indeed, 'every drive is virtually a death drive', Lacan states in 'Position of the unconscious'. At times, for Lacan, this is because the drive pursues its own extinction; at others, it is because it involves the subject in repetition, and sometimes because it seeks something *beyond* pleasure: the ineffable, impossible, overwhelming *jouissance*; it does not know how to stop.

But the lamella is informed by Freud's hard science as well: the glutinous vision of a self-reproducing life-substance from which the 'I' has been extracted. Freud (1920) describes 'splintered fragments of living substance' creeping and autonomous (pp. 26–27). Lacan adds this to imagery he has noted in *Seminar I*, Freud's description of the libido as 'given off to the object-cathexes much as the body of an amoeba is related to pseudopodia which it puts out' (Freud, 1914, p. 75). In addition to all this, Lacan has his own interest in Weismann. As early as *Seminar I*, Lacan has been exploring 'the notion of the immortality of the germ-plasm', an immortality on which the mortal individual is 'parasitic', 'worth nothing alongside the immortal substance hidden deep inside it ... which authentically and substantially represents such life as there is' (1988, p. 121).

One of the most remarkable features of the lamella is its name, which manages to combine elements of all the above. In English, the term *lamella* is most commonly found in zoology – although also botany and anatomy – to label a thin scale, layer of bone or a filmy tissue. In humans, *lamellae* is the anatomical term given to the precursors of the prepuce (the foreskin in men, or protective tissue around the clitoris in women) during the development of reproductive organs; Lacan (2014) had spoken at length on circumcision in the previous year's seminar with regards to our anxiety-riddled relationship to the 'lost-object'. Richard Boothby (1991), in his own commentary on Lacan's text, informs the reader that, 'Literally speaking, the word "lamelle" refers to the thin folds of flesh forming the gills of bivalve molluscs, such as clams or oysters (in the class Lamellibranchia)' (p. 237). Paul Allen Miller (1998) notes that lamella, in French, would sound like the diminutive of *lame* (blade), itself evoking the act of division in the myth. Darian Leader (2003) unearths another layer of semantic resonance when he notes that in ancient burial practices: 'Lamellae were thin gold plates or foils buried with a cadaver and containing instructions and passwords for use in the next world' (p. 46).[17]

In truth, all are connected by the humble omelette. In 'Position of the Unconscious', a paper delivered in 1960 at a colloquium at Bonneval Hospital and rewritten in 1964, the year of *Seminar XI*, Lacan sets out the terrifying, B-movie potential of the slimy, autonomous lamella at greater length, bestowing it with a punning synonym: *hommelette*.[18] A website on food-related words explains that the omelette is named after the kitchen pan in which it was originally cooked: the spelling 'omelette' evolved in old French from *une amelette*: a wide, flat frying pan. *Amelette* itself can be traced back to the Latin *lamella* meaning 'thin layer' or 'slender leaf'. This refers to the iron from which a blacksmith would have hammered out the earliest frying pan.[19] So 'lamella' represents hard metal and slimy substance in one.

Hommelette is more than just a pun, however; it is a reminder of the concept's significance. It reminds us that, at issue, is what starts the drive in the first place. 'This *hommelette*, as you will see, is easier to animate than primal man, in whose head one always had to place a homunculus to get it working' (Lacan, 1977, p. 197). Lacan's homunculus mocks the failure of ego-psychology to break from what Lacan sees as a *pre-scientific* model of the mind – the *I* of the *cogito*, as he puts it, mistaken for 'the homunculus who has long been represented whenever one has wished to practise psychology … the presence, inside man, of the celebrated little fellow who governs him, who is the driver, the point of synthesis, as we now say' (p. 141). This is the 'Ego' as explanation, as supposedly accounting for our needs and desires. Part of the message behind Lacan's bad pun is that the lamella is to be opposed to any anthropomorphic model of human will; in fact, it is in no way an *hommelette*: a homunculus, familiar, internal, self-willed. What *starts* the mechanism, making it tick, pulling the trigger – the question that plagued Freud – is not an innate driver but the initial split.

It is in this way that the lamella's role shifts line by line. If the passages on the lamella appear opaque even by Lacan's standards, it is worth recognizing the extent to which he has gone out of his way to make them so, confusing conceptual boundaries at every turn. He has fun with it. You can plug it into the body: it can, and indeed must, attach to the rims of the erogenous zones; it is 'a force field', a *surface* which can be turned inside out. Whenever we think we have grasped it, a new detail or metaphor arises to defeat both the visual and theoretical imagination. Lacan evokes the placenta, the amoeba, he toys with the bizarre pun *hommelette*, and just when we have identified the lamella as a form of lost object, 'what the sexed being loses in sexuality', it becomes the libido itself, a force, an organ and a myth: 'This lamella, this organ, whose characteristic is not to exist, but which is nevertheless an organ' (2007, p. 718).

It is mythical. This is perhaps the most challenging aspect of the lamella: when, after all our work, we're told not to consider it real after all. But it is clear that, to Lacan at least, this is essential. One week after he has introduced the lamella to the eleventh seminar, Lacan relives the moment. The libido is the essential organ in understanding the nature of the drive, he asserts.

> This organ is unreal. Unreal is not imaginary. The unreal is defined by articulating itself on the real in a way that eludes us, and it is precisely this that requires that its representation should be mythical, as I have made it.
>
> *(1977, p. 205)*

Lacan takes the underlying issue that troubled Freud, the exact status of the libido, and places it in the foreground. Freud struggled to reconcile a theory of memories and narratives with a model based on the circulation of energetic force. For Lacan, who places greater attention on language, the danger is even more pronounced. A probing of the category of myth itself is one solution to this predicament. As Ellie Ragland (1996) puts it: 'In trying to decipher the "myth" of libido, Lacan ended up redefining myth' (p. 201).

Lacan's recourse to myth often comes alongside frustration at those who see his structuralist approach as neglecting the dynamic, libidinal element of Freudian theory. 'At a time that I hope we have now put behind us, it was objected that in giving dominance to structure I was neglecting the dynamics so evident in our experience', he complains in *Seminar XI*, following the introduction of the lamella (1977, p. 203). And his original turn to Aristophanes in 'Position of the unconscious' is prefaced by a similar complaint:

> As for sexuality, which people would like to remind me is the force we deal with and that it is biological, I retort that analysts perhaps have not shed as much light as people at one time hoped on sexuality's mainsprings .... I will try to contribute something newer by resorting to a genre that Freud himself never claimed to have superseded in this area: myth.
>
> *(2007, p. 716)*

In support of this interpretation of Freud, Lacan seizes on moments such as Freud's comment in his *New Introductory Lectures* (1933a): 'The instincts so to say are our mythology. Instincts are mythical entities, magnificent in their indefiniteness' (p. 95). This is repeated in Freud's comment to Einstein, with regards to the death drive: 'Does not every science come in the end to a kind of mythology like this? Cannot the same be said today of your own physics?' (1933b, p. 211).

As Lacan continues to probe this concept of myth – that it describes necessary but non-existent forces – the question of how it might have an *effect* returns. In 'On Freud's "Trieb"', Lacan draws upon Freud's statement regarding mythical drives again:

> The drives are our myths, said Freud. This must not be understood as a reference to the unreal. For it is the real that the drives mythify, as myths usually do: here it is the real which creates desire by reproducing in it the relationship between the subject and the lost object.
>
> *(2007, p. 723)*

This cryptic assertion hinges on the Lacanian concept of the real. In Lacan's tri-partite scheme of real, symbolic and imaginary, the real describes all that lies beyond the latter two categories: what escapes language; what cannot, therefore, be imagined. Just as the lamella flies off when a new life is established, the real is what is expelled when a signifier becomes attached to a piece of existence; it is the bit that that signifier fails to capture (Bailly, 2009). As such, the real is not outside of the symbolic but a structural feature of it: its limit. It is what cannot be assimilated in the chain of signifiers, yet, in its exclusion, it drives their circulation. (It bears a direct relation to Freud's theories of trauma and repression, particularly as elaborated in *Beyond the Pleasure Principle*: repetition as a failed attempt to master loss, to process what consciousness resists as impossible.) In this way, it arises whenever we explore *how* the subject is attached to the symbolic order. And it is this relationship on the border of the symbolic and the real that Lacan suggests the drives 'mythify', i.e. embody, bestow with narrative form. This is the value of Aristophanes' myth of Eros, very clearly concerned with lost objects, and very clearly a myth.

The truth of myths

Something about Aristophanes' tale foregrounds the idea of myth itself, inducing the self-consciousness heard when Freud and Lacan refer to it: 'I will take the liberty of setting a myth before you'; 'it is of so fantastic a kind – a myth rather than a scientific explanation'.

When Freud turns to other myths it is different: Narcissus and Oedipus find themselves in a more ambiguous category, evoking psychological truths that come to eclipse their mythical sources.

Aristophanes' myth, however, seems to draw attention to its artifice. It is a crowd pleaser, its seductive simplicity plain to see. For A. E. Taylor (1966), 'the whole tale of the bi-sexual creatures is a piece of gracious Pantagruelism …. Plato's serious purpose must be looked for elsewhere' (p. 209). Christopher Gill (1999), in his edition of the *Symposium*, suggests, 'It is more like an intellectual's idea of a myth or an Aesopic fable' (p. xxiii). It is, literally, the myth of a comedian. As Lacan is keen to note, Plato not only invites to the symposium a comic playwright, but one known for lampooning Socrates. And Lacan (2015) has an explanation for this curiosity: Plato has a 'clown', a comedian in place, because 'Love is a comical feeling …. [This] is so essential and indispensable that it is why there is in the *Symposium* a presence that, for a long time, commentators were never able to explain, that of Aristophanes' (pp. 33–4).

We have seen the purpose this might serve in the overarching philosophical scheme of the *Symposium*. But the role of myth itself in Plato's dialogues is more complex than simply standing for error. Plato is the first writer known to have exploited the category of myth self-consciously (Dowden, 1992). Aristophanes' myth stands beside Diotima's myth (of Penia and Poros), the myth of Er (a legend that concludes Plato's *Republic*) and of Atlantis (the name of a fictional island mentioned within an allegory on the hubris of nations in Plato's works *Timaeus* and *Critias*) (see Kirk, 1974). While the philosopher excludes poetry from his Republic, it seems myth still has a purpose to serve.

Myths are more than just unreal. They carry weight. In Ancient Greek, *Muthos* (literally 'utterance') originally referred to traditional tales of gods and heroes. In Aristotle's *Poetics*, *muthos* refers to the plot of a play, contrasted with *logos* meaning 'analytical statement' or 'theory' (13/14).[20] From this came an exaggerated sense of myth as untruth, *Muthoi* as stories rather than statements. But a traditional tale is not to be dismissed. The elements that attach to the idea of myth over the centuries are that they are stories with pre-literary roots and cultural significance. It is central to the definition of myth that they are told, passed on, and they are somehow important. G. S. Kirk (1974) distinguishes myth from fables and folktales in this manner: myths are not just good stories, but also bearers of important messages about life.

It seems there is something *within* myth, in contrast to an analytic statement that wears its value on the outside. A myth *demands* things – recounting, for one – and this is central to its power. As Richard Armstrong (2005) puts it: 'A myth is not a final narrative, but one that thrives in retelling; it is not a static repository of truth so much as a way of processing truth in narrative form' (p. 146). There is a sense of function here: 'productive', 'thrives', 'processing'. We can elaborate on Armstrong's statement by asking: what exactly is occurring when a myth 'thrives'? How can something, especially something old and fictitious, continue to produce meaning? Could the meaning be unpacked (becoming a theory, for example) and the outer coating of myth itself be put aside? The possibility feels unlikely, perhaps because there is a sense that myth arises where other means of expression would not suffice. But the question of a relationship between its surface properties and underlying 'meaning' remains. Myth is doing something.

To take another step towards understanding the value of myth, we can ask what it is that might need 'processing' in this way. Psychoanalysis suggests that it is not 'truth' itself that needs 'processing', rather it is problems. Lacan benefits from a thinker who put this at the heart of a new approach to myth itself: Claude Lévi-Strauss (1908–2009). In a series of works between 1949 and 1964, Lévi-Strauss had revolutionized anthropology and, central to this, the study of myth – his structuralist method holding out the promise of a new rigour amongst the humanities generally.[21] Previous to Lévi-Strauss, the study of myth sought historical origins – this was where the 'truth' of myths could be found, through a genealogical archaeology, to origins, sources, historical events, personages, allegory, gods, rituals. But, for Lévi-Strauss, applying the insights of structural linguistics, the meaning of a myth is to be found in the composition of its parts. This composition responds to an underlying conceptual challenge, a problem resistant to a logical solution. The myth 'solves' this crux through a repetition of the problem within narrative. More than just a comfort, it is a psychological mechanism.

The similarity to Freud's theory of repetition as a response to an event that we can't psychologically process is no coincidence. In *Tristes Tropiques* (1955), Lévi-Strauss describes geology, Marxism and psychoanalysis as his 'three mistresses'. The mistresses have in common 'a process of decoding' whereby 'the operation of understanding consists of reducing apparent reality to its hidden dimension' (Rossi, 1974, p. 7).[22] That Freud is more to Lévi-Strauss than just one amongst a handful of influences is evident in the centrality of Oedipus to Lévi-Strauss' developing theory of myth. In demonstrating that myth responds to an underlying contradiction that can't be resolved by other means, Lévi-Strauss takes Oedipus, and Thebes more broadly, as his example. He surveys the interlocked Theban tales – Oedipus marrying his mother, Antigone attempting to bury her brother, and so on – and concludes that the common theme is a failure to properly manage 'blood relations' (i.e. by killing your father and sleeping with your mother). This is bound to a deeper concern with the nature of our creation, he argues, underlying episodes such as Cadmus' killing of the dragon, and Oedipus' defeating of the Sphinx. The Sphinx and the dragon are both traditionally chthonian beings that must be killed before mankind can be born from the earth. His conclusion is that the issue, repeated from Cadmus to Antigone, has to do with lingering ideas about 'the *autochthonous origin* of mankind' (pp. 215–216). And he cites Pausanius, the second-century geographer who records a widespread belief that humans first arose like plants.

For Lévi-Strauss, two troubling questions underlie the Oedipus myth: the initial concern, 'is one born from one or from two', is shadowed by a second, derivative issue: 'Is the same born out of the same or out of something that is different?' (Grigg, 2006, p. 54). For Lévi-Strauss (1963), the

Oedipus myth has to do with 'the inability, for a culture which holds the belief that mankind is autochthonous ... to find a satisfactory transition between this theory and the knowledge that human beings are actually born from the union of man and woman' (p. 216).[23] In a move that will inspire Lacan, he positions Freud's theory of the Oedipus complex as another telling of the myth itself:

> Although the Freudian problem has ceased to be that of autochthony *versus* bisexual production, it is still the problem of understanding how *one* can be born from *two*: how is it that we do not have only one procreator, but a mother plus a father?
>
> (p. 217)

Lacan himself will be interested in the Oedipus complex as a fantasy – as a solution to something more troubling which remains beneath, un-mythologized.

All this informs Lacan's enthusiasm for the category of myth when he finds Plato employing it and seeks to compete. In the lamella's first outing, in 1960, Lacan, with a clear echo of Lévi-Strauss, describes the lamella as providing 'a symbolic articulation ... rather than an image' (2007, p. 718).[24] How do you conceptualize something that can't be *imagined*? Lacan's answer, thanks to Lévi-Strauss, is through myth. In his paper 'The neurotic's individual myth', Lacan (1979) has already appropriated the term 'individual myth' from Levi-Strauss's 'The Effectiveness of Symbols' (1949), stating: 'Myth is what provides a discursive form for something that cannot be transmitted through the definition of truth' (p. 407).[25] Plato bolsters this approach, opening the door to a re-appropriation of the mythical more generally. He provides a precedent for *creating* myths to articulate the impossible. Lacan expresses his admiration for this self-conscious use of myth: 'What is remarkable,' he claims, 'is precisely this rigor which ensures that when one engages with, when one locks into the plane of myth, Plato always knows perfectly well what he is doing or what he makes Socrates do.' Lacan (2015) refers to the theories of a nineteenth-century philologist, Ulrich von Wilamowitz-Moellendorff:

> Certain people have stressed it, Wilamowitz-Moellendorff for one – that there is a difference in register between what Socrates develops with his dialectical method and what, in Plato's testimony, he presents us in the form of myth .... When one arrives, and in plenty of fields other than

love, at a certain terminus regarding what can be obtained at the level of *episteme* or knowledge, myth is necessary in order to go further.

It is quite conceivable to us that there is a limit to knowledge, assuming that the latter is what can be accessed by purely and simply bringing the law of the signifier into play. In the absence of far-reaching conquests based on experiments, it is clear that in many domains – and even in domains in which we have no need for such conquests – it is urgent to give myth the floor.

(pp. 118–19)

For Lacan, 'beyond the *episteme*' becomes 'beyond the symbolic order' (i.e. beyond what language can reasonably contain and map out: the zone of the real). This is why he is interested in Plato's own response to this 'beyond': 'And in all of Plato's work, in the *Phaedo*, the *Timaeus*, and the *Republic*, myths arise when Plato needs them in order to fill the gap in what can be assured dialectically' (p. 119).[26] Limits and gaps carry significance in Lacanian theory: gaps in truth, in knowledge, in the subject itself. Consciousness cannot abide them, so their site becomes marked by invention: stories, desires, narratives underpinning desires, desires underpinning selfhood – anything to sustain at least the *promise* of wholeness and completion somewhere. Love is the ultimate filling of a gap with fantasy. It is mythical in its grandiosity and demands a myth to underpin it – western culture testifies to that. Lacan is keen to note that Plato contributes his own myth to this tradition. He introduces a myth regarding the birth of love which, Lacan (2015) notes, 'is found only in Plato's work', showing that a writer of Plato's era 'is altogether capable of forging a myth, a myth that has must have been enthusiastically handed down through the ages for it to function as such' (p. 120). Love, Plato says, is the son of Poros (expediency) and of Penia (poverty). Penia had visited a banquet in order to beg and came across Poros, asleep in the garden outside. She lay down beside him and conceived Eros who is, consequently, poor but enterprising (Plato, *Symposium*, 178). Lacan, once again not to be outdone, provides his own myth of love – love as an impossible harmony – in *Seminar VIII*, with due self-consciousness. 'To illustrate it for you, I will take the liberty of completing my image and of truly making it into a myth' (2015, p. 52). He describes a hand reaching towards an object: a piece of fruit or a rose or a log:

> If, in the movement of reaching, drawing, or stirring, the hand goes far enough toward the object that another hand comes out of the fruit,

> flower, or log and extends toward your hand – and at that moment your hand freezes in the closed plenitude of the fruit, in the open plenitude of the flower, or in the explosion of a log which bursts into flames – then what is produced is love.
>
> (p. 52)

This is all well and good, but he continues:

> Consider what I mean to emphasize with this myth. Every myth is related to the inexplicable nature of reality [*réel*], and it is always inexplicable that anything whatsoever responds to desire.
>
> (p. 52)[27]

Lacan's myth of love highlights its own improbability. The myth self-evidently masks a failure of possible reciprocation, and in doing so draws attention to its function *as* myth – a narrative in place of an impossibility. Jean-Michel Rabaté (2001) describes Lacan's myth as 'a rare effusion of lyricism', which is precisely the point: it is an artful, self-conscious fantasy of impossible symmetry (p. 142). To demonstrate the same point, Žižek (1997) likes to cite an advert rather than a myth but it is performing essentially the same function: a princess kisses a frog and it turns into a prince. The prince kisses the princess and she turns into a beer. The miracle is that desire should even *seem* symmetrical between someone desiring a whole Other and someone desiring a part object. 'Truth's first imagining or invention is Love', Lacan states (2015, p. 51). Truth, like love, structured as a fiction, as a veil for a failure of reciprocity, for a gap.

Myth does not just cover the gap but, remembering Lévi-Strauss's analysis, it *processes* an underlying impossibility by repeating, and thereby refiguring, it. Hence Lacan's concluding statement above: 'It is the real that the drives mythify …. It is the real which creates desire by reproducing in it the relationship between the subject and the lost object.' The real opens up a theoretical space for something which is unreal and yet has effect. In 'Position of the unconscious', Lacan explains that the lamella must be called unreal 'in the sense in which the unreal is not the imaginary and precedes the subjective realm it conditions (2007, p. 718).' 'Conditions' is the verb via which we move to a model closer to that of trauma: the impossible pressing in upon the possible. It arises alongside developments in Lacan's use of the concept of the real. Before 1964, the real is still loosely associated with some sense of an 'ultimate reality', but in *Seminar XI* it clearly becomes the 'impossible real': having been entirely excluded from consciousness it gains its power to effect (see Chiesa, 2007).[28] It impinges.

This, finally, provides an answer to the question of desire's 'mainspring'. Desire, in its dynamic of lack and need, reproduces an *original* loss of which we are not even conscious: the real 'creates desire by reproducing in it the relationship between the subject and the lost object' (Lacan, 2007, p. 723). This relationship is something we cannot depict for ourselves other than through myth, an intangible loss pressing in upon consciousness, forming the structure of desire itself. Armed with Plato and Lévi-Strauss, Lacan returns to the two problems we saw driving Freud's theoretical excursion: the nature of the libido and the source of sexual desire. In the mythical nature of the first, he finds a solution for the second. This is established in *Seminar XI*'s myth of the lamella, but it has been prepared for in his extended encounter with Plato's *Symposium* three years earlier, Plato read through the prism of *Beyond the Pleasure Principle* and the work of August Weismann. It allows Lacan to locate sexuality's mainsprings in mortality. Aristophanes' myth validates this transition.

One final implication of Lacan's theory is that desire is removed not only from questions of reproduction but also from gender itself. 'The link between sex and death, sex and the death of the individual, is fundamental', Lacan (1977) states, and to this he adds a fundamental qualification regarding sexuality: 'Existence, thanks to sexual division, rests upon copulation, accentuated in two poles that time-honoured tradition has tried to characterize as the male pole and the female pole' (p. 150).[29] Lacan's phrasing is significant: It is only 'time-honoured tradition' that has tried to establish 'male' and 'female' as the two poles of sexed reproduction. Sex itself only 'takes up the other lack, which is the real, earlier lack, to be situated at the advent of the living being' (p. 205). It is the myth, strung across the traditional, sexuated poles, by which we come to terms with a division deeper than gender itself.

This is why Lacan's return to Aristophanes in *Seminar XI* bridges chapters on 'the drive' and 'the Other'. Sex is found in the Other, here denoting the field of language and culture. Sexual difference is a game of *fort-da* that replicates but never resolves an original loss. A favourite reference of Lacan's is the tale of Daphnis and Chloe, found in a third-century romance by the Greek writer Longus, in which two naive young lovers seek instruction as to what they are meant to do together (1977; see also 2007). There is no innate genital drive, no human sexuality without the external network of symbols and stories to tell it where to go.

Aristophanes' myth of Eros proves popular over the centuries because it so powerfully seems to convey a truth about desire, lack and completeness. We've seen how, for Freud, it becomes inextricably entangled with his own questions over the logic of sexuality. But its original role as a fable to be corrected by Diotima carries a warning. Plato knew that the phenomenon of desire was not sufficiently explained by its various objects. These account for neither its origins nor its ultimate ends. He saw that desire is endless and, in some way, bound to our finitude. Pleasure points to something beyond sex, whether the material immortality of reproduction or the immortal values of which physical reproduction is a reflection. Without recourse to a world of Forms, however, Freud's abstract drive causes problems, collapsing back into the cul-de-sac of narcissism (desire as a return to self) and eventually forcing the formulation of a 'death drive' (desire caught in a repetitive cycle). For Lacan, the mortal longing which led Plato to the realm of Forms leads to an equivalently inexhaustible drive founded on inherent, mortal lack. This fuels his interest in the *Symposium*. Aristophanes' myth is even more valuable still, because Lacan intends to exploit the category of myth itself. An understanding of myth is necessary for his confrontation with Freud's scientific aspirations, but it also mirrors sexuality more broadly, responding to a conceptual problem that is insoluble by any other means.

Notes

1 'Science makes use of the word "libido"' (p. 45), he writes, introducing it. Libido is derived from the Latin for wish or desire. Freud claimed to have borrowed it from the neurologist Albert Moll, but it appears prior to Moll's work in early letters and manuscripts sent by Freud to his friend and intellectual companion in the formative years of psychoanalysis, Wilhelm Fliess.
2 This would have been noticeable at the time of its composition; the passage contains the only reference to female homosexuality in ancient Athenian writing (Plato, Symposium, 25, n. 72).
3 Freud himself uses the familiar designation 'Uranism', derived from the *Symposium*, in *Three Essays* (1905, 49, n. 2). Equally, this has been central to long-running criticism of Plato's dialogue. See Philo of Alexandria on the *Symposium*'s pederasty as against 'nature' to the extent that it threatened the end of civilization (Hunter, 2004, p. 121).
4 This figure of the Androgyne had deep roots in Freud's culture (see Furness, 1965). In this tradition, the androgynous figure represents an overcoming of sex differences. For Rilke, the limitations of individuality itself are surmounted. It is a mystic and transcendent phenomenon. Raymond Furness notes that in the medieval Cabbala (a key source for Boehme) Adam is originally both male and female, reflecting the androgynous unity of the Gnostic God.
5 See Sheldrake (1994). Modern 'energy' provided a unifying principle for the various components of a seventeenth-century mechanical universe: gravitation, magnetism and so on.

6 Nachmansohn (1915) begins by criticizing Jung's expanded definition of libido, and then argues that Plato's notion of Eros is closer to Freud's version: according to Plato, Eros (Love) is above all the instinct of sex or propagation.
7 Frankland (2006) hears an echo of Goethe in this use of Eros, specifically an allusion to the opening monologue of *Faust* (p. 47): 'Eros, which holds together everything in the world'. See also Freud's Goethe prize speech: 'Goethe always rated eros high, never tried to belittle its power, followed its primitive and even wanton expressions with no less attentiveness than its highly sublimated ones and has, as it seems to me, expounded its essential unity throughout all its manifestations no less decisively than Plato did in the remote past' (1927, p. 210).
8 Spencer (1900) combined insights from Coleridge's essay 'The Theory of Life' – itself derivative from Schelling's *Naturphilosophie* – with a generalization of Karl Ernest von Baer's law of embryological development (it is Spencer who first uses the term 'survival of the fittest'); see also Ellenberger (1981).
9 Compare the secular god Logos that Freud supports in *Future of an Illusion* (1927); again, knowledge of the 'laws of reality' displaces the purely *narcissistic* 'omnipotence of thoughts.' Oedipus had been associated with science since before Freud's adoption of the myth. The French philosopher Philippe Lacoue-Labarthe (2003) writes that 'before becoming ... the figure of desire *and* science, Oedipus was already a figure ... a figure in philosophy, and the figure of philosophy' (p. 8). Armstrong (2005) hears this undertone in the Leonardo study, the idea of science as 'a means of oedipal self-assertion, a way of escaping the dangerous implications of feminization – emasculation, passivity, sensuality – through a masculine rivalry over knowledge of Mother Nature' (p. 241). If knowledge involves confronting and coming to terms with our origins from two parents of different sex, there is a natural fit. See also Dean and Lane (2001) on the ominous 'alignment of autoeroticism, homosexuality and narcissism' in the Leonardo essay.
10 Furness (1965) describes Jung's projection of the *animus* and *anima* within us all as the most significant twentieth-century manifestation of the Androgyne.
11 The classical pair of opposites was, in fact, *Eros–Neikos* (Love–Strife), and *Bios–Thanatos* (Life–Death), but not *Eros–Thanatos* (Ellenberger, 1981). But the importance of evolutionary biology for Freud suggests why equating *Eros* and *Bios* is valuable. The equation of love and life allows for a sense of progress and assimilation under the banner of Eros, while death as a form of 'strife' preserves a sense of fragmentation.
12 Freud's main source for the science is Alexander Lipschütz, *Warum wir Sterben* (*Why we Die*) (1914). Lipschütz describes a range of experiments on protista undertaken in the previous couple of decades including those conducted by Émile Maupas, who disproved Weismann: Paramecium *can* continue indefinitely.
13 As Aristophanes describes, the original, 'whole' humans were terrible in their strength and vigor; they had great ambitions and made an attack on the gods. The story told by Homer about Ephialtes and Otus, how they tried to climb up to heaven to attack the gods, really refers to them. In Homer's account, Ephialtes and Otus were huge humans who planned to overthrow the gods by piling mountains on each other. They were destroyed by Apollo, Zeus' son (Homer, Odyssey, 11.307–20).
14 There is no evidence that she is a historical figure. On the significance of her being female, see Halperin (1990).
15 Gill (1990) argues that this type of interpretation expresses a distinctively modern interest in individuality.
16 For example, Lacan also uses the rare word *scissiparous* meaning reproduction by fission: 'it is, like the amoeba in relation to sexed beings, immortal – because it

survives any division, any scissiparous intervention'. Georges Bataille (1957 [1986]), in *Erotism* a few years earlier, uses the rare *scissipare/scissiparité* to describe reproduction by splitting as he presents reproduction itself as a form of growth feeding off an excess energy in life, but it is growth that threatens us by not being our *own*. This is part of the work's abiding concern with the relationship between death and sexuality, with its own clear echoes of *Beyond the Pleasure Principle*. The chapter 'Sexual Plethora and Death' involves a prolonged comparison of sexual and asexual reproduction (see Roudinesco, 1997, who covers the relationship between Lacan and Bataille extensively). The work has a clear impact on Lacan's *Ethics of Psychoanalysis* seminar of 1959–60 (Žižek, 2006), but given Lacan's medical training, one might expect the direction of influence is from Lacan to Bataille.

17 For a description of gold lamellae found in a Greek grave, see Graf (1993).
18 Lacan (2007) describes the autonomous *hommelette* at far greater length, before stating that 'I will now change [its name] to a more decent one, "lamella" (of which the word '*omelette*' is, in fact, but a metastasis)' (p. 719).
19 *Lamella* is a Latin diminutive form of *lamina*, which to the ancient Romans meant 'a flake of metal', 'a thin plate' (it is the source of *laminated*).
20 Vernant (1957) argues that philosophy ceases to be myth in order to become philosophy.
21 See *Les Structures élémentaires de la parenté* (1949); *Tristes Tropiques* (1955); *Anthropologie structurale* (1958); *Le Cru et le cuit* (1964).
22 According to Doniger (2009), 'Lévi-Strauss is indebted to Freud for many things: for the concept of ambivalence that underlies his theories of contradiction and paradox, for the structural use of inversion and so forth. His debt is patently evident, particularly in one of his last books, *The Jealous Potter* (1985), in his use of such Freudian terms as "secondary elaboration", for glosses of the symbolism of myth, and 'upward displacement' for the substitution of parts of the head for the lower parts of the body …. In his analysis of the myth of Asdiwal, Lévi-Strauss refers to latent content and unconscious categories (The Story of Asdiwal, 1967)' (1976, pp. 146–97). More relevant still is his emphasis on the importance of irrational forces as a basis of myth. See also Grigg (2006). Hénaff (2009) notes that the father of one of Lévi-Strauss's classmates worked closely with Marie Bonaparte; Lévi-Strauss read Freud 1925–30.
23 He refers to Pausanius (VIII, XXIX, 4) on the ability of the sun to produce human life from wet ground.
24 For a concise account of Lévi-Strauss's significance for Lacan's thoughts on myth, see Leader (2003). The anthropologist is, of course, a very real presence at Lacan's seminars, present in both the second and the eleventh, and responsible for the eleventh happening at all. For a book-length study of the relationship, see Zafiropoulos (2010).
25 Leader (2003) also notes a very Lévi-Straussian formulation in *Seminar IV*: 'a way of confronting an impossible situation by the successive articulation of all the forms of the impossibility of the solution' (p. 38).
26 On this subject, see Brisson (1999), although Brisson argues that Plato saw *logos* as vastly superior; see also Detienne (1986).
27 Leader (2003): 'Although Lacan does not cite the reference, this odd metaphor is in fact adapted from the work of the thirteenth-century mystic Ramón Lull' (p. 45).
28 Roudinesco (1997) finds the influence of Bataille here: 'Bataille's ideas on the impossible and heterology, deriving from them a concept of the "real" seen first as "residue" and then as "impossible"' (p. 136).
29 In *Seminar XVII* (1991, p. 75), he associates *sexus* (sex) with *secare* (cut).

References

Armstrong, R. (2005) *A Compulsion for Antiquity: Freud and the Ancient World*, Ithaca, Cornell University Press.
Bailly, L. (2009) *Lacan: A Beginner's Guide*, Oxford, Oneworld.
Bataille, G. ([1957] 1986) *Erotism: Death and Sensuality* (trans. M. Dalwood), San Francisco, City Lights.
Boehlich, W. (1989) *Sigmund Freud: Jugendbriefe an Eduard Silberstein: 1871–1881*, Frankfurt, Fischer.
Boothby, R. (1991) *Death and Desire: Psychoanalytic Thinking in Lacan's Return to Freud*, London, Routledge.
Brisson, L. (1999). *Plato the Myth Maker*, Chicago, Chicago University Press.
Chiesa, L. (2007) *Subjectivity and Otherness: A Philosophical Reading of Lacan*, Cambridge, MA, MIT Press.
Darwin, C. (1861) 'On the two forms, or dimorphic condition, in the species of Primula, and on their remarkable sexual relations', *Journal of the Proceedings of the Linnean Society of London (Botany)*, vol. 6, pp. 77–96.
Dean, T. and Lane, C. (2001) *Homosexuality and Psychoanalysis*, Chicago, Chicago University Press.
Detienne, M. (1986) *The Creation of Mythology*, Chicago, Chicago University Press.
Doniger, W. (2009) 'Theoretical and actual approaches to myth', in Wiseman, B. (ed.) *The Cambridge Companion to Lévi-Strauss*, Cambridge, Cambridge University Press, pp. 196–216.
Dowden, K. (1992) *The Uses of Greek Mythology*, London, Routledge.
Ellenberger, H. (1981) *The Discovery of the Unconscious*, New York, Basic Books.
Frankland, G. (2006) *Freud's Literary Culture*, Cambridge, Cambridge University Press.
Freud, S. (1894) 'The neuro-psychoses of defense', in Strachey, J. (ed.) *The Standard Edition of the Complete Psychological Works of Sigmund Freud*, vol. 3, London, Hogarth Press, pp. 43–70.
Freud, S. (1895) *Project for a Scientific Psychology*, in Strachey, J. (ed.) *The Standard Edition of the Complete Psychological Works of Sigmund Freud*, vol. 1, London, Hogarth Press, pp. 283–411.
Freud, S. (1905) *Three Essays on the Theory of Sexuality*, in Strachey, J. (ed.) *The Standard Edition of the Complete Psychological Works of Sigmund Freud*, vol. 7, London, Hogarth Press, pp. 125–323.
Freud, S. (1910) 'Leonardo da Vinci and a memory of his childhood', in Strachey, J. (ed.) *The Standard Edition of the Complete Psychological Works of Sigmund Freud*, vol. 11, London, Hogarth Press, pp. 59–137.
Freud, S. (1913) *Totem and Taboo*, in Strachey, J. (ed.) *The Standard Edition of the Complete Psychological Works of Sigmund Freud*, vol. 13, London, Hogarth Press, pp. 1–163.
Freud, S. (1914) *On Narcissism: An Introduction*, in Strachey, J. (ed.) *The Standard Edition of the Complete Psychological Works of Sigmund Freud*, vol. 14, London, Hogarth Press, pp. 67–101.
Freud, S. (1920) *Beyond the Pleasure Principle*, in Strachey, J. (ed.) *The Standard Edition of the Complete Psychological Works of Sigmund Freud*, vol. 17, London, Hogarth Press, pp. 1–63.
Freud, S. (1921) *Group Psychology and the Analysis of the Ego*, in Strachey, J. (ed.) *The Standard Edition of the Complete Psychological Works of Sigmund Freud*, vol. 18, London, Hogarth Press, pp. 65–143.
Freud, S. (1927) *Future of an Illusion*, in Strachey, J. (ed.) *The Standard Edition of the Complete Psychological Works of Sigmund Freud*, vol. 21, London, Hogarth Press, pp. 3–57.

Freud, S. (1933a) *New Introductory Lectures*, in Strachey, J. (ed.) *The Standard Edition of the Complete Psychological Works of Sigmund Freud*, vol. 22, London, Hogarth Press, pp. 1–183.
Freud, S. (1933b) 'Why war?', in Strachey, J. (ed.) *The Standard Edition of the Complete Psychological Works of Sigmund Freud*, vol. 22, London, Hogarth Press, pp. 197–217.
Furness, R. (1965) 'The androgynous ideal: Its significance in German literature', *Modern Language Review*, vol. 60, pp. 58–64.
Gill, C. (1990) 'Platonic love and individuality', in Loizou, A. and Lesser, H. (eds) *Polis and Politics: Essays in Greek Moral and Political Philosophy*, Aldershot, Gower Press, pp. 69–88.
Gill, C. (1999) 'Introduction', in *Plato – The Symposium*, London, Penguin.
Graf, F. (1993) 'Dionysian and Orphic eschatology', in Carpenter, T. and Faraone, C. (eds) *Masks of Dionysus*, Ithaca, Cornell University Press, pp. 239–258.
Grant, I. H. (2006) *On an Artificial Earth: Philosophies of Nature after Schelling*, London, Continuum.
Grigg, R. (2006) 'Beyond the Oedipus complex', in Clemens, J. and Grigg, R. (eds) *Jacques Lacan and the Other side of Psychoanalysis: Reflections on Seminar XVII*, Chapel Hill, Duke University Press, pp. 50–68.
Halperin, D. M. (1990) *Before Sexuality*, Princeton, Princeton University Press.
Hankinson, R. J. (1995) 'Science', in Barnes, J. (ed.) *The Cambridge Companion to Aristotle*, Cambridge, Cambridge University Press, pp. 140–167.
Hatfield, E. and Walster, G. W. (1978) *A New Look at Love*, Lanham, University Press of America.
Hénaff, M. (2009) 'Lévi-Strauss and the question of symbolism', in Wiseman, B. (ed.) *A Cambridge Companion to Claude Lévi-Strauss*, Cambridge, Cambridge University Press, pp. 177–195.
Homer, *The Odyssey*, trans. Richmond Lattimore (1967), New York, Harper Collins.
Hunter, R. (trans.) (2004) *Plato – The Symposium*, Oxford, Oxford University Press.
Jones, E. (1953) *The Life and Work of Sigmund Freud*, New York, Basic Books.
Jung, C. G. (1991) *Transformations and Symbols of the Libido*, London, Routledge.
Kirk, G. S. (1974) *The Nature of Greek Myths*, London, Penguin.
Klein, M. (1967) *Contributions to Psychoanalysis*, London, Hogarth Press.
Kochhar-Lindgren, G. (1993) *Narcissus Transformed: The Textual Subject in Psychoanalysis and Literature*, University Park, Penn State University Press.
Lacan, J. (1977) *Seminar XI: The Four Fundamental Concepts of Psychoanalysis* (ed. J.-A. Miller, trans. A. Sheridan), London, Penguin.
Lacan, J. (1979) 'The neurotic's individual myth', *Psychoanalytic Quarterly*, vol. 48, no. 3, pp. 405–425.
Lacan, J. (1988) *Seminar I: Freud's Papers on Technique (1953–1954)* (ed. J.-A. Miller, trans. J. Forrester), Cambridge, Cambridge University Press.
Lacan, J. (1991) *Seminar XVII: The Other Side of Psychoanalysis* (ed. J.-A. Miller, trans. R. Grigg), New York, Norton.
Lacan, J. (2007) *Écrits: The First Complete Edition in English* (trans. B. Fink), New York, Norton.
Lacan, J. (2014) *Seminar X: Anxiety* (ed. J.-A. Miller, trans. A. R. Price), London, Polity Press.
Lacan, Jacques (2015) *Seminar VIII: Transference* (ed. J.-A. Miller, trans. Bruce Fink), London, Polity Press.
Lacoue-Labarthe, P. (2003) 'Oedipus as figure', *Radical Philosophy*, vol. 118, pp. 7–17.
Lamarck, J.-B. (1815–1822) *Histoire naturelle des animaux sans vertèbres*, Paris, Verdière.
Leader, D. (2003) 'Lacan's myths', in Rabaté, J.-M. (ed.) *The Cambridge Companion to Lacan*, Cambridge, Cambridge University Press, pp. 35–49.

Lévi-Strauss, C. (1949) 'L'efficacité symbolique', *Revue de L'Histoire des Religions*, vol. 135, no. 1, pp. 5–27.
Lévi-Strauss, C. (1963) *Structural Anthropology*, vol. 1 (trans. Claire Jacobson and Brooke Grundfest Schoepf), St Ives, Penguin.
Lévi-Strauss, C. (1976) *Structural Anthropology*, vol. 2 (trans. Monique Layton), New York, Basic Books.
Lipschütz, A. (1914) *Warum wir Sterben*, Stuttgart, Frankh'sche Verlagshandlung.
Ludwig, P. W. (2002) *Eros and Polis: Desire and Community in Greek Political Theory*, Cambridge, Cambridge University Press.
Miller, P. A. (1998) 'The classical roots of post structuralism', *International Journal of the Classical Tradition*, vol. 5, no. 2, pp. 204–225.
Nachmansohn, M. (1915) 'Freud's Libidotheorie verglichen mit der Eroslehre Platos', *Internationale Zeitschrift für Psychoanalyse*, vol. 3, pp. 65–83.
Nussbaum, M. (1979) 'The speech of Alcibiades: a reading of Plato's *Symposium*', *Philosophy and Literature*, vol. 3, no. 2, pp.131–172.
Ovid, *Metamorphoses*, trans. Mary Innes (1955) London, Penguin.
Plato, *The Symposium*, trans. C. Gill (1999) London, Penguin.
Rabaté, J-M. (2001) *Psychoanalysis and the Subject of Literature (Transitions)*, New York, Palgrave Macmillan.
Ragland, E. (1996) 'An overview of the real, with examples from seminars I and II', in Feldstein, R., Fink, B. and Jaanus, M. (eds) *Reading Seminars I and II*, Albany, SUNY Press, pp. 192–211.
Reidel-Schrewe, U. (1994) 'Freud's debut in the sciences', in Gilman, S. L., Birmele, J., Geller, J. and Greenberg, V. D. (eds) *Reading Freud's Reading*, New York, New York University Press, pp. 1–22.
Roudinesco, E. (1997) *Jacques Lacan* (trans. B. Bray), New York, Columbia University Press.
Sallis, J. (1999) 'Secluded nature: The point of Schelling's reinscription of the Timaeus', *Pli: Warwick Journal of Philosophy*, vol. 8, pp. 71–85.
Sheldrake, R. (1994) *The Rebirth of Nature: The Greening of Science and God*, Rochester, Inner Traditions.
Small, H. and Tate, T. (2003) *Literature, Science, Psychoanalysis 1830–1970: Essays in Honour of Gillian Beer*, Oxford, Oxford University Press.
Spencer, H. (1900) *First Principles*, New York, Appleton & Company.
Rossi, I. (ed.) (1974) *The Unconscious in Culture: the Structuralism of Claude Lévi-Strauss in Perspective*, New York, Dutton.
Sulloway, F. (1992) *Freud: Biologist of the Mind*, Cambridge, Harvard University Press.
Taylor, A. E. (1966) *Plato, the Man and His Work*, London, Methuen.
Vernant, J-P. (1957) *Myth and Thought among the Greeks*, London, Routledge and Kegan Paul.
Weismann, A. (1889) *Essays upon Heredity and Kindred Biological Problems*, Oxford, Clarendon.
Zafiropoulos, M. (2010) *Lacan and Lévi-Strauss or The Return to Freud* (trans. J. Holland), London, Karnac.
Žižek, S. (1997) *The Plague of Fantasies*, London, Verso.
Žižek, S. (2006) *Parallax View*, Cambridge, MA, MIT Press.

3
CREATION AND CASTRATION
Making something out of nothing

> And Heaven came, bringing on night and longing for love, and he lay about Earth spreading himself full upon her. Then the son from his ambush stretched forth his left hand and in his right took the great long sickle with jagged teeth, and swiftly lopped off his own father's members and cast them away to fall behind him. And not vainly did they fall from his hand; for all the bloody drops that gushed forth Earth received, and as the seasons moved round she bore the strong Erinyes and the great Giants with gleaming armor, holding long spears in their hands and the Nymphs whom they call Meliae all over the boundless earth.
>
> *Hesiod,* Theogony *(174–186)*

Introduction

Nowhere is myth more valuable than when we seek to explain beginnings. To minds most comfortable with cause and effect, absolute beginnings are, with the pun intended, difficult to conceive. Tales of the universe confront the greatest challenge of all: how to account for the appearance of existence itself. Perhaps for this reason, the Ancient Greeks considered stories of creation to be the prototypical poetic genre. Hesiod's *Theogony* is not only the fullest surviving account of the ancient Greek gods but also the fullest surviving demonstration of the archaic poet's function. And when the poet sings, he sings of castration.

If the value of creation myths is clear, less clear is the value, across several traditions, of making creation so bloody, associated with transgression, punishment and mutilation. Aristophanes' violent myth of love's origin, explored in the previous chapter, belongs in a large family of stories, the most significant of which is given at the very start of the *Symposium* itself. While Phaedrus has begun proceedings by describing Eros as parentless, the source of all that subsequently appears, Pausanius points out that there are two cosmological accounts of Eros. In one, it is true, he is parentless – this is the older Eros – Orphic Eros, which we have heard Jung (1991) comparing to the primal, universal 'libido'.[1] He exists peacefully alongside the original cosmic entities, Ouranos (sky), Khaos (air) and Gaia (earth). But this original harmony ends, in a startlingly proto-oedipal scene, with the castration of Ouranos by his son, Kronos. Kronos cuts off Ouranos' genitals and throws them behind him (Hesiod, *Theogony*, 178–187; see also Vernant, 1990). The drops of blood unleash conflict and division. In the universe that results from this act, there are now two sexes, along with gendered desire personified by Aphrodite. Aphrodite is assisted by the younger Eros and Himeros (Longing).

Ouranos and Kronos emerge from a tradition of creation myths. In a Hittite version of a Hurrian tale from the mid-second millennium BC, Kumarbi deposes the sky god Anu by biting off his phallus; he swallows it and becomes pregnant with an all-powerful storm god, equivalent to the sky and weather god Zeus.[2] Parricide and castration rear their heads in the Egyptian myth of Osiris. In his groundbreaking work of comparative mythology, *The Golden Bough* (1894), Sir James Frazer pursues these themes into myths of renewal more broadly: Adonis, Attis, Tammuz, all spirits of vegetation associated with incest who are violently punished (Adonis, for example, the product of incest between Myrrha and her father Cinyras, is castrated by his father the boar). The imprint of this tradition, of course, can be seen in the tragedy of Oedipus, the myth Freud chooses to explain our own psychological origins.

As a genre, tragedy is defined by its endings, yet if we ask what it does for psychoanalysis, it is bound to beginnings – to a struggle with beginnings that Freud shares with mythology. This is the context for a provocative strand of Lacan's teaching explored in this chapter: his self-identification as a 'creationist'. Lacan repeatedly declaims the superiority of a creationist outlook over any developmental or evolutionary scheme. To his progressively minded trainee analysts, disciples of Freud and Darwin, he declares:

> no one can think, except in creationist terms. What you take to be the most familiar model of your thought, namely, evolutionism, is with you, as with all your contemporaries, a form of defence, of clinging to

religious ideals, which prevents you from seeing what is happening in the world around you.

(2008, p. 156)

This may seem at first bizarre, a betrayal of Freud's passionate attachment to Darwinian evolution, but it responds to yet another knotty issue in Freud's work. Freud's metaphors of evolution mask problems of chronology and genesis that he never entirely solves and that Lacan, once again, intends to confront head on. The problem concerns first causes, specifically how to account for an *initial* traumatic event when it is only in relation to *past* events that something is traumatic. This is a problem so deep that, as Lacan recognizes, Freud's struggles with it drive the development of psychoanalysis itself.

The spontaneous universe

The problem of first causes arises when Freud moves from a purely physical account of the mind to a psychoanalytical one. At the end of 1895 he abandons the mechanical model of psychology found in the *Project* notes, referring to it in a letter to Fliess as 'pure balderdash' (Jones, 1953, p. 420). In the following year, in his paper on the origins of hysteria, he introduces the term *psychoanalysis*. A new kind of origin is now situated at the source of all neuropathologies: incidents of childhood abuse. It is in these he claims to have found the *'caput Nil'*, the source of the Nile (Freud, 1896). Then, two years later, he abandons this theory, citing lack of therapeutic success as well as concern, given the prevalence of hysteria, over accusing so many fathers of abuse. He also has a growing sense that the unconscious cannot, in fact, distinguish between fact and fiction (Masson, 1985). Out of this grows a theory of infantile sexuality centred on fantasy and, ultimately, the Oedipus complex, a *universal fantasy*.[3] But, in explaining an individual's psychology, there was still a need for biographical narrative to play its part, therefore still the need for an initiating *incident*. Jung had argued that there were hysterias in which reminiscences played no part, being 'organic' or 'hereditary' in character. Freud maintains the importance of a personal trauma, one that allows, of course, for interpretation.

Yet the chronology of development becomes increasingly complex. The initiating event is traumatic yet, in Freud's theory, traumatic events are so because they refer back to a previous experience. One attempt at pinning down an original moment in which trauma is created involves the concept of 'primal scenes'. These involve a child's witnessing of a sex act. The first and most famous example occurs in Freud's (1918) case study of the 'Wolf Man', Sergei Pankejeff. Pankejeff's depressive illness is traced back to an incident at the age of one and a half when he witnessed his parents having sex. But 'primal scenes' such as these turn out to have an ambiguous status. Again, the 'reality' problem rears its head. The question of whether or not it is credible that Pankejeff actually saw this (Freud refers to it as an 'imaginary trauma') returns Freud to the issue of truth and fiction that forced him from the seduction theory into the development of the Oedipus complex:

> I should myself be glad to know whether the primal scene in my present patient's case was a phantasy or a real experience; but, taking other similar cases into account, I must admit that the answer to this question is not in fact a matter of very great importance.
>
> (p. 97)[4]

This is a bold statement. But Freud's insouciance is given the lie by years of theoretical wrestling. As Lacan (1977) himself comments (regarding the Wolf Man case), Freud 'applies himself in a way that can almost be described as anguish, to the question – what is the first encounter, the real, that lies behind this phantasy?' (p. 54). The psychological trauma can only be conceived of as arising from something already there, the reminiscence of the first scene. But how is this possible – that something can be already there, traumatic in and of itself rather than in relation to any previous experience? Where would it get its meaning for the subject? We are left with a choice between an infinite regression or an arbitrary stop at whichever moment we choose to represent the beginning (Laplanche and Pontalis, 1993).

In *Totem and Taboo* (1913), Freud suggests that the origins of fantasies may be found in prehistoric times. Fantasies could be inherited experiences from 'the primeval times of the human family' (p. 371). To this end, he introduces a new concept, that of the *Urphantasien*, primal (or original) fantasy. This allows him to draw, once again, on the realm of evolutionary biology via the concept of 'phylogenesis':

> A child catches hold of this phylogenetic experience where his own experience fails him. He fills in the gaps in individual truth with prehistoric truth; he replaces occurrences in his own life by occurrences in the life of his ancestors.
>
> (1918, p. 97)

The term *phylogenesis* was coined by biologist and artist Ernst Haeckel (1834–1919) to describe the evolutionary development of a species over time.[5] Haeckel popularized Darwin's work in Germany and developed the 'recapitulation' theory that fascinated Freud, according to which the biological development of an individual organism reflected its species' entire evolutionary development.[6] It is in this context that Freud introduces the myth of the primal horde as a possible origin of Oedipal guilt and the incest taboo. In wording reminiscent of his move to Aristophanes' account of Eros in *Beyond the Pleasure Principle*, he concedes ignorance before an apologetic swerve to a myth: 'I must, however, mention one other attempt at solving it. It is of a kind quite different from any that we have so far considered, and might be described as "historical"' (1913, p. 125).[7] Freud recounts Darwin's hypothesis regarding the social state of primitive man. In this, a jealous, older male has a monopoly over females until he is deposed and killed by a younger male. This new victor drives out the other younger males, preventing interbreeding. And these exiled males, establishing their own hordes, may outlaw sexual relations within the group for defensive, jealous reasons. This would ground the incest taboo and its associated Oedipal psychology in a (pre)historical event. Tellingly, Freud (1921) refers to it as 'the *scientific myth* of the father of the primal horde' (p. 135). 'Scientific myth' is as good an 'origin' as Freud will find. But even he acknowledges the difficulty of establishing which came first, exogamy (the forbidding of marriage within the social group) or totemism (the symbolism by which the group is defined).

There is another approach Freud takes to this problem of temporality, however. This line of speculation unsettles chronology itself via the concept of *Nachträglichkeit*, 'afterwardness', which Ernest Jones translates as 'deferred action.' *Nachträglichkeit* is a way of accounting for events that become sexualized, and therefore traumatic, only *after* the event: a retrospective activation of sexual content.[8]

Yet the problem of first cause is exacerbated. Crucially, for our interests, the need for a deferred action applies not just with regards to specific cases of individual trauma, but to the general formation of the ego itself. We return to the problem discussed in the previous chapter, that of an initial objectless Eros within an infant yet to develop a sense of self, one that must somehow be converted to an ego-centred, object-seeking libido (even if its first object is narcissistic).

> We are bound to suppose that unity comparable to the ego cannot exist in the individual from the start: the ego has to be developed. The

auto-erotic instincts, however, are there from the very first; so there must be something added to auto-erotism – a new psychical action – in order to bring about narcissism.

(Freud, 1914, pp. 76–77)

Freud (1905) admits that to speak of an 'originary' kind of narcissism in any literal rather than mythical sense, is to 'look across a frontier, which we may not pass' (p. 84). As with the universe as a whole, therefore, an origin for the ego must be located over the border of time itself. Lacan, however, says we *can* look across the frontier. The 'something added to auto-erotism', the 'new psychical action' is supplied by the mirror stage.

'A conspiracy against time'

Lacan is conscious of what he's doing when he returns to Freud's problem with chronology, and is ready to tackle it at its base. As early as his thesis, Lacan had described the Freudian theory of primary narcissism as 'confused' and 'obscure' (Borch-Jacobsen, 1991, p. 249). When, in *Seminar II*, he notes that the problem of converting initial objectless libido to sexual libido 'is an extremely knotty one for [Freud] to resolve', he continues: 'this idea confirms the usefulness of my conception of the mirror-stage' (Lacan, 1991, p. 14). There must be a moment when the ego is formed and begins to function. He quotes Freud's positing of '*eine neue psychische Aktion … zu gestalten*' as evidence that 'in the development of the psyche, something new appears' (1988, p. 115).

It is the abruptness of this 'something new appears' that it will be Lacan's task to convey and protect against Freud's own attachment to development. The mirror stage is centred on an event: an infant of 3–18 months before a mirror, seduced by the unity of its image. It will found its own imagined unity on this pleasing image, repressing the sense of chaotic fragmentation that defined its previous experience. More broadly, the term 'mirror stage' describes the structure which extends beyond this particular moment to include the child's absorption into the larger social order as a whole, an order that provides its own tools with which to construct a singular, coherent identity. It does, then, have an aspect of developmental narrative. But the evolution of the concept itself demonstrates the effort Lacan makes to keep the mirror stage distinct from developmental ideas and to retain a sense of instantaneity.

The origins of Lacan's mirror stage theory can be found in experiments by physiologist Willhelm Preyer and psychologist Charlotte Buhler, but the theory owes its greatest debt to the psychologist Henri Wallon, who himself relied on previous work by Darwin (Borch-Jacobsen, 1991). Wallon describes a similar occurrence before a mirror, but in his account it is an *'episodic* process' of development.[9] There is no mention of Wallon in Lacan's (1938) article on the family complexes or the paper on the mirror stage. Wallon extensively quotes Darwin; Lacan does not. Lacan (2007) attributes to the philosopher and psychologist James Baldwin an approximate periodization that in fact does belong to Darwin: 'This event can take place, as we know from Baldwin's work, from the age of six months on' (p. 75). All this is part of a process of substitution. Instead of Darwinism, there is structuralism. Lévi-Strauss is quoted in the revised 'mirror stage' paper of 1949 (a note directs us towards his essay 'L'efficacité symbolique' of the same year). By now, the mirror stage has come to signify the Lacanian model of consciousness generally, rather than acting as an account of psychological development (Dosse, 1997). It acquires a mythical spontaneity, logical rather than chronological (Forrester, 1990; Lacan, 1988). Over the course of the 1950s, it becomes less and less associated with a specific moment and more emblematic of our entry into the symbolic order (see 'The subversion of the subject' 1977).

There is a fundamental tension between structuralism and chronology. A structural interpretation derives meaning – of a text, a tribe, etc. – through an analysis of synchronous relations between units, i.e. its structure in the present rather than its origins and history. This synchronicity is central to structuralism's appeal. Lévi-Strauss (1971) identifies in myth itself, 'something better than time regained, time abolished' which he then asserts is a fundamental trait of mankind: 'a conspiracy against time' (p. 542). It is certainly fundamental to the appeal of science. Hans Gadamer (1975) describes the aim of science as being the objectification of experience so that it no longer contains any historical element. Severed from any supposed 'roots', signs become, in themselves, arbitrary, their meaning only found in their relationships. As Lévi-Strauss says himself of his great influence, 'the Saussurean principle of the *arbitrary character of linguistic signs* was a prerequisite for the accession of linguistics to the scientific level'. And Lacan, in turn, celebrates the 'synchrony of mythemes' as structuralism's great inheritance from Saussure's linguistic revolution.[10]

Once again, for Lévi-Strauss, a confrontation with psychoanalysis is deliberate. When he asserts that it was the arbitrary character of linguistic signs that raised linguistics to the scientific level, this is in the course of criticizing Jung's theory of archetypes, with its attribution of inherent meaning to words and symbols. And it is not just Jung who receives criticism. In the last volume of *Mythologiques* (Lévi-Strauss, 1971) psychoanalysts are criticized generally for connecting the structure of a collective or individual work to what they falsely call its origin. And in chapter 6 of *Tristes Tropiques* (1955), Lévi-Strauss turns to psychoanalysis's interest in the origin of myth specifically and describes this approach as flawed.

Lévi-Strauss's confrontation with Freud becomes more complex still when he (1949) returns to Freud's enquiry in *Totem and Taboo* regarding the origin of the incest taboo and identifies the prohibition of incest with the birth of language. According to this scheme, we leave the rest of nature behind when we adopt a coded system: the structure of kinship necessary to identify incestuous relationships. But insofar as this structure is at once a universal feature of early humans, yet not a biological or natural phenomenon, it must somehow arise spontaneously – out of nowhere, so to speak.

The identification of language and incest gives Lacan a means of elaborating his own solution to the problem of origins. The significant implication of Lévi-Strauss's notion of the elementary structure, Lacan (1991a) sees, is that there are no means 'starting from the natural plane, of deducing the formation of this elementary structure' (p. 29). There is nothing 'natural' about kinship laws, no biological accounting for them. 'In the human order, we are dealing with the complete emergence of a new function, encompassing the whole order in its entirety.' And he calls this 'a universe': 'The symbolic order from the first takes on its universal character …. As soon as the symbol arrives, there is a universe of symbols …. It's not for nothing that Lévi-Strauss calls his structures *elementary* – he doesn't say *primitive*' (p. 29). Lacan (2007) takes care to emphasize the difficulty in conceiving of this 'emergence': 'The creation of the symbol, as [Lévi-Strauss] stressed, must be conceptualized as a mythical moment rather than as a genetic moment' (p. 319).

This is the context for his assertions of creationism in *Seminar II*. 'With the symbolic order there are absolute beginnings, there is creation', he announces (Lacan, 1991, pp. 291–292). Discussion leads, naturally enough, to consideration of Biblical creation, the nature of St John's Greek *logos* compared to the Hebrew *Dabar* (the Word). And Lacan is evidently happy to encourage parallels, encouraged by the felicitous presence of a Father Beirnaert in the audience.

In *Seminar II*, so fiercely does Lacan guard the synchronous, spontaneous nature of the symbolic order against ideas of development that persist in psychoanalysis that even the word 'stage' becomes suspect, passed over in favour of the less hierarchical 'mirror phase'. An audience member at the

École Normale Supérieure objects: 'I don't see how, in describing the formation of intelligence up to the age of three or four, one can do without stages' (Lacan, 1977, p. 64). They argue that one needs stages to understand the procession of defence phantasies, phantasies of castration, fear of mutilation. Lacan seizes on the reference to castration, for a revision of this concept will be his weapon against adaptive, teleological accounts of human psychology. Castration is *structural* and foundational: 'The description of the stages, which go to form the libido, must not be referred to some natural processes of pseudo-maturation, which always remains opaque' (p. 64). Rather: 'The stages are organized around the fear of castration … the introduction of sexuality is traumatizing – this is a snag of some size – and it has an organizing function for development. The fear of castration is like a thread that perforates all the stages of development' (p. 64).

So, while one explanation of Lacan's creationism is the spontaneity it brings, bound to a structuralist approach, castration brings in another aspect, a relationship between something and nothing. Lacan's creation is creation *ex nihilo*.

Lacan's creation *ex nihilo*: touching the void

The concept of castration centres psychological development on a terrifying drama regarding presence and absence, being and nothingness. As such, it gives psychoanalysis its own relationship with ontology. Nothingness is not just a concept for psychoanalysis, it is a personal trauma. Lacan uses the concept of nothingness to associate several discrete areas of Freud's thought, linking castration anxiety itself with concepts of repression and negation, foreclosure (from Freud's *Verwefung*, repudiation, used by Lacan to describe the rejection of a signifier from the symbolic order altogether) and, of course, death. This creates a bridge to his own work, defined by the signifier. The signifier itself is bound to absence (the absence of the thing itself) and therefore castration. Signifiers place us in an intimate relationship with non-existence. The castrating bar of signification falls between the word and the concept it represents, which is itself forever divided from the thing. When we enter the mirror stage, this severance characterizes the structure of our selves.

Heidegger is a crucial influence here, and the intellectual figure behind much of Lacan's return to Greek philosophy (see Roudinesco, 2014). Heidegger's (1927) concept of Being-toward-death (*Sein-zum-Tode*) presents death as a phenomenon woven into the structure of human experience, already part of us rather than simply an event on the horizon. Lacan knew Heidegger's work intimately and the man himself personally (see Roudinesco, 1990). From 1953's 'Individual's myth', references to Heidegger can be found when Lacan seeks to articulate 'the symbolic abolition', the disappearance of the signified beneath the signifier, linking the 'symbolic order' and the death instinct (Marini, 1992).

Heidegger, in his essay 'The Thing', had explored being, non-being and creation via the example of a potter and a vase. The potter's creation or the vase stands for an original deed, one that necessitates the creation of a void in order for the void to then hold the 'fullness' of water or wine. Lacan borrows this image in *Seminar VII* to describe the relation of the signifier to nothingness. The vase's shape embodies a primordial signifier arising alongside the void itself: 'the fashioning of the signifier and the introduction of a gap or a hole in the real is identical' (2008, p. 151). It is as such that we are in 'a domain of creation *ex nihilo*, insofar as it introduces into the natural world the organization of the signifier' (p. 264). This allows him to describe the notion of the death drive, somewhat startlingly, as a 'creationist sublimation' (p. 262). Again, Lacan is seizing the opportunity to identify death with nothingness, signifiers with creation. In doing so he joins two distinct concerns in *Beyond the Pleasure Principle*: the instinct to repeat (identified with the chain of signifiers that make up the symbolic order) and the 'death' of the death drive, presented as the absence which underlies the chain:

> As soon as we have to deal with anything in the world appearing in the form of the signifying chain, there is somewhere – though certainly outside of the natural world – [that] which is the beyond of that chain, the *ex nihilo* on which it is founded and articulated as such.
>
> (p. 262)[11]

As discussed above, it is the radically arbitrary nature of signs, divorcing them from supposedly natural origins or meanings, that grants structuralism its scientific status. But the arbitrary is itself an odd, threatening category to humans who instinctively seek meaning – never more so than when we turn to the sign that represents ourselves.

> There is, in effect, something radically unassimilable to the signifier. It's quite simply the subject's singular existence. Why is he here? Where has he come from? What is he doing here? Why is he going to disappear? The signifier is incapable of providing him with the answer.
>
> (pp. 179–180)

This returns us to the conceptual challenge of sexual reproduction discussed in the previous chapter. It is our existence as a (arbitrary, *ex nihilo*) signifier that seems so at odds with our biological origins. Lacan discusses the conceptual challenge and the role it plays in psychosis and neurosis (both involving struggles with sexed identity) in *Seminar III*.

> There is ... one thing that evades the symbolic tapestry, it's procreation in its essential root − that one being is born from another. In the symbolic order procreation is covered by the order instituted by this succession between beings. But nothing in the symbolic explains the fact of their individuation, the fact that beings come from beings. The entire symbolism declares that creatures don't engender creatures, that a creature is unthinkable without a fundamental creation. In the symbolic nothing explains creation.
>
> (p. 179)

Two attempts at softening the radical contingency of this creation particularly vex Lacan. One is the Jungian theory of archetypes in which the sudden appearance of the signifier is transformed into the 'symbol' emerging naturally from the collective unconscious: 'the archetype makes the symbol into the blossoming of the soul', Lacan (2007, p. 392) complains.[12] The other false comfort is the concept of evolution. When Lacan encounters President Schreber engaged in his own struggle with the idea of creation, he highlights Schreber's clutching at evolutionary theory as a defence mechanism. Schreber tries to maintain the appearance of a rational modern man, responding to the sudden appearance of his hallucinations 'with ideas that are more familiar to the man he assures us he is, as if there were any need for it: a *gebildet* German of the Wilhelmine era, raised on Haeckelian metascientism'; Schreber even provides 'a list of readings, an occasion for us to fill out, by reading them, what Gavarni somewhere calls a courageous idea of Man' (pp. 466–467). Paul Gavarni, referred to by Lacan, was a nineteenth-century French caricaturist. What is being caricatured is someone not dissimilar to Freud. Schreber presents himself as a *Gebildet* (cultured) German up to date with the cutting edge of nineteenth-century evolutionary theory, seeing it as part of a broader progressive historical outlook. Without recourse to the insights of structuralism, he turns to the science of his time to explain creation.

It is the complacent anthropocentrism of this 'courageous idea of Man' that Lacan takes to task in the second seminar:

> Implicitly, modern man thinks that everything which has happened in the universe since its origin has converged on this thing which thinks, creation of life, unique, precious being, pinnacle of creation, which is himself, with this privileged vantage-point called consciousness.
> This perspective leads to an anthropomorphism which is so deluded that one has to start by shedding the scales from one's eyes, so as to realize what kind of illusion one has fallen prey to. This is a newcomer for humanity, this idiocy of scientific atheism.
>
> *(1991, p. 48)*

Where, for Freud, Darwinism represents the promise that we might ground speculative thought in biological and anthropological fact, for Lacan Darwinism is more often the means by which an overarching narrative has been imposed on the human: a narrative of progress and belonging. In *Seminar II*, the psychoanalyst Octave Mannoni discusses Darwin in relation to Gestalt psychology (which posits that the operational principle of the brain is holistic and self-organizing).[13] Lacan responds:

> The idea of living evolution, the notion that nature always produces superior forms, more and more elaborated, more and more integrated, better and better built organisms, the belief that progress of some sort is immanent in the movement of life, all this is alien to [Freud], and he explicitly repudiates it .... It is his experience of man which guides him ... of a fundamental conflict, in man.
>
> *(1991, pp. 78–79)*[14]

This demands a playing of Freud against himself, for it is an exaggeration, to say the least. We have seen how Darwin provided Freud with an ideal of scientific progress. But Lacan is wary of development in multiple senses. As well as his theoretical issues with narratives of individual adaptation, there is a deep-seated distaste at a self-satisfied modernity. Freud (1916–17) had famously placed psychoanalysis as the third of the great blows to humanity's self-esteem, following the discoveries of Copernicus and Darwin. Lacan (2007) dares to question the supposedly humbling effect of these thinkers: 'In any case, it is not because of Darwin that men believe themselves to be any less the best among the creatures, for it is precisely of this that he convinces them' (p. 674). Lacan's critique is sometimes explicitly ideological: 'Lots of things have been made to fit within the political myth of the "struggle for life" [English in original]. If it was Darwin who wrought it, that was because he came of a nation of privateers, for whom racism was the basic industry' (1988, p. 177). And again: 'Darwin's success seems to derive from the fact that he projected the predations of Victorian society and the economic euphoria that sanctioned for that society the social devastation it initiated on a planetary scale' (2007, p. 98). Darwinism can serve as an alibi for the worst of mankind, and facilitate self-blindness.

Lacan's most common ground for attack is more abstract, if no less heartfelt. The theory of evolution obscures the multiple ways in which archaic superstitions and prejudices about the workings of the mind remain. And, given Freud's evolutionary interests, this is prevalent amongst analysts themselves.

> The idea of creation is consubstantial with your thought. You cannot think, no one can think, except in creationist terms. What you take to be the most familiar model of your thought, namely, evolutionism, is with you, as with all your contemporaries, a form of defence, of clinging to religious ideals, which prevents you from seeing what is happening in the world around you.
>
> *(2008, p. 156)*

Evolutionism as a clinging to religious ideals may seem a peculiar idea. But Rob Weatherill (1999) expresses the sentiment powerfully via the notion of a narcissism writ large: this is what he describes as 'the global mirror-stage', a comforting belief that our present stage of development is close to the epitome of evolution (Schreber's courageous, anthropocentric idea of Man) and that this process itself was set in motion just after the Big Bang 'when the fundamental laws of physics were set at values that would ultimately offer the possibility of evolution to not only life but consciousness and self-consciousness'. This is the so-called 'Anthropic Principle' – the miracle that the universe suits us: 'Connectedness, Gaia: somehow we *belong*, mind and consciousness are as much part of the universe as are the stars .... There is no lack, no gap, no void, only global narcissism – "the universe knew we were coming"' (pp. 216–217).[15]

Again, Plato and Aristotle allow Lacan to draw out the philosophical implications of our beliefs. In *Seminar VIII*, recalling the previous year's seminar and 'the creationist structure of the human *ethos* ... the *ex nihilo* which subsists at its heart', Lacan (2015) draws a contrast with what he calls Plato's '*Schwärmerei*': 'Plato's *Schwärmerei* consists in having projected the idea of the Sovereign Good onto the impenetrable void', in having 'Good' rather than 'void' occupy 'the centre of our being' (p. 5).

104 Creation and castration

Lacan borrows the term *Schwärmerei* from Kant (*Schwärmerei*, meaning excessive sentimentality, from *schwärmen*, to swarm).[16] *Schwärmerei* here represents the masking of a fundamental lack. Plato fills the *nihilo* with a notion of the Good: the idea that there is a higher value underpinning material existence and giving it meaning. Yet it is Aristotle who introduces an even more dangerous form of denial with his idea that the 'good' is manifest in *design*. Lacan locates this proto-scientific conversion in the *Nicomachean Ethics* where 'although it maintains this notion of sovereign good, it profoundly changes its meaning'. The good is in nature, in the stars, 'absolute, uncreated, incorruptible' (p. 4).

Plato and Aristotle take individual stances on creation; both posit first cause arguments but of very different kinds. In the *Laws* (Book X), Plato argues that motion in the world and the Cosmos requires some kind of *self-originated* action to start it off. In the *Timaeus*, he posits a 'demiurge' of supreme wisdom and intelligence as the creator of the Cosmos, fulfilling this function, even if Platonists have never been able to decide to what extent his account of the divine craftsman is metaphorical or literal (Most, 2003). For Aristotle (in his *Physics* and *Metaphysics*), the 'prime mover' underwrites the *order*, not the origin. First causes are not first in a chronological sense, they are first in the sense of being ultimate; they are where explanations come to a stop (*Posterior Analytics*, I 24, 85b27). Aristotle argues *against* a finite universe (and therefore 'creation' as described by Plato), the very need for an 'efficient cause' being its flaw.

It is this Aristotelian 'first cause' that Lacan (2014) describes as 'a deaf and blind mover to what it sustains, namely the whole cosmos' (pp. 198–199).[17] God has been smuggled back in. In *Seminar X*, Lacan compares Aristotle's first cause to the pre-Socratic philosophy of Anaxagoras, who saw *Nous*, the cosmic mind, creating order out of originally undifferentiated matter. Both install an implicit (anthropomorphic) consciousness in existence. That is why

> the creationist perspective is the only one that allows one to glimpse the possibility of the radical elimination of God.
>
> It is paradoxically only from a creationist point of view that one can envisage the elimination of the always-recurring notion of creative intention as supported by a person. In evolutionist thought, although God goes unnamed throughout, he is literally omnipresent. An evolution that insists on deducing from continuous process the ascending movement which reaches the summit of consciousness and thought necessarily implies that that consciousness and that thought were there at the beginning. It is only from the point of view of an absolute beginning, which marks the origin of the signifying chain as a distinct order … that we do not

find Being [*l'être*] always implied in being [*l'étant*], the implication that is at the core of evolutionist thought.

(2008, p. 264)

A recognition of design seduces us with its implicit teleology: the universe was waiting for us to appreciate it; meaning is already installed. What infuriates Lacan (or at least provokes his act of intellectual irritation) is that this becomes injected into the very tradition that should uphold the radical contingency of creation: Christianity. When Thomas Aquinas (*c.*1225–1274) adapted Aristotle's arguments, he interpreted the First Cause, inevitably, as God: 'All things which are diversified by the diverse participation of being, so as to be more or less perfect, are caused by one First Being, who possesses being most perfectly' (*Summa Theologica*, I, 44).[18] Everything that is created strives for its own perfection in accordance with this.

Theories of creation have epistemological implications. Thomas inherits from the Greeks what Lacan (2014) calls the 'myth of the psychological origin of knowledge' (p. 199). According to this, knowledge of the world is the most natural of things because it is simply a true recognition of the created order of which we are part. Lacan (1998) holds the Pre-Socratic Parmenides responsible for initiating this idea (see Braungardt, 2002). In *On Nature*, his only known work, Parmenides describes reality ('what-is') as one: change is impossible and existence is timeless, uniform. Appearances, therefore, represent false conceptions. As such, he was the first to express a vision of truth as a return to the unity beneath appearances, a return of thought to its home, after wandering into an erroneous world of multiplicity. Thought was indivisible from being.

All this had an unmistakable influence on Plato and subsequently Aristotle, and gives rise to a correspondence theory of truth: truth as an accurate mirror of reality in the mind of the knower.[19] This is augmented by Christianity, Aquinas (*De Veritate*) in particular, and with it the belief that the reason for the intelligibility of reality is the presence of a subject (in some way similar to us) on the other side: God. The idea that truth is a perfect equation of world and intellect becomes central to the defences of 'rational' Christianity (see Braungardt, 2002).

For Plato and the tradition of Aristotelian Christianity he spawns, 'Form [Ideas] is the knowledge that fills being' (Lacan, 1998, p. 120). For Lacan, this is a narcissistic projection.

> For Aristotle's philosophy to have been reinjected by Saint Thomas into what one might call the Christian conscience, if that had any

meaning, is something that can only be explained by the fact that Christians – well, it's the same with psychoanalysts – abhor what was revealed to them. (p. 114)

What was revealed to them, in Lacan's reading of Genesis, is the underpinning of nothingness that haunts creation, the creation that is *ex nihilo*. The psychoanalytic equivalent he has in mind here is, of course, resistance to the full implications of the death drive as he interprets it: the Lacanian theory of a self split from within, founded on an arbitrary signifier.

Neither Christianity nor psychoanalysis acknowledges the full implications of their own theories. Thomism not only rests on the unwarranted assumption of an intelligible world, but it eliminates the *subjective* dimension of truth – that 'truth' describes a subjective *experience* of coherence, not an objective correspondence (Braungardt, 2002). It masks the split between the subject and the world but, equally, the split (born of the mirror stage) within the subject themselves without which there would be no desire for truth in the first place (see chapter 1).[20]

Lacan (1998) claims his own theme is 'the discordance between knowledge and being' (p. 120). His is also concerned with an active appreciation of *non*-being. In a Parmenidean universe, there is no room for nothingness: matter is eternal, it is one with thought; non-being cannot be thought so therefore cannot be. This is the precise opposite of the Lacanian universe. For Lacan, non-being can be thought all too easily – indeed, it is forced upon us by the nature of our existence. The reality of non-being is heard in myth and literature, from Oedipus' pronouncement that 'not to be born surpasses all reckoning' (Sophocles, *Oedipus at Colonus*, l.1225) to Hamlet's wondering whether 'to be, or not to be' (Shakespeare, *Hamlet*, Act III, Scene 1).[21]

Having dismissed Parmenides, Lacan introduces another pre-Socratic philosopher in order to set up a distinction: 'Parmenides was wrong and Heraclitus was right' (1991, p. 114). We have seen how, in his doctrine of eternal unity, Parmenides was wrong. The role of Heraclitus in rescuing psychoanalysis brings us to a universe that is not just born spontaneously, not just born from a void, but born wrong.

The flawed universe

> There is something originally, inaugurally, profoundly wounded in the human relation to the world.
>
> *Jacques Lacan (1991, p. 167)*

A universe defined by an irreparable split demands its own type of creation myth. Creation becomes fall: the start not just of existence, but its problems. This is a distinct tradition that brings with it the sense of a universe defined by guilt, founded on a crime: a cosmological viewpoint that is, naturally, of interest to Freud. Freud's consideration of a cosmological fault attracts Lacan's interest and provides another example of Freud's classicism serving Lacan's philosophical project.

Freud is interested in the idea of original sin, and conscious that his theory has aligned itself with a way of seeing the universe itself, and hopefully thrown light on its psychological rationale. An original killing of a primal father, an internalization of guilt, would account for the traditions collated and compared by Sir James Frazer in *The Golden Bough*, tales that attract Freud's interest in *Totem and Taboo*. Freud (1913) turns in particular to the constellation of myths centred on dismemberment. In his own Frazerian excursion, Freud sees these giving rise to the Persian god Mithras (and eventually Christ) as doctrines of original sin are elaborated, before entering Pre-Socratic philosophy itself as a sense of unity destroyed:

> The doctrine of original sin was of Orphic origin. It formed a part of the mysteries, and spread from them to the schools of philosophy of ancient Greece. Mankind, it was said, were descended from Titans who had killed the young Dionysus-Zagreus and had torn him to pieces. The burden of this crime weighed on them. A fragment of Anaximander relates how the unity of the world was broken by a primeval sin, and that whatever issued from it must bear the punishment. The tumultuous mobbing, the killing and the tearing in pieces by the Titans reminds us clearly enough of the totemic sacrifice described by St. Nilus – as, for the matter of that, do many other ancient myths, including, for instance, that of the death of Orpheus himself.
>
> *(pp. 153–154)*

The Titans, St Nilus and Orpheus are all involved in scenes of brutal *sparagmos*: ritual dismemberment (St Nilus describes the sacrifice of camels by Bedouins of the Sinai desert). In the case of the philosopher Anaximander (c.610–c.546 BC), the primeval sin Freud refers to is individual existence itself. In Anaximander's only surviving fragment, there is already a sense of the cosmological tragic: individual elements of existence must perish and return back into the Boundless because this individual existence is an injustice to the universe. 'And the source of coming-to-be for existing things is that into which destruction, too, happens, according to necessity; for they pay penalty and retribution to each other for their injustice according to the assessment of Time' (Kirk and Raven, 1957, p. 117).

Freud's immediate source for his interests here is Jacob Burckhardt's *History of Greek Civilization* (1818–97). In a study of Freud's reading, Mitchell-Boyask (1994) notes Freud's interest in a particular passage of Burckhardt's *History*, evident in repeated pencil marks. In this passage, Burckhardt is arguing that the progression of the Greek gods, from Ouranos to Zeus, was a belated product of the imagination. The Greeks only ever actually believed in the Zeus-ruled Olympians, he suggests, and the dynasties of Kronos and Ouranos were projected backwards 'as prehistory'. Mitchell-Boyask notes this as a potential source for the concept of retroactive fantasies generally (Burckhardt describes the imaginative projection of the Greeks as *Phantasie*). But of equal interest is the nature of what is being cast back: a fundamental incestuous conflict and originary castration identified with the imposition of mortality. In this account of existence, Burckhardt writes, misery and evil stem from the castration of Uranos, 'the great sin in the divine world, from which come all the things which cause anxiety for mankind, the first of which is *Schickslatod* (fated death)' (in Mitchell-Boyask, 1994, p. 45). It is while he is reading Burckhardt that Freud is developing the Oedipus complex. In a letter to Fliess during the composition of *The Interpretation of Dreams*, Freud writes: 'For relaxation I am reading Burckhardt's *History of Greek Civilization*, which is providing me with unexpected parallels' (pp. 30–31). Mitchell-Boyask notes that Freud marks the passage on *Schicksaltod* with a double line in the margin (a mark he rarely used) and in lead pencil, not red as elsewhere in the volume, suggesting that he returned to it at a later date, recognizing its significance for his own work: a myth concerning a struggle between a father and a son leading to a castration and, as a result, the introduction of *Angst* to the world.

Plato cites the castration of Ouranos by Kronos (in Hesiod, *Theogony*, 180–181) in the *Republic* as an example of bad mythology and castigates Hesiod (along with Homer) for their misrepresentation of gods and heroes (377e). Plato's criticism is not so much that their myths are false, but that their stories are unhelpful, providing misleading metaphors for existence (378a) (see also Dowden, 1992). His preferred mythology is one that would show the gods as unchanging and benign, responsible for all that is good in the world but not for the evil (any evil in Plato's world would be the product of error, ignorance) (382e; 379c).

Plato's gods underwrite a vision of the universe and man's place in it. In a Platonic universe, there is no originary and fundamental fault. Any division, such as that between subject and the world, is a mark of error, and therefore retains the possibility of reunion if we only rid ourselves of illusion. It is this promise that the Neoplatonists preserve. Neoplatonism was a tradition of philosophy arising in the third century AD, influenced both by Plato and by the Platonic tradition that thrived during the six centuries following his death. Its founder Plotinus (AD 204–270), like Parmenides, presented the first principle of reality as an inexpressible unity, the source and the end of all existing things. Plotinus' disciple Proclus (AD 485) stated 'The One is God'.

There is an element of creationism in Neoplatonic thought, however, in so far as the One transcendent absolute still needs to engender the universe of multiplicity. Neoplatonists turn to myth to picture how the universe with which we are familiar should arise from this perfect, original unity. What is striking is the relationship their creation myth bears to Lacan's mirror stage – and the conscious effort Lacan will have to put in to maintain his distance.

As Freud describes in *Totem and Taboo*, the Neoplatonic philosophers inherit the myths of the mystery cults. Plotinus' followers depicted the emergence of multiplicity as 'the fall into the mirror of Dionysus'. According to myth, Dionysus had been conceived by the adulterous coupling of Zeus and Semele. Zeus's jealous wife, Hera, sends the Titans, a primeval race of godlike giants, to kill the child. To distract the infant Dionysus while they perform the execution, the Titans give him a mirror; while he is admiring his image they capture him and tear him to pieces.[22] Neoplatonists used this motif of the mirror to express the passage from the One to the many (Vernant, 1990).

A mirror is an ingenious solution to the problem of how one might become two. The symbolism of the myth could be taken further. For Neoplatonists, the mirror of Dionysus represented the material world itself (see Bull, 2001). In support of this interpretation, Proclus suggested that when Plato stated that the surface of the world was created smooth, he meant that it had a reflective surface like a mirror. Plotinus had something similar in mind when he claimed that it was when the original immortal souls saw their images in 'the mirror of Dionysus' that they descended from unity into material multiplicity.

Inevitably, the figure of Narcissus lurks at the origins of this mythology, entwined with Dionysus and his mirror. A story is preserved in the *Hermetica*, Egyptian-Greek wisdom texts from the second and third centuries AD: Man, seeing the beauty of God's creative workmanship, separated himself from the Father and descended into the sphere of generation. He stooped down, and seeing in the 'water' of earth the reflection of his own beauty, he fell in love with it and sought to cohabit with it.

> In his love for it, he wrapped himself about it and became married unto it. And for this cause man above all creatures is double; mortal because of his body, and immortal because of his celestial part. Immortal and having power over all things, he yet suffers mortal experience and is subject to Fate and Destiny.
>
> (Kuhn, 2007)

The fifteenth-century Italian scholar Marsilio Ficino translated the *Hermetica* and interpreted Plato as part of a sixteenth-century revival of Neoplatonism. He borrows from Aristophanes' myth of Eros in constructing his own Neoplatonic creation myth: souls as originally created were whole but, through aspiring to equal God they fell, divided, lost their supernatural facilities, and entered bodies. But Plotinus *rescues* Narcissus-Dionysus from their violent division. Crucially, in his philosophy, reunion *is* possible (Vernant, 1990). For Plotinus' disciples, Narcissus became a model for reflective reason, the possibility of using the mind to reflect on truth and so reunite with original Being. In this sense the fall is a *felix culpa*, without which there would be no process of reunification for us.

This reveals two very different traditions of cosmic dualism: one that retains an emphasis on potential harmony, one associated with an enduring schism (Kristeva, 1989).[23] In so far as Lacan's theory of the mirror stage betrays clear echoes of the Neoplatonic myth, he must negotiate the opposing connotations. Indeed, in an intriguing *London Review of Books* essay, Malcolm Bull (2001) suggests that the parallels between Plotinus and Lacan may be more than coincidental. The 1930s, when Lacan first developed his theory of the mirror stage, was a time when Neoplatonism was undergoing a revival in France under the leadership of Emile Berthier at the Sorbonne; Bergson also brought Neoplatonism into contemporary philosophical debate, and the belief that there were affinities between his philosophy and that of Plotinus enhanced its status. Bull points out one further possible source for Lacan's interest in the myth of Dionysus Zagreus and its Neoplatonic interpreters in a book Lacan refers to in his *Ethics* seminar: Erwin Rohde's *Psyche* (1890–94), a monumental study of Greek cult practices and the associated conception of the soul, which had been translated into French in 1928 (Lacan, 2008, recommends that all psychoanalysts read it at least once). Bull concludes that while the general fascination with Neoplatonism had waned by the 1950s and 1960s, Lacan's references to Plotinus in the seminars testifies to his enduring interest.

Lacan's emphasis on disjunction suggests the importance for him of clarifying that his mirror stage does not hold out the promise of potential reunification and harmony. The event before the mirror is presented by Lacan as the moment when an inescapable discrepancy opens up between the unified image of the reflection and the experiential fact of our uncoordinated body. We gain an idealized image of ourselves as unified but, insofar as it is merely an image, a rupture is created: fantasy splits from the real.

Lacan establishes a tone of tragic violence in his own 'myth'. We are cursed by being born too soon, and the initial months of dim chaos haunt the apparently unified ego that subsequently arises. Lacan (2007) adds a powerful cosmological element to Wallon's developmental scheme, asserting that, in man, the 'relationship to nature is altered by a certain dehiscence at the very heart of the organism, a primordial Discord betrayed by the signs of malaise and motor uncoordination of the neonatal months' (p. 78). *Dehiscence* is a technical term describing the breaking of a wound along a surgical suture. Lacan goes on to talk about the 'fragmented body' (*corps morcelé*), as a term he has introduced, describing the 'aggressive disintegration of the individual' (p. 78) in dreams, fantasies and symptoms. It is one of the earliest original concepts to appear in Lacan's work: a sense of violent fragmentation experienced by the infant for which the mirror image is a balm (p. 85). Yet the ego that arises from the mirror stage is haunted by this original chaos and it returns in images of castration and dismemberment. In the 'mirror stage' paper of 1949, Lacan refers to 'a primordial Discord', twice evoked with references to the paintings of Hieronymus Bosch, 'an atlas of all the aggressive images that torment mankind' (p. 85). Marini (1992) unearths one possible early influence on this line of thinking in Lacan's reference to a 'Saturnine complex' in his first paper delivered to the Société Psychoanalytique de Paris, 'From Impulsion to Complex' (from the name of the god that devours his children in the cosmological myth with which this chapter opens), which would correspond to the nightmare of the fragmented body.

It is, as ever, the death drive to which Lacan turns when seeking to underwrite the fundamentally inharmonious nature of being human. This is the context for Lacan's (2007) declaration in favour of Heraclitus in 'Aggressivity in psychoanalysis': the death drive is 'a "negative" libido that enables the Heraclitean notion of Discord, which the Ephesian believed to be prior to harmony, to shine once more' (p. 94). Heraclitus regarded existence as made up of conflicting elements (he regarded the soul as being a mixture of fire and water, with fire being the noble part of the soul, and water the ignoble part). He presents a fundamentally disrupted universe – disruption *prior* to harmony, compared to one that is good, whole, One. Where Parmenides argued for unchanging, unitary existence, Heraclitus famously asserted that the only constant was change itself.

This is the value to Lacan of Freud's pre-Socratics. In 1937, Freud had acknowledged that his theory of the life and death drives corresponds to the cosmological theory of the pre-Socratic philosopher Empedocles. He equated Empedocles' terms *philia* and *neikos* (unity/ strife) with Eros and the death drive.[24] Lacan takes advantage of this. He depicts Freud, in a pre-Socratic narrative, 'starting from the royal principle of the Logos' [the talking cure], but led by the force of his insights 'from structure … to rethink the deadly Empedoclean antinomies' (2007, p. 432). Again, in 'Instance of the letter', Freud's 'new conception', the death drive, is identified with 'the conflict of the two principles to which the alternation of universal life was subjected by Empedocles of Agrigentum in the fifth century BC' (p. 261).

In *Seminar II*, a seminar extensively concerned, as we've seen, with Freud's split from Jung and his subsequent formulation of the death drive, Lacan (1991a) depicts Freud attempting to save 'some kind of dualism at all costs' at the very moment when this dualism 'was crumbling in his hands, and when the ego, the libido, etc., all of that was tending to produce a kind of vast whole, returning us to a *philosophy of nature*' (p. 37). With *Naturphilosophie* lingering, Lacan knows how careful one has to be to ensure that Eros is never allowed to operate on its own, like a Parmenidean or Neoplatonic original force: 'the tendency to union … is only ever apprehended in its relation to the contrary tendency, which leads to division, to rupture, to a redispersion …. These two tendencies are strictly inseparable. No notion is less unitary than that' (p. 79).

There is, as ever, a contemporary context for this battle over man. In his 'Response to Jean Hyppolite's commentary on Freud's "Verneinung"', Lacan (2007) claims that Freud's repeated references to pre-Socratic doctrines 'do not simply bear witness to a discreet use of notes on his reading … but rather to a properly metaphysical apprehension of what were pressing problems for him' (p. 319). Lacan has been drawn once more to consider the subject's founding relationship to being and non-being, and his point in referring to Freud's pre-Socratics is to argue that Freud does not in any way anticipate 'the modern development of a philosophy of existence' (p. 319). His target here is existentialism, a dominant movement of the time, and therefore a key opponent, in so far as it places the human at the centre: 'a humanism that is – don't you think? – somewhat pedestrian' (p. 470).

Sartre had devoted part of the last chapter of *Being and Nothingness* (1943) to a critique of Freud, and the construction, instead, of an 'Existential Psychoanalysis'. Lacan wants to show that there are deeper truths in Freud's work than those alighted on by existentialism. The underlying truths of psychoanalysis do not relate to relationships between humans, but to that between the human and existence itself. It is something fundamentally problematic about human psychology that makes the distance from any more optimistic 'humanism' so crucial. His ally against existentialism is Heidegger himself (Lacan translated Heidegger's 'Logos', which deals in particular with Heraclitus). In an intellectual environment dominated by Sartre, Heidegger's thought had been interpreted as a form of existential anthropology (see Heidegger, 1997; Roudinesco, 1997, pp. 222–23). But in his 1946 *Letter on Humanism*, Heidegger argues for a need to go back beyond 'Western reason' to Parmenides and Heraclitus. He accuses existentialism of a 'forgetting of being'.

This shows the influence, once more, of Kojève, who had presented Heidegger as reaffirming a sense of 'non-relation', of division between the human and the world, thought and being – a sense introduced into modern philosophy by Kant, but which Hegel mistakenly sought to mend (see Badiou, 2006; Drury, 1994, Kojève, 1968, 1982). Non-relation is pitted against myths of unity. As we've seen, implicit in cosmological models are theories of the mind. The universe is split and it is man who has thrown a spanner in the works.

> That's the great discovery of analysis – at the level of the generic relation, bound up with the life of the species, man already functions differently. In man, there's already a crack, a profound perturbation of the regulation of life. That's the importance of the notion introduced by Freud of the death instinct.
>
> (Lacan, 1991, p. 37)

Man as a creature capable of returning to the Good, the Light, to wholeness in God is a false depiction. So is 'a confused, unitary, *naturalistic* conception of man, of the ego' (p. 37). Against these myths of reunion, man 'introduces the idea of *asymmetry*' (p. 38). Asymmetry is key to the Lacanian universe. It is 'an utter and complete misunderstanding of Freud's thought' to regard 'the Discord of the life and death instincts ... as the play of a couple of forces that are homologous in their opposition' (2007, p. 505). In *Television* (1990), Lacan mocks this idea of promised wholeness with a familiar example, bridging the personal and cosmological: 'The mystical One whose crude equivalent is given to us through its comical other – Aristophanes, to name him, strutting his stuff in Plato's *Symposium* – presenting the beast-with-two-backs that he accuses Zeus, who is not responsible for it, of bisecting' (p. 23). We are back at the *Symposium*. That Aristophanes' circle-people might stand as a cosmological model (as we've seen attempted by Neo-Platonism) is mocked. But, Lacan goes on, it is so seductive that even Freud 'stumbles on this point' by presenting Eros and Thanatos as apparently co-dependent: 'because his allegation with respect to Eros, insofar as he opposed it to Thanatos, as the principle of "life" is that of unifying, as if, apart from a brief coiteration, one had ever seen two bodies unite into one' (p. 23).

Freud's metapsychology should be understood, not according to the potentially balanced opposition of Eros and the death drive, but in terms of the asymmetric pairs that define Lacan's theory: concord and discord, unity and multiplicity, finite and infinite. Žižek (2005) expands on the danger implicit in the concept of the death drive. The introduction of Thanatos as a cosmic principle, 're-establishing the pacifying harmonious vision of the universe as the battlefield of the two opposing principles', is actually '*an attempt to cover the true trauma*', which is the 'ontological fault' in the universe, the 'break' that disrupts its functioning and makes it not whole, not consistent (p. 214). And, with this insufficiency, drives it. Again, fracture provides cause. Lacan's mirror stage is not about reflection; it is a myth of illusion born of desperation, and it is this difference that makes it a beginning rather than an end.

The accidental universe

Creationism without gods arrives eventually at some sense of the accidental – an initiating event that is not a *fiat*, neither caused nor commanded. But a beginning that is an accident acquires a strange status, accidental in origin yet necessary in retrospect. This is similar to the status of Freud's pre-histories. The peculiar character of the primal 'historical event', John Forrester (1980) writes, 'whether primal murder or primal scene – is that its historicity grants it the status of being accidental yet "necessary"' (p. 107). Once the primal event has occurred, it becomes foundational; its exclusion from consciousness founds the shape of consciousness itself. Hence, in Charles Shepherdson's (2000) account, the 'original murder' of the father must be cast 'not as a real event but as a structural characteristic that would account for the very emergence of historical time' (p. 95). As in all cases of traumatic repetition,

> What repeats is ... something that somehow 'never took place', a past that was never 'present', which does not mean that it is merely nothing, a figment of the imagination or a purely mythical event, but rather that it happens without happening ... or like the murder of the father, the traumatic event that is recounted in the story of the primal horde in *Totem and Taboo*, an event which occurred, as Freud tells us, before history as such, before the beginning of historical time, in a mythical moment that explains how time in fact began.
>
> *(p. 95)*

But how? Lacan explores this sense of the accidental yet necessary via two classical concepts, the *clinamen* (swerve) from Lucretius' cosmological poem *De Rerum Natura*, and *tuche* (chance) from Aristotle's theory of cause presented in the *Physics*. I will consider the function these serve for Lacan as a conclusion to this exploration of his creationism and a bridge into the next chapter's extended look at causality and tragedy in psychoanalysis.

Again, *Seminar XI*, where both terms appear, sees the concerns of earlier seminars bolstered by classical and philosophical references. As in the second seminar, Lacan (1977) asserts: 'The very originality of psychoanalysis lies in the fact that it does not centre psychological ontogenesis on supposed *stages* – which have literally no discoverable foundation in development observable in biological terms' (p. 63). He continues:

> If development is entirely animated by accident, by the obstacle of the *tuche*, it is in so far as the *tuche* brings us back to the same point at which pre-Socratic philosophy sought to motivate the world itself.
> It required a *clinamen*, an inclination, at some point.
>
> *(p. 63)*

Lacan is unusual in bringing the two concepts together but correct in seeing both as attempts to imagine cause outside of a system. Lucretius was an atomist, a follower of the Greek Epicurus who had inherited from the original atomist Democritus a theory of purely physical causation. This seemed to leave no room for free will. In response, Democritus introduced a minimal degree of *un*-necessitated movement in atoms – the *clinamen* (in Greek, *parenklisis*), a tiny 'swerve' or 'deviation' from their trajectory too small to generate macroscopic chaos but sufficient to leave the future undetermined.[25] Once this space of undetermined occurrence was opened up it proved useful in explaining the other great challenge to determinism: creation, how the chain began.[26]

The term *tuche* is drawn from Aristotle's *Physics*, which Lacan claims is 'the most elaborate [theory] that has ever been proposed on the function of cause'. Aristotle divides cause into four categories (material, formal, efficient and final). But, finding that none of these cover the concept of the *accidental*, he introduces two new concepts: *automaton*, spontaneous happenings in nature, and a sub-category of *automaton*: *tuche*, a specific kind of chance happening referring to events we might consider lucky or unlucky.[27] It amounts to 'chance for objects' and 'chance for subjects'. Lacan (1977) uses them more in the sense of *automaton* to describe the structural system that engenders repetition and *tuche* as the trauma which lies *behind* the repetitive system, driving it; *behind* what repeats 'as if by chance'. *Automaton* belongs to the mechanical, deterministic model of existence; *Tuche* represents the eruption of something else into it, something unassimilable, beyond the structure of consciousness but whose absence shapes consciousness itself.

To elaborate further on this odd status, Lacan describes Democritus trying to designate the *clinamen* and having to bend language to his purpose ('thus showing you that from what one of my pupils called the archaic stage of philosophy, the manipulation of words was used just as in the time of Heidegger' (p. 64)). Democritus writes: '*it is not an μηδέυ, but a δευ*' (pp. 64)

The Greek word μηδέυ means 'nothing'. But, as Lacan points out, δευ is a coined word, sliced from the end: a δευ suggests a 'thing' but it is not the Greek for a 'something' (p. 64). Not something and not nothing. The philosophical context for this is Democritus' belief that atoms and the void in which they move have equal claims to true existence. Both must play their part. But this 'inclination'/ *clinamen* belongs to neither. It appears to require a category of its own.

Curiously, Lacan makes a mistake. Democritus never does discuss the *clinamen* or *parenklisis*. It was introduced by Epicurus only after, and in response to, Aristotle's *criticisms* of Democritus. It is possible that, consciously or unconsciously, Lacan is attributing the term to Democritus because he wants to discuss the subsequent Heideggerian wordplay that does belong to the Greek (Monk, 1993). And he wants this because the wordplay pertains to something between existence and non-existence but which might have a causal effect. In this it begins to resemble the real: no thing, yet not nothing.

This is an opportunity to glance at one of the most subtle critiques of psychoanalysis, and probably the deepest and most extended engagement with the triangular relationship between Freud, Lacan and Greek philosophy: Derrida's reading of psychoanalysis. Derrida returns to the role of chance in psychoanalysis and Greek philosophy, specifically via reference to Lucretius and the *clinamen*. The Greek references provide him, as they do Lacan, with the means of isolating conceptual problems. In *Mes Chances*, Derrida (1984) wields chance against psychoanalysis itself. He quotes Freud's essay 'Telepathy': 'I believe in external (real) chance, it is true, but not in internal (psychical) chance.' Derrida sees this exclusion of chance as affirming Freud's project of founding psychoanalysis as a positive science, a tradition he sees Lacan sustaining:

> Lacan follows Freud to the letter on this point, when he says that a letter always arrives at its destination. There is no chance in the unconscious. The apparent randomness must be placed in the service of an unavoidable necessity that in fact is never contradicted.
>
> (p. 24)[28]

Derrida's criticism may be valid against the symbolic, automaton unconscious of 'Seminar on "The Purloined Letter"', but Lacan's continued probing of cause and trauma will result in the more complex understanding of chance, the unconscious and necessity in *Seminar XI*. Lacan, with Aristotle, recognizes the need for there to be something beyond the system. Lacan's solution is to take Aristotle's recognition of its conceptual difficulty and align it with his own category of the impossible, in which we find the trauma that can't be processed but, by very virtue of its 'impossibility', has an effect. This is the real of *Seminar XI*:

> The real is beyond the *automaton*, the return, the coming-back, the insistence of the signs, by which we see ourselves governed by the pleasure principle. The real is that which always lies behind the *automaton*, and it is quite obvious, throughout Freud's research, that it is this that is the object of his concern ...
>
> (1977, p. 53–54)

The *tychic* (as Lacan renders the adjectival form of *tuche*) remains as a permanent challenge to the supposed completeness of the *automaton* network/the unconscious/the symbolic order. It is a way of returning to the fundamental traumas that Freud found so difficult to situate in time and to rearticulate them according to a structural model. It is also a response to the potentially static self-enclosure of this model. Derrida's criticism throws light on why it was necessary for Lacan to develop his theory of the unconscious over the decades: an 'effective' real becomes necessary once the unconscious becomes structural, in order to provide a space from which something beyond structure (comparable to the gods or accident) can impinge, troubling and driving the chain.[29]

Throughout this chapter, we've seen that creationism is important to Lacan because it responds to problems in Freud's theory. The spontaneity of the mirror stage, as a structuralist 'myth', provides one solution. It is crucial, however, to maintain a sense of inherent asymmetry. This is the significance of Lacan's further emphasis on creation *ex nihilo* and his repeated dismissals of philosophies promising any potential harmonizing of opposed forces. The Lacanian unconscious, as system/language/universe, is always already complete, arising outside of developmental time. As such, it returns Lacan to the problem of giving a chronological account of trauma. This is where Lucretius and Aristotle prove useful. The struggles of Greek and Roman materialist philosophers with the concept of prime movers grant Lacan a resource with which to attempt his own thinking about the limit of a system. They allow him to embrace the paradoxes of Freud's category of the primal: events that are at once necessary and accidental, a category that is always traumatic in so far as it lies beyond our structure of comprehension. This, finally, is where we find creation, even if, as the next chapter shows, a *first* cause is just the start of the problem.

Notes

1 'I would remind the reader of the cosmogenic significance of Eros in Hesiod, and also of the Orphic figure of Phanes, the Shining One, the First-Created, the "Father of Eros"' (Jung, 1991, pp. 137–8). This Eros can be traced to Hesiod's *Theogony*, the main classical source for cosmological accounts: 'Only Hesiod in his *Theogony* went beyond the few obscure hints in Homer to attempt a systematic account. And in order to do so he seems to have had to have recourse to archaic oriental myths' (Most, 2003, p. 308).
2 See Kirk (1974) on castration analogues.
3 Freud's first mention of the idea of the Oedipus complex is in a letter to Wilhelm Fleiss (see Freud, 1897, 1900).
4 There is some debate regarding a possible distinction between 'fantasy' and 'phantasy.' I do not differentiate here but have left quotations in original spelling; see Steiner (1993). James Strachey points to the *OED*'s differentiation of fantasy ('caprice, whim, fanciful invention') and phantasy ('imagination, visionary notion'). But Klein (1997) uses the spelling to identify phantasy as a mental phenomenon

between the conscious and unconscious realms – one that, from infancy onwards, serves as a bridge between somatic experience and the outside world.
5 Haeckel also coined the term *ecology* and discovered the kingdom of microorganisms he named Protista. He was one of the first to consider psychology as a branch of physiology.
6 The theory is summarized in the phrase 'ontogeny recapitulates phylogeny'. Haeckel's *Generelle Morphologie* (1866) synthesized Darwin with *Naturphilosophie* and with the progressive evolutionism of Jean-Baptiste Lamarck.
7 Freud quotes Frazer in a footnote: 'Thus the ultimate origin of exogamy, and with it of the law of incest … remains a problem nearly as dark as ever' (Frazer, 1910, p. 165).
8 The concept first appears in 'Project' and *Studies on Hysteria*, both 1895 (Freud 1895a and 1895b). Laplanche (1976) credits Lacan with recovering the concept. In his 'Rome report', Lacan picks the word out in the Wolf Man paper (in German and in italics, in its adverbial form). He suggests a translation, the *après coup*, though says in a footnote that this is weak. The concept is taken up by Laplanche and Pontalis in 1964 in 'Fantasme originaire' and in 1967 in *Vocubulaire de psychanalyse*, which contains a complete article on the *après coup*. Here, Laplanche claims that it arises in Freud's 1894 case of Elizabeth von R, then reappears in 'Project' before its appearance in the Wolf Man case, where it is connected specifically with traumatism. This concept has received some significant theoretical attention, not least because of the interest in it demonstrated by both Lacan and Derrida; see Derrida's 1966 lecture on Freud, 'Freud and the scene of writing' (Derrida, 2002). The concept can be seen to open the way to his explorations of the *architrace* and *différence* (see Forrester, 1980).
9 The term *stade du miroir* appears in Henri Wallon's 1931 article, *Comment se développe chez l'enfant la notion de corps proper* (Rabaté, 2003).
10 In 'Structure, Sign and Play', Derrida (2002) famously locates the work that goes into all this: 'the neutralization of time and history' that structure compels, the need for any structure to break 'with its past, its origin and its cause'. Derrida quotes Lévi-Strauss on language that it 'could only have been born in one fell swoop' (p. 291).
11 In a similar vein, Lacan (2007) describes the idea of a return to the inanimate in *Beyond the Pleasure Principle* as a metaphor: we should recognize in it 'the margin beyond life that language assures the human being of due to the fact that he speaks' (p. 680).
12 The relationship between Lacan and Jung is complex, and far from being defined by a simple dismissal of Jungian theory on Lacan's part: both are heirs to Freud seeking to free psychoanalysis from biologism; they knew each other personally, and Lacan had done an internship at Jung's Bergholzi clinic (see Roudinesco, 1990).
13 Gestalt is from the German for the essence or shape of an entity's complete form; Gestalt psychology is discussed in Lacan's (2007) paper on the mirror stage. On Lacan's use of 'Gestalt', see Nobus (1999).
14 Of course, the elegance of Darwin's theory is that it doesn't depend upon an active 'nature', just chance mutation and survival.
15 One of the first works to explore the anthropic principle is Paul Davies (1982). Surveying the range of apparently miraculous accidents that have led to the emergence of life, it concludes with an investigation of the anthropic principle, considering how much of what we see around us is a consequence of the presence of observers in the universe.
16 For Kant, it denoted fanaticism (see 'Essay on the maladies of the head' (1764) in Louden and Zöller, 2011) or the enthusiasm of those who ground philosophical projects on what they believe is revelation. Kant (1766) himself uses it against Neoplatonists; Swedenborg is also a specific target (see Lipscomb and Krueger, 2010).

17 Lacan compares it to the Anaxagorian *nous* ('Mind') as an ordering force in the cosmos.
18 Aquinas cites Plato directly: 'Every being in any way existing is from God .... Hence Plato said (*Parmenides*, xxvi) that unity must become before multitude; and Aristotle said (*Metaphysics*, ii, text 4) that whatever is greatest in being and greatest in truth, is the cause of every being and of every truth; just as whatever is the greatest in heat is the cause of all heat' (*Summa Theologica*, I, 44),
19 See Aristotle's *Metaphysics*, Plato's *Cratylus*, *Sophist*, and *Theaetetus*; see also Prior (1969), Drury (1994) and Kojève (1968).
20 Interestingly, a key work on this is by a figure who may have been an influence on Lacan: a long essay on final causality – 'an ultimate ordering'. Etienne Gilson (1984) was a French medievalist and Thomist 'who transformed Thomism and medieval studies in general for a generation of French intellectuals' (Pound, 2008, pp. 89–90), including Baruzi. For possible influence on Lacan, see Pound (2008) and Labbie (2006). See also Roudinesco (1997) on the influence of Jean Baruzi, a rationalist Catholic thinker who taught Lacan and brought about a 'transition in Lacan's thinking' (p. 12).
21 *Hamlet* and *Oedipus at Colonus* are both discussed in Lacan (1991).
22 The other baubles given by the Titans include a spinning top, knuckle-bones and a doll with jointed limbs.
23 'The *reflection* of which Narcissus became enamored and which led him to his death became the fundamental topos of a thought that parted with ancient philosophy to nourish speculative thinking' (Kristeva, 1989, p. 105). Drury (1994) suggests another context for Lacan's interests here, and see Bataille (1985) on the Manichean aspects of Gnosticism.
24 Empedocles died about six years before Plato was born (see Frankland, 2006).
25 See Lucretius, *The Nature of Things* (*De Rerum Natura*), though some confusion remains, as we still wouldn't have free will, just chaos. One solution put forward is that the self is autonomous and the swerve accounts for its *creation*.
26 *De Rerum Natura* is a poem Lacan associates with this issue, the problem of beginnings. In *Seminar II*, considering, once again, the possible *origin* of the forces that move us, Lacan (1991a) quotes the Roman poet Lucretius; he writes: 'In the end, at this existential level, we can only talk about the libido satisfactorily in a mythical way – it is the *genitrix, hominum divumque voluptas*. That is what Freud is getting at. In former days what returns here used to be expressed in terms of the gods, and one must proceed with care before turning it into an algebraic sign' (p. 227). The Latin is from the first line of *De Rerum Natura* and it refers to Venus: 'Progenitor, object of ecstasy of men and gods.' The question of Venus' place in *De Rerum Natura* is much debated, as Epicureans insisted that the gods played no causal role in the lives of men. Venus, as the ultimate universal life-source in a fiercely materialist account of life, is clearly intended to be symbolic. But of what? The invocation may be a formality, but it's also clear that 2000 years ago Lucretius was facing precisely the same difficulties in positing an *origin*. It is in this context that Lacan makes the parallel. An algebraic sign can appear a fit substitute for divine forces until you get to the question of their beginning.
27 Richard Sorabji (1980) suggests that 'four causes' would be better translated as 'four explanations' (p. 40).
28 This can be seen in line with Derrida's (2002) earlier criticism of Lévi-Strauss and structuralism generally, its simultaneous dependence on, and elision of 'chance' in its project to abolish time and origin from its analyses.
29 In his essay 'Causality in science and psychoanalysis', Verhaeghe (2002) distinguishes between an early Lacan associated with the deterministic linguistic unconscious, and a later one concerned with the drive and the real, in which causality is less straightforward.

References

Aquinas, T., *Summa Theologica*, trans. The Fathers of the Dominican Province (1911), Notre Dame, Ave Maria Press.
Aquinas T., *Disputed Questions on Truth (Quaestiones disputatae de Veritate)*, trans. R. W. Milligan (1952–1954), Chicago, Chicago University Press.
Aristotle, *Metaphysics*, trans. Hugh Lawson-Tancred (1998), London, Penguin. Classics
Aristotle, *Physics*, trans. R. Waterfield (2008), Oxford, Oxford World Classics.
Aristotle, *Posterior Analytics*, trans. J. Barnes (1994) Oxford, Clarendon Press.
Badiou, A. (2006) 'Lacan and the Pre-Socratics', in Žižek, S. (ed.) *Lacan: The Silent Partners*, London, Verso, pp. 7–16
Bataille, G. (1985) 'Base materialism and Gnosticism', in Stoekl, A. (ed.) *Visions of Excess: Selected Writings 1927–1939*, Minneapolis, Minnesota University Press, pp. 45–52.
Borch-Jacobsen, M. (1991) *Lacan: The Absolute Master*, Stanford, Stanford University Press.
Braungardt, J. (2002) 'Thinking and being: Lacan versus Parmenides' [online]. Available at http://braungardt.trialectics.com/philosophy/my-papers/lacan-parmenides/ (accessed 21/3/14).
Bull, M. (2001) 'Hate is the new love', *London Review of Books*, vol. 23, no. 2, pp. 23–24.
Davies, P. (1982) *The Accidental Universe*, Cambridge, Cambridge University Press.
Derrida, J. (1984) 'My chances/mes chances: A rendezvous with some Epicurean stereophonies', in Smith, J. H. and Kerrigan, W. (eds) *Taking Chances: Derrida, Psychoanalysis and Literature*, Baltimore, Johns Hopkins University Press, pp. 1–32.
Derrida, J. (2002) *Writing and Difference* (trans. A. Bass), London, Routledge.
Dosse, F. (1997) *The History of Structuralism*, vol. 1 (trans. D. Glassman), Minneapolis, University of Minnesota Press.
Dowden, K. (1992) *The Uses of Greek Mythology*, London, Routledge.
Drury, S. B. (1994) *Alexandre Kojève: The Roots of Postmodern Politics*, New York, St Martin's Press.
Forrester, J. (1980) *Language and the Origins of Psychoanalysis*, New York, Columbia University Press.
Forrester, J. (1990) *The Seductions of Psychoanalysis: Freud, Lacan and Derrida*, Cambridge, Cambridge University Press.
Frankland, G. (2006) *Freud's Literary Culture*, Cambridge, Cambridge University Press.
Frazer, J. (1894) *The Golden Bough*, London, Macmillan & Co.
Frazer, J. (1910) *Totemism and Exogamy*, London, Macmillan & Co.
Freud, S. (1895a) *Project for a scientific psychology*, in Strachey, J. (ed.) *The Standard Edition of the Complete Psychological Works of Sigmund Freud*, vol. 1, London, Hogarth Press, pp. 283–387.
Freud, S. (1895b) 'Studies on hysteria', in Strachey, J. (ed.) *The Standard Edition of the Complete Psychological Works of Sigmund Freud*, vol. 2, London, Hogarth Press, pp. 1–305.
Freud, S. (1896) 'The aetiology of hysteria', in Strachey, J. (ed.) *The Standard Edition of the Complete Psychological Works of Sigmund Freud*, vol. 3, London, Hogarth Press, pp. 189–223.
Freud, S. (1897) 'Extracts from the Fleiss papers', in Strachey, J. (ed.) *The Standard Edition of the Complete Psychological Works of Sigmund Freud*, vol. 1, London, Hogarth Press, pp. 175–281.
Freud, S. (1900) *The Interpretation of Dreams*, in Strachey, J. (ed.) *The Standard Edition of the Complete Psychological Works of Sigmund Freud*, vols 4–5, London, Hogarth Press, pp. 1–627.

Freud, S. (1905) *Three Essays on the Theory of Sexuality*, in Strachey, J. (ed.) *The Standard Edition of the Complete Psychological Works of Sigmund Freud*, vol. 7, London, Hogarth Press, pp. 125–323.
Freud, S. (1913) *Totem and Taboo*, in Strachey, J. (ed.) *The Standard Edition of the Complete Psychological Works of Sigmund Freud*, vol. 13, London, Hogarth Press, pp. 1–163.
Freud, S. (1914) *On Narcissism: An Introduction*, in Strachey, J. (ed.) *The Standard Edition of the Complete Psychological Works of Sigmund Freud*, vol. 14, London, Hogarth Press, pp. 67–101.
Freud, S. (1916–17) *Introductory Lectures (Part III)*, in Strachey, J. (ed.) *The Standard Edition of the Complete Psychological Works of Sigmund Freud*, vol. 16, London, Hogarth Press, pp. 243–462.
Freud, S. (1918) 'From the history of an infantile neurosis', in Strachey, J. (ed.) *The Standard Edition of the Complete Psychological Works of Sigmund Freud*, vol. 17, London, Hogarth Press, pp. 1–123.
Freud, S. (1921) *Group Psychology and the Analysis of the Ego*, in Strachey, J. (ed.) *The Standard Edition of the Complete Psychological Works of Sigmund Freud*, vol. 18, London, Hogarth Press, pp. 65–143.
Freud, S. (1937) *Analysis Terminable and Interminable*, in Strachey, J. (ed.) *The Standard Edition of the Complete Psychological Works of Sigmund Freud*, vol. 23, London, Hogarth Press, pp. 209–254.
Gadamer, H. (1975) *Truth and Method*, New York, Seabury.
Gilson, E. (1984) *From Aristotle to Darwin and Back Again: A Journey in Final Causality, Species and Evolution* (trans. J. Lyon), South Bend, Notre Dame University Press.
Heidegger, M. (1927) *Sein und Zeit*, Tübingen, Max Niemeyer Verlag.
Heidegger, M. (1997) 'Letter on humanism', in Farell, D. (ed.) *Basic Writings*, New York, Harper & Row.
Heidegger, M. (1998) 'Plato's doctrine of truth', in McNeill, W. (ed.) *Pathmarks*, Cambridge, Cambridge University Press, pp.155–182
Hesiod, *Theogony*, trans. H. G. Evelyn-White (1914) Cambridge, Harvard University Press.
Jones, E. (1953) *The Life and Work of Sigmund Freud*, New York, Basic Books.
Jung, C. G. (1991) *Transformations and Symbols of the Libido*, London, Routledge.
Kant, I. (1766) *Dreams of a Spirit Seer Elucidated by Dreams of Metaphysics*, n.p, n.p.
Kirk, G. S. (1974) *The Nature of Greek Myths*, London, Penguin.
Kirk, G. S. and Raven, J. E. (1957) *The Presocratic Philosophers*, Cambridge, Cambridge University Press.
Klein, M. (1997) *Envy and Gratitude and Other Works*, London, Vintage.
Kojève, A. (1968) *Essay on the History of Reason, Vol. 1 (Essai d'une histoire raisonée de la philosophie païenne)*, Paris, Gallimard.
Kojève, A. (1982) *Heidegger's Parmenides* (trans. A. Schuwer and R. Rojcewicz), Indianapolis, Indiana University Press.
Kristeva, J. (1989) Narcissus: the new insanity', in *Tales of Love* (trans. L. S. Roudiez), New York, Columbia University Press.
Kuhn, A. B. (2007) *Lost Light: Interpretation of the Ancient Scriptures*, Minneapolis, Filiquarian Publishing.
Labbie, E. (2006) *Lacan's Medievalism*, Minneapolis, University of Minnesota Press.
Lacan, J. (1938) 'Les complexes familiaux', *republished in* Autres écrits (2001), Paris, Le Seuil.
Lacan, J. (1977) *Seminar XI: The Four Fundamental Concepts of Psychoanalysis* (ed. J.-A. Miller, trans. A. Sheridan), London, Penguin.
Lacan, J. (1988) *Seminar I: Freud's Papers on Technique (1953–1954)* (ed. J.-A. Miller, trans. J. Forrester), Cambridge, Cambridge University Press.

Lacan, J. (1990) *Television* (trans. D. Hollier, R. Krauss, A. Michelson), New York, W. W. Norton & Co.
Lacan, J. (1991) *Seminar II: The Ego in Freud's Theory and in the Technique of Psychoanalysis* (ed. J.-A. Miller, trans. J. Forrester), New York, Norton.
Lacan, J. (1998) *Seminar XX: Encore – On Feminine Sexuality: The Limits of Love and Knowledge* (ed. J.-A. Miller, trans. B. Fink), New York, Norton.
Lacan, J. (2007) *Écrits: The First Complete Edition in English* (trans. B. Fink), New York, Norton.
Lacan, J. (2008) *Seminar VII: The Ethics of Psychoanalysis* (ed. J.-A. Miller, trans. D. Porter), London, Routledge.
Lacan, J. (2014) *Seminar X: Anxiety* (ed. J.-A. Miller, trans. A. R. Price), London, Polity Press.
Lacan, Jacques (2015), *Seminar VIII: Transference* (ed. J.-A. Miller, trans. Bruce Fink), London, Polity Press.
Laplanche, J. (1976) *Life and Death in Psychoanalysis*, Baltimore, Johns Hopkins University Press.
Laplanche, J. and Pontalis, J.-B. (1964) 'Fantasme orignaire, fantasmes des origines, origine du fantasme', *Les temps modernes*, 19, pp. 1833–1868.
Laplanche, J. and Pontalis, J.-B. (1967), *Vocabulaire de la psychanalyse*, Paris, Presses Universitaires de France.
Laplanche, J. and Pontalis, J.-B. (1993) 'Fantasy and the origins of sexuality', in Steiner. R. (ed.) *Unconscious Phantasy*, London, Karnac, pp. 107–144.
Lévi-Strauss, C. (1949), *Les Structures élémentaires de la parenté [The Elementary Structures of Kinship]*, Paris, La Haye.
Lévi-Strauss, C. (1955), *Tristes tropiques*, Paris, Libraire Plon.
Lévi-Strauss, C. (1971) *L'Homme nu (Mythologiques 4)*, Paris, Libraire Plon.
Lipscomb, B. B. and Krueger, J. (2010) *Kant's Moral Metaphysics: God, Freedom and Immortality*, Berlin, De Grueter.
Louden, R. B. and Zöller, G. (eds) (2011) *Immanuel Kant – Anthropology, History and Education*, Cambridge, Cambridge University Press.
Lucretius, *The Nature of Things*, trans. Alicia Stallings (2007), London, Penguin Classics.
Marini, M. (1992) *Jacques Lacan: The French Context* (trans. A. Tomiche), Piscataway, Rutgers University Press.
Masson, J. M. (1985) *The Complete Letters of Sigmund Freud to Wilhelm Fliess, 1887–1904*, Cambridge, MA, Harvard University Press.
Mitchell-Boyask, R. N. (1994) 'Freud's reading of classical literature and classical philology', in Gilman, S. L., Birmele, J., Geller, J. and Greenberg, V. D. (eds) *Reading Freud's Reading*, New York and London, New York University Press.
Monk, L. (1993) *Standard Deviations: Chance and the Modern British Novel*, Stanford, Stanford University Press.
Most, G. W. (2003) 'Philosophy and religion', in Sedley, D. (ed.), *The Cambridge Companion to Greek and Roman Philosophy*, Cambridge, Cambridge University Press, pp. 300–322.
Nobus, D. (1999) *Key Concepts of Lacanian Psychoanalysis*, New York, Other Press.
Pound, M. (2008) *Žižek: A Very Critical Introduction*, Grand Rapids, Eerdmans.
Prior, A. N. (1969) *Encyclopedia of Philosophy*, vol. 2, New York, Macmillan.
Rabaté, J.-M. (2003) *Cambridge Companion to Lacan*, Cambridge, Cambridge University Press.
Roudinesco, E. (1990) *Jacques Lacan and Co.* (trans. J. Mehlman), Chicago, Chicago University Press.
Roudinesco, E. (1997) *Jacques Lacan* (trans. B. Bray), New York, Columbia University Press.

Roudinesco, E. (2014) *Lacan: In Spite of Everything* (trans. G. Elliot), London, Verso.
Sartre, J.-P. (1943) *L'être et le néant*, Paris, Gallimard.
Shakespeare, W. (2008), Greenblatt, S. (ed.) *The Norton Shakespeare*, London, Norton.
Shepherdson, C. (2000) 'Telling tales of love: Philosophy, literature and psychoanalysis', *Diacritics*, vol. 30, no. 1, pp. 89–105.
Sophocles (2004) *The Three Theban Plays*, trans. R. Fagles, London, Penguin.
Sorabji, R. (1980) *Necessity, Cause and Blame: Perspectives on Aristotle's Theory*, London, Duckworth.
Steiner, R. (1993) *Unconscious Phantasy*, London, Karnac.
Verhaeghe, P. (2002) 'Causality in science and psychoanalysis', in Glynos, J. and Stavrakakis, Y. (eds) *Lacan and Science*, London, Karnac, pp. 119–147.
Vernant, J.-P. (1990) *Before Sexuality*, Princeton, Princeton University Press.
Weatherill, R. (1999) *The Death Drive: New Life for a Dead Subject*, London, Karnac.
Žižek, S. (2005) 'The swerve of the real', in Bartsch, S. and Bartscherer, T. (eds) *Erotikon: Essays on Eros, Ancient and Modern*, Chicago: Chicago University Press, pp. 213–217.

4

EXPLOITING TRAGEDY

Psychoanalysis, fate and free will

> If we began to think of Oedipus, for example, as just extremely unlucky, psychoanalysis would be a very different thing.
>
> *Adam Phillips (1995, p. 17)*

Psychoanalysis and fate

Oedipus is more than just unlucky. The oracle knows from the beginning how events will unfold. Indeed, the very attempt made by his parents to forestall his fate – by abandoning the child with a spike through its foot – proves to be the means of its realization; it leads, via an apparent coincidence (Oedipus unwittingly meeting his father at the crossroads and killing him) to the prophecy's fulfilment. If luck appears to be involved, then that is due to Oedipus' (and our own) misperception. It belongs to the human point of view, not to the gods.

It is via Oedipus that tragic drama becomes central to psychoanalysis. If psychoanalysis took Oedipus as just extremely unlucky, it would lose recourse to the myth as a demonstration of universal desires, one that endorses the authority of psychoanalytic theory itself. Oedipus does not live out only his own fate, but ours too. His story reflects a fundamental human phenomenon, even if it took psychoanalysis to develop this into a theory, thereby offering a means of interpretation. Fate is never entirely separable from questions of knowledge and power (and ignorance and powerlessness). This is the knowledge and power that must keep notions of luck at bay. In the words of William Kerrigan: 'Fate pulls unfolding time back into the past and precedent. It drives out chance from a reign of law. It interprets everything' (Smith and Kerrigan, 1984, p. xiii).

Interprets too much? And interpreted by whom – who occupies this position of oracle? This chapter explores the role of tragedy in the work of Freud and Lacan, with regards to the light it throws on the relationship between psychoanalysis, fate and free will. Hingeing on this is the question of a psychoanalytic cure: to what extent can we free ourselves from forces that determine us? Freud's Oedipus is bound to fate on his first psychoanalytic appearance, in a letter to Freud's friend Wilhelm Fliess. Freud is contemplating making the Oedipus complex universal, 'in spite of all the objections that reason raises against the presupposition of fate' (Masson, 1985, p. 272). Fate constitutes an ultimate power over which we cannot exercise control. Cautiously, as Oedipus develops in *The Interpretation of Dreams* (1900), Freud compares the effects of the unconscious to 'the *daemonic* powers' that ancient peoples attributed to the soul.[1] Scholar of Greek mythology and contemporary of Freud Walter Burkert defines *daimon* as 'occult power, a force that drives man forward where no agent can be named ... the veiled countenance of divine activity ... something like fate, but without any person who plans and ordains being visible' (in Winter, 1999, p. 313).

Freud is conscious of the ominous ground to which he has brought his discipline. Yet his attempts to avoid a totally determinist account fall back into fatefulness. He notes that people finding themselves repeating undesirable situations will sometimes describe their predicament as 'being pursued by a malignant fate or possessed by some "daemonic" power', but psychoanalysis takes the view that their fate is 'for the most part arranged by themselves and determined by early infantile influences' (1920, p. 21). We escape from one version of fate into another: a fate of our own making. At least, here, chance can play a role. In a letter of 1911, contemplating this issue of psychoanalysis's position with regards to fate, Freud writes, '*daimon kai tuche* (fate and chance) and not one *or* the other are decisive' (Freud, 1960, p. 292). This does little, however, to restore our self-determination: both fate and chance render us helpless. Tragedy can identify the two phenomena, as we've seen in the case of Oedipus' 'chance' encounter with his father. Romeo and Juliet, to provide a more recent example, may be 'star crossed' but Romeo's killing of Tybalt and his failure to get the message about Juliet's faked death appear products of pure chance, and this enhances the tragic effect. The plays are tragic in so far as individual will proves inadequate against the universe generally. More sinister still, this will may be complicit in fulfilling destinies of which the individual themselves remains ignorant.

Freud approaches Oedipus from within a long tradition of thinking about, and with, tragedy, one that leads from Aristotle to Hegel and Nietzsche, probing the strange appeal of this genre in relation to the question of man's freedom. Like myth, tragedy appears to bring with it a form of knowledge. It conveys a sense of the inexorable, of paradox, a dark universalism and a vision of mankind, cloaked in religiosity, ceremony and awe. It is also foundational, at the root of European civilization.[2] As such, the inclusion of Sophocles in psychoanalytic theory lends intellectual weight at the very least. But this very prestige has fuelled criticisms of psychoanalysis. Having freed us from the old gods, Freud seems to deny us our freedom and individuality once again. And he borrows the gravitas of one of western culture's founding art forms as if this itself lent credence. In her critique, 'Psychoanalysis as "necessity": Freud's "tragic" theories of the psyche, gender and cultural history', Sarah Winter (1999) argues that this co-option of tragic drama cunningly positions psychoanalytic truth itself as a tragic necessity. That Sophocles in particular had a privileged place in the nineteenth-century classical pantheon does much to explain Oedipus' inclusion in psychoanalysis.[3] In Freud's hands, tragic *pathos* legitimizes a theory 'based on the primacy of unconscious determination and guilt'. It also 'designates a set of experiences and moral questions' (p. 19) in relation to being human over which psychoanalysis will claim authority.

The 'truth effect' of psychoanalysis, as Winter puts it, depends upon demonstrating that Sophocles' *Oedipus* is compelling because the oracle laid the same curse upon us as upon the tragic hero. Freud engineers a double act of *anagnorisis* (recognition), at once individual and cultural. Any resistance on our part is anticipated: of course we're bound to object, the complex touches on our deepest fears and desires. We are caught in a trap of guilt and denial before we are even capable of acting freely. And all this is founded on one ancient play.

Tragedy's 'cultural specificity' is one of the most effective weapons wielded against psychoanalysis's supposedly universal theory:

> Psychoanalytical theory never analyses the historical reasons for the authority of Greek tragedy in Western cultures, and neither does it address tragedy's formal and cultural specificity, because tragedy must operate as a medium of psychoanalytic cross-cultural and transhistorical translations, and as support for institutional claims about the necessary conditions of subjectivity.
>
> *(p. 114)*

128 Exploiting tragedy

Winter draws on the philological expertise of the French classicist Jean-Pierre Vernant to support her critique. Vernant's seminal readings of tragedy reinvigorated twentieth-century classicism. They are explicitly a corrective to those of Freud and his followers, contained in a series of hugely influential essays: 'Oedipus without the complex' (1967), 'The historical moment of tragedy in Greece' (1968), 'Ambiguity and reversal' (1970) and 'Intimations of the will in Greek tragedy' (1972). In these, we see philology fighting back against psychoanalysis's hijacking of classical texts. As 'Oedipus without the complex' asks on its first page:

> In what respects is it possible that a literary work belonging to the culture of fifth-century Athens, itself a very free transposition of a much more ancient Theban legend dating from before the institution of the city-state, should confirm the observations of a doctor on the patients who throng his consulting rooms at the beginning of the twentieth century?
> *(Vernant and Vidal-Naquet, 1981, p. 63)*

Miriam Leonard (2005), in a critical study of psychoanalysis that builds on Winter's own, refers to Vernant's 'blanket rejection of psychoanalysis' (p. 113) in this essay. Vernant historicizes Oedipus, arguing that undue focus on the themes of incest and parricide overlooks the significance of the drama in the context of the fifth-century polis, one bound to unique historical and ideological circumstances. Tragedy belongs, Vernant argues, to a new political subjectivity tied to the development of democratic Athens, its citizens now autonomous, legally bound entities. The tragic genre emerges just as myth begins to lose its political authority, reflecting a transitional period and its clash of values (Vernant and Vidal-Naquet, 1981).

Vernant pours particular derision on a psychoanalytic study by Didier Anzieu (1966). Anzieu's analysis ranges from Oedipus to Kronos and then on to several other myths, finding in them a universal theme of incest and castration. It is a decidedly odd-sounding reading ('In repossessing his mother [Oedipus] rediscovers that first happiness that he lost when he was so early separated from her', for example).[4] Vernant writes: 'According to Anzieu almost all Greek myths reproduce, in the form of an infinite number of variants, the theme of incestuous union with the mother and murder of the father' (Vernant and Vidal-Naquet, 1981, p. 71). Oedipus just sets the seal on this general trend. This is another criticism common in attacks on psychoanalysis: its universalism is reductionist. Vernant complains that 'in this mythology as presented by Anzieu … it is impossible for the Greek specialist to recognize the legends with which he is familiar. They have lost their distinctive features and character and their own specific field of application' (p. 71). Likewise, Winter (1999) objects that the Lacanian interpretation of Oedipus as a figure of the unconscious history of the subject 'overlooks both the multiple and contradictory formulations of agency and causality explored in Sophocles' plays' (p. 20). Leonard (2005) portrays psychoanalytic theory as tendentious. For its adherents,

> The child's contingent circumstances within the family coincidentally reproduce the oedipal situation, and thus lead the child to repeat Oedipus' 'tragedy of specificity' through the structural limitations of object choice. What was once considered fate (*daimon*) is now considered chance (*tuche*), but the end result is the same.
>
> (p. 52)

Leonard's argument rests on the wry 'coincidentally', this large 'coincidence' that links each individual's unique circumstance with Ancient Greek tragedy. She extends this line of criticism to Lacan, by setting up a parallel between fate and '*tuche*' (a parallel supported by Freud's own association: *daimon kai tuche*). But Aristotle's problematic category of chance serves a more complex role for Lacan than as a reinterpretation of the Freudian *daimon*. Rather, as part of Aristotle's interrogation of cause generally, it represents a fundamental challenge to our comprehension of causality.

A return to Aristotle's *Physics* shows the extent to which *tuche* is already involved with the question of free will and determinism, and how, therefore, it allows Lacan to confront their apparent incompatibility as it arises in psychoanalysis. Lacan, with Aristotle, recognizes the issue as one related to perception. This chapter demonstrates the ways in which this is in line with the concerns of tragic drama itself. Tragedy's place in psychoanalysis need not be defined by its concern with fate, death or parricide but by its interrogation of cause and the struggle humans have in reconciling a limited human point of view with one that encompasses the entirety of events: the view of the gods.

The tragic point of view

Aristotle against science

> They did not want to look on the naked face of luck (*tuche*), so they turned themselves over to science (*techne*). As a result, they are released

> from their dependence on luck; but not from their dependence on science.
>
> Hippocrates, On Science *(late fifth-century BC)*
> *(in Nussbaum, 1986, p. 19)*

Aristotle is considered the founder of empirical research, 'the first genuine scientist in history', according to the Encyclopædia Britannica (2008, p. 12), and the first to construct a comprehensive system of philosophy. A long tradition ascribes to Aristotle a Baconian vision of scientific and philosophical method, avoiding subjective interpretation in his pursuit of natural laws. As such, we should expect him to eliminate ideas of chance from his philosophy, along with all other superstitions and purely subjective phenomena. But a closer look at Aristotle's project reveals his true interests as being more subtle and complex. He is interested in the act of perception itself, and keeps within his consideration the desire for knowledge that shapes it. And it is this that leads him to explore the idea of the *tychic*, in that it belongs to our perception of the world, and of cause.

Where the other category of chance happenings he describes, the *automaton*, covers all things that occur without a clear cause, the *tychic* applies only to 'beings who can do well or ill, in the sense either of faring or acting so' (Aristotle, *Physics*, 197b10).[5] Aristotle reserves *tuche* for moral creatures, but the qualifying factor is not so much our ability to act morally as to interpret significance. As examples of the *tychic* he considers lucky and unlucky coincidences: going shopping and coming across someone who owes you money; being attacked by robbers at a well that you have only visited because you ate something spicy (*Metaphysics*, 6.3, 1027a29–b14; *Physics*, 196b33; see also Hankinson, 1995). It seems *tuche* is never an actual cause in itself, he concedes, rather a property of these chains of events (i.e. an *interpretation* of causality as it bears upon our circumstances).

It is in this respect that the concept belongs to a broader concern of Aristotle's: the role of point of view in supposed 'truth'. As he states in the *Nicomachean Ethics*, we can't investigate things as *haplos* – simple, without qualification – but only how they are to us (*Physics*, 196b24–25; see also Shew, 2008). In a similar vein, Martha Nussbaum (1986) draws attention to Aristotle's use of the word *phainomena*, usually translated as 'observed facts', 'data of perception' or almost anything but what it literally means: 'appearances', or the frequently interchangeable 'what we believe' or 'what we say' (p. 241). Nussbaum argues that, with this term, Aristotle was purposefully confronting an earlier philosophical tradition in which 'appearances' had been understood as the opposite of 'the real' or 'the true' (the Greek for truth, *aletheia*, meaning 'what is revealed', 'what is brought out from concealment'; Plato inherits this tradition from Parmenides). Aristotle sets himself apart from this ideal, establishing a more phenomenological approach. It is as such that Heidegger (1998) describes Aristotle's *Physics* as 'the hidden, and therefore never adequately studied, foundational book of western philosophy' (p. 185).

Is chance a subjective or objective phenomenon? The concept demands, in the view of one modern commentator, that we unhinge ourselves from these categories, along with the categories of empirical and conceptual (Winslow, 2007). It is as such that Melissa Shew (2008), in her study of chance in Aristotle's philosophy, sees the notion of *tuche* problematizing the *logos* (knowledge) in the way that all *paradoxa* challenge the complacency of *endoxa* (beliefs generally accepted).[6] Aristotle recognizes it as an *aporia*, an irresolvable internal contradiction. He presents it as an attempt to give a *logos* to something which exceeds the *logos*.

Aristotle and Lacan share this scepticism with regards to the extent that scientific accounts may ever be all-encompassing. It is impossible to speak the whole truth, Aristotle states, even if it is also impossible to miss it entirely:

> Each thinker makes some statement about the natural world, and as an individual contributes little or nothing to the inquiry; but a combination of all conjectures results in something considerable. Thus in so far as it seems that Truth is like the proverbial door which no one can miss, in this sense our study will be easy; but the fact that we cannot, although having some grasp of the whole, grasp a particular part, shows its difficulty.
>
> (*Metaphysics*, 2.993b)

Lacan himself, at the beginning of *Television*, declares: 'I always speak the truth. Not the whole truth, because there's no way to say it all. Saying it all is literally impossible: words fail. Yet it's through this very impossibility that the truth holds onto the real' (1990, p. 7). Lacan devotes a lot of consideration to the ideals, and self-deception, of a science that promises the whole truth, in particular its illusion of transparency. Modern science depends upon keeping the questioning subject out of the equation, so to speak.

What does all this have to do with tragedy? Interestingly, both Shew and Nussbaum see this concern with the impossible challenge of objectivity as having an influence on Aristotle's admiration for tragic drama, granting it place of honour in the education of citizens in both the *Poetics* and *Politics*.

Nussbaum (1986) connects this to 'the general anthropocentrism of his ethics .... His rejection of the Platonic external "god's eye" standpoint leads him to turn, for moral improvement, not to representations of divine non-limited beings, but to stories of *human* activity' (p. 378). Shew (2008) sees his praise of tragedy as specifically bound to the *tychic*. The concept, she argues, plays an important role in the *Poetics*. It is through tragedy, Aristotle argues, that a person realizes 'the radical contingency of her lot' (p. 3), its provisional and random nature. This will be the nub of Lacan's own defence of tragedy's place in psychoanalytic theory, hence the value of having Aristotle's terminology in his tool kit.

Humans vs gods

> I am a child of *tuche*.
> Sophocles, Oedipus Tyrannos *(l.1080) (*The Theban Plays*))*

Sophocles' play *Oedipus Tyrannos* is purposefully constructed to explore the role of chance, fate and human interpretation. The concept of *tuche* recurs explicitly at crucial moments, one of several elements that turns the play itself into an extended exploration of point of view

Vernant (Vernant and Vidal-Naquet, 1981) himself is the first to discuss this thread, identifying it with the transitional historical moment he sees as defining tragedy. In 'Tensions and Ambiguities in Greek Tragedy', he portrays the tragic figure as being caught between competing modes of fate: *daimon* or divine intervention, and ethos, or human character. 'Tragic culpability' reflects, on one hand, 'the ancient religious concept of crime-defilement, *hamartia*, sickness of the mind, the delirium sent by the gods', and, on the other, 'the new concept in which the guilty one, *hamarton*, and, above all, *adikon* [unjust], is defined as one who, under no compulsion, has deliberately chosen to commit a crime' (pp. 28–30, 41–42). As we've seen, it is central to Vernant's analyses that tragedy arises during a period in Greek culture when concepts of individual agency are evolving. At this point in history, 'human and divine levels [are] ... distinct enough to be set in opposition. But if drama is to be tragic it is also necessary that these two levels should continue to be seen as inseparable' (p. 21). Individual will is now a powerful force, while deriving its true meaning 'by becoming an integral part of an order that is beyond man and eludes him' (p. 22). Vernant cites the surviving fragment of Heraclitus as evidence of this, '*ethos anthropos daimon*' (p. 13). In a literal sense, this means 'character in man is *daimon*'. But the syntactical symmetry of the Greek opens up multiple interpretations. Heraclitus could be implying that it is his character, in man, that one calls *daimon* (i.e. fate is actually just character) or, conversely, that what one calls character in man is in reality a *daimon*, a possession of sorts. Today, Vernant says, they are seen as mutually exclusive. But the existence of psychoanalysis might lead us to qualify this assertion.

Ruth Padel (1992), in *In and Out of the Mind: Greek Images of the Tragic Self*, describes Greek tragedy inheriting the sense of a world run by conflicted divinities. It is a cosmos reflecting our own human division. Padel provides a possible etymology for *daimon* itself: *daio*, I divide. Dionysus, the god most identified with Greek tragedy, is associated with an original division in the universe (the Fall into the Mirror explored in the previous chapter).[7] But the presence of gods causes a subtler division, one between human and divine levels of interpretation, and it is this in which Vernant is interested.

The multiple levels of meaning are powerfully revealed by humans' use of language. Words and phrases intended to mean one thing are translated into new senses by a context of which the speaker is unaware. Vernant presents the word *tuche* in *Oedipus Tyrannos* as an example. When the herdsman who saved Oedipus as an infant arrives as a messenger in Thebes, and reveals that Oedipus is not the natural son of Polybus and Merope, Jocasta sees the truth: she has married her son. The prophecy has come true, he is doomed. But Oedipus himself remains oblivious. He misreads Jocasta's reaction as distaste for his apparently inferior background:

> I must unlock the secret of my birth.
> The woman, with more than woman's pride, is shamed
> By my low origin. I am the child of Fortune
> The giver of good, and I shall not be shamed
>
> *(ll. 1078–81)*

Paida tes Tyches, tes eu didouses – 'the child of Fortune, the giver of good'. At the beginning of the play, the priest describes Oedipus as *Tuche*, the city's Good Luck (l.52). It is this interpretation that blinds Oedipus in the lines above. Tiresias comes to see that Oedipus is the *victim* of fortune/*tuche* not its beneficiary (l.442). On the hinge of this word – alongside that of *pharmakos* (meaning both 'medicine' and 'poison', depending on context) – the highest (godlike) becomes equivalent to the lowest, cure interchangeable with curse, saviour with scapegoat.

Vernant, for this reason, draws attention to tragedy's use of puns and chiastic reversals that underpin the dramatic situation with linguistic ambiguity. Double-entendres are prevalent: 'no literary genre of antiquity made such full use of double entendre as did tragedy, and *Oedipus Tyrannos* contains more than twice as many ambiguous expressions as Sophocles' other plays' (Vernant and Vidal-Naquet, 1981, p. 14). The effect of dramatic irony brought about by this wordplay establishes the distance and inherent difference between actor and audience.

> It is only for the spectator that the language of the text can be transparent at every level in its polyvalence and with all its ambiguities. Between the author and the spectator the language thus recuperates the full function of communication that it has lost on the stage between the protagonists in the drama .... The language becomes transparent and the tragic message comes across ... only if he relinquishes his earlier convictions, accepts a problematical vision of the world and, through the dramatic spectacle, himself acquires a tragic consciousness.
>
> *(p. 18)*

This is the lesson of tragedy. As egotistical, self-orientated humans, we are caught between modes of interpretation, one of which will always be devastating.

> Seen from a human point of view, Oedipus is the leader with second sight, the equal of the gods; considered from the point of view of the gods he is blind, equal to nothing. Both the reversal of the action and the ambiguity of the language reflect the duality of the human condition which, just like a riddle, lends itself to two opposite interpretations. Human language is reversed when the gods express themselves through it. The human condition is reversed – however great, just and fortunate one may be – as soon as it is scrutinized in relation to the gods.
>
> *(p. 93)*

The duality of the human condition does not so much describe two forces within us as two means of perceiving our lot. It is this that made Oedipus 'exemplary of the human condition for the Greeks' (Winter, 1999, p. 108). And, of course, this duality is reinforced by tragic drama's own position between secular entertainment and religious ceremony, one performed for the gods themselves (as heard in the title of Patricia Easterling's 1997 study,

'A show for Dionysus'). The original setting itself, the Theatre of Dionysus Eleuthereus in Athens, with its steeply tiered rows surrounding the stage, enacts the contrast.

It is worth considering, briefly, how the full resonance of this condition is lost in the transition from pagan to Christian thought. Christianity, of course, also recognizes parallel levels of meaning, mortal and divine, but dismisses the lower, human point of view entirely. Augustine, on the border of the classical and Christian worlds, rejected a tragic vision of life, seeing 'fate' and 'chance' as inconsistent with divine providence.[8] The wisdom of the Christian God trumps human experience entirely. Boethius defined medieval thought on the subject when, in his *Consolations*, he has Lady Philosophy demonstrate that the very idea of misfortune masks the true state of affairs in a universe designed by reason. Philosophy raises us above the perception of individual fate.[9] God's all-encompassing gaze eliminates the concept of luck, but, also eliminated, is the ambivalence responsible for so much of tragedy's power: the open, uncertain place of man in the universe; the possibility of human triumph. A sense of man's powers is needed if we are to feel pathos when humans are defeated by forces beyond their control. Tragedy has heroes, with what seem to the audience as almost god-like powers, and seductively god-like egos – the very egos that blind them to their fate.

It is this blindness that aligns Vernant's reading of tragedy with Lacan's own. The conflicting modes of interpretation that give tragic drama its force, one from the individual's point of view, one that recognizes the structures in which they are entrapped, defines Lacanian theory of subjecthood generally. Against the idea of an adequate (heroically self-willed) ego, transparent to itself, he describes one that is fundamentally oblivious to its own truth. 'The unconscious is this subject unknown to the self, misapprehended, misrecognized, by the ego', as Lacan writes in *Seminar II* (1991, p. 59). For Lacanian psychoanalysis, 'there's no such thing as a knowing subject' (1988, p. 126), which would mean simultaneously actor, audience and gods. This would be a contradiction in terms; a subject is a point of view.

In fact, Lacan's theory and Vernant's share more than a few points in common. In the following section I explore this relationship further, as Lacan extends his enquiry into tragedy and point of view, in particular the perception attributed to the gods. This takes us back to the issue of cause more generally, and the *tychic* as a concept that allows Lacan to elaborate the philosophical underpinnings of tragic self-blindness. It leads to Lacan's introduction of a third god, neither pagan nor Christian: 'the god of scientific atheism'.

Gaps in the system

In *Seminar XI*, the *tychic* is closely allied to the real. Lacan (1977) introduces the concept of *tuche* in the course of arguing against a line of criticism: the reproach that psychoanalysis constitutes a retreat from reality. On the contrary, he argues, 'no praxis is more orientated towards that which, at the heart of experience, is the kernel of the real' (p. 53). This, of course, is the real as what threatens the sufficiency of the symbolic, representing the moment when a system is exposed as being based on a denial. One such system is that of causality itself.

> The phases of the moon are the cause of tides .... Or again, miasmas are the cause of fever – that doesn't mean anything either, there is a hole, and something that oscillates in the interval. In short, there is cause only in something that doesn't work.
>
> (p. 22)

Lacan acknowledges he is on well-trodden philosophical ground. He refers to Kant's *Prologomena* and the recognition of 'the gap that the function of cause has always presented to any conceptual apprehension' and describes the problem as 'an embarrassment to philosophers' (p. 21) and to science. In the previous year's seminar, Lacan had identified the 'progress' of science with the gradual elimination of the idea of 'cause' from explanations. In its place come scientific 'laws', accounting for the connection between one event and the next but not bothering itself with the strange gap between them.[10] Lacan notes: 'Cause is to be distinguished from that which is determinate in a chain, in other words *the law*' (Fink, 1995, p. 22). Law may describe, it predicts, but it cannot itself fill the gap between events. Cause is an *aporia*.

Verhaeghe (2002) writes on this at length in his essay, 'Causality in science and psychoanalysis'. The scientific dream of the Complete Causal System, in which everything can be accounted for, becomes a nightmare 'once one asks the question of the cause of the cause'. What joins the moon and the tide is, of course, gravity. But where is the causation itself? Cause is a narrative with which a sequence of events are understood, an interpretation but not a physical event. It will not fill the hole we have papered over. 'Cause is a concept that, in the last resort, is unanalyzable – impossible to understand by reason' (Lacan, 1977, p. 21). Verhaeghe (2002) writes: '*tuche*, chance, functions as the trauma underlying this nightmare' (p. 121). In the supposed elimination of chance and the causal gap, we also obscure the desire for a complete, unified (*automaton*/mechanical) system – a psychological need, the creative well-spring, that cannot be acknowledged if science is to remain 'scientific'. This is Lacan's argument in *Seminar X*:

> The cause always arises in correlation with the fact that something is omitted in the consideration of knowledge, something which is precisely the desire which animates the function of knowledge. Every time the cause is invoked, in its most traditional register, it is in a way the shade, the pendant, of what is the blind spot in the function of this knowledge itself.
>
> *(2014, p. 198)*

'Cause' betrays the subjective, human element – the very human desire (for meaning) underlying the quest for objective knowledge. This function of knowledge is the desire we touched on in chapter 1: knowledge as 'suture' to close the gap between subject and world, rendering our sight objective. But the notion of 'cause' is subjective, an interpretation. Aristotle, faced with the need to underpin the concept, devises a Final Cause, the natural 'end' of all existence towards which it flows. Without it, we find a worrying absence at the centre of the causally structured world.

Seminar XI is a seminar of gaps. Lacan (1977) approaches the problem of cause via the mystery of the unconscious. Those who consider the unconscious to be 'dynamic' are substituting 'the most common kind of mystery for a particular mystery – in general, force is used to designate a locus of opacity' (p. 21). The seminar also, famously, considers a gap in the field of the visible (us). All involve some implicit unifying power: causation, consciousness, the gaze. When it falters we see the usually hidden effort any system has to make to appear complete and sufficient. In this sense, the *tychic* denotes the point in a system where it looks back at us, exposing the (unconscious) work that goes into subjecthood.

This is especially clear in the case of the visible. In *Seminar XI*, *tuche* is introduced at the end of the first section, on 'The unconscious and repetition', but discussion continues into the next chapter, 'The split between the eye and the gaze'. Lacan (1977) writes: 'It is at the level that I call the stain that the *tychic* point in the scopic function is found' (p. 77). Vision itself presents us with a sense of objectivity, a totality in which we see everything, but not the 'point of view' itself. This is the stain. We are the elided gap in the field of the visible: 'in the so-called waking state, there is an elision of the gaze' (p. 75). It is in this sense that the gaze is *tychic*, and as such it reminds us of our limited point of view. It is why, while it may seem 'self-evident' to go 'from perception to science ... it is a way that analytic experience must rectify' for 'it avoids the abyss of castration' (p. 77), i.e. the fact that fantasies of coherence are born from a situation of division and fragmentation. It is the elided gaze underpinning sight that forces Lacan, finally, to situate the psychoanalytic 'point of view' away from the self-assurance of science:

> That is why we should try to avoid, by our interventions in the session, allowing the subject to establish himself on this level. On the contrary, we should cut him off from this point of ultimate gaze, which is illusory.
>
> (p. 77)

This is important because 'the level of reciprocity between the gaze and the gazed at is, for the subject, more open than any other to alibi'. The analyst must avoid finding themselves used as an alibi for an identity, a substitute for the ultimate gaze underwriting objectivity – and objective identity – in order to bring the patient's attention to the determining forces that go into making a subject in the first place.

In the eyes of God

'The true formula of atheism is not *God is dead* ... the true formula of atheism is *God is unconscious*' (Lacan, 1977, p. 59). The God of 'scientific atheism' is unconscious – passing no judgements, making no commands – but still present, holding everything together, underwriting the coherence of the world. In *Seminar X*, Lacan (2014) speaks of 'the correlation between this omnipotence and something which is, as I might say, all seeingness':

> Whatever an obsessional testifies to you in his remarks ... you can be quite persuaded that *qua* obsessional he still believes in God, I mean that he believes in the God that everybody or almost everybody in our cultural arena believes in without believing in him, namely this universal eye that is brought to bear on all our actions.
>
> (p. 285)

This universal eye is the fantasy of both science and fate (see the god's eye view of tragedy). Both represent a timeless knowledge that trumps the limited, time-bound perspective of an individual. It is this difference between a human, temporal perspective and one that incorporates all time that leads Lacan into a reconsideration of fate, and provokes his own return to Sophocles' Theban plays.

Time is the most decisive property distinguishing human perception of the world from that of the gods. In 'Tensions and ambiguities in Greek tragedy', Vernant writes:

> Perhaps the essential feature that defines [tragedy] is that the drama brought to the stage unfolds both at the level of everyday existence, in a human, opaque time made up of successive and limited present moments, and also beyond this earthly life, in a divine omnipresent time that at every instant encompasses the totality of events, sometimes to conceal them and sometimes to make them plain but always so that nothing escapes it or is lost in oblivion. Through this constant union and confrontation between the time of men and the time of the gods, throughout the drama, the play startlingly reveals that the divine intervenes even in the course of human actions.
>
> (Vernant and Vidal-Naquet, 1981, pp. 18–19)

The theme of time is manifest both in the very design of tragedy, with each play intended to represent continuous action over the course of one day ('a single revolution of the sun', Aristotle, *Poetics*, V), and in its content. 'Time sees all', the Chorus declares in *Oedipus Rex* (1213–14). Edith Hall (1997) describes time as 'the only conceptual benchmark by which Sophocles' mortals can fully understand their difference from divinity' (p. ix). The power of Creon or Oedipus or Clytemnestra will inevitably pass, but the sovereignty of the gods is immune to time's passing. There is an echo of this difference of perspective in the Sphinx's riddle to Oedipus (what walks on four legs in the morning, two in the afternoon and three in the evening): it is riddlesome because it presents human life on a different scale.

Time vividly distinguishes a subject's point of view from one overlooking existence as a whole. This provides Lacan with a solution to the problem of repetition that had troubled Freud in *Beyond the Pleasure Principle*. In acts of irrational repetition we find an example of humans apparently controlled by something beyond their will – a space Freud filled with another autonomous, seemingly mythopoeic force within us, the death drive.[11] Lacan translates a temporal repetition into a spatial one. Repetition is how the temporal, diachronic human experiences the structure in which he is fixed.[12] At the opening of 'The split between the eye and the gaze' in *Seminar XI*, Lacan (1977) riffs etymologically on *Wiederholung* (repetition) and its root in *holen* (to haul):

> *To haul, to draw.* To draw what? Perhaps, playing on the ambiguity of the word in French, to draw lots (*tirer au sort*). This *Zwang*, this compulsion, would then direct us towards the obligatory card – if there is only one card in the pack, I can't draw another.
>
> *(p. 67)*

The comparison is an everyday one from the world of card tricks. We are invited to pick a card and insert it back into the pack. The pack is shuffled and then, as if by magic, the same card appears. We have to consider whether what seemed an act of free choice on our part was really free (a trick deck of cards?). The impression (to the ignorant) is of magical forces, but the true cause is the structure that entraps us: 'If the subject is the subject of the signifier – determined by it – one may imagine the synchronic network as it appears in the diachrony of preferential effects' (p. 67). One may imagine the structure of the symbolic order appearing, from our temporal point of view, as repetition. Lacan extends his (linguistic) trickery even further:

> It is the very structure of the network that implies the returns … this is the figure that Aristotle's *automaton* assumes for us. Furthermore, it is by *automatisme* that we sometimes translate into French the *Zwang* of the *Wiederholungszwang*, the compulsion to repeat.
>
> *(p. 67)*

Via the French, *automatisme* (automatic reflex), the compulsion in repetition compulsion (*Zwang* in Freud's German), can be linked to Aristotle's Greek *automaton*, now denoting an automatic force within us (see Freud, 1894). The effects of existing within the symbolic order may seem accidental, but this is a different phenomenon to *tuche*, which is truly unaccountable, and lies outside of the structure altogether. Lacan clarifies this theory in 'Position of the unconscious' (delivered in 1960 but rewritten in 1964, the year of *Seminar XI*):

> The effect of language is to introduce the cause into the subject. Through this effect, he is not the cause of himself; he bears within him the worm of the cause that splits him. For his cause is the signifier ….

> As an effect of language, in that he is born of this early split, the subject translates a signifying synchrony into ... primordial temporal pulsation ....
>
> (2007, p. 708)[13]

Tragedy exposes us to both points of view, synchronic and diachronic. It allows us to play God, experiencing fate from within and without. Aristotle's theory of cause allows Lacan to return to Freud's exploitation of tragedy with a new emphasis: the symbolic order as a form of fate, installing a foreign power within us while also representing an external structure in which we're trapped. This leads Lacan to another Sophoclean play, *Oedipus at Colonus*, via which he attempts his own approach to the question of 'cure'.

Innocent guilt

Secret speech

> It was a *sublime* thought, to suffer punishment willingly even for an inevitable crime, and so to prove one's freedom by the very loss of this freedom, and to go down with a declaration of free will.
>
> Friedrich W. J. Schelling, Tenth Letter, Letters on Dogmatism and Criticism, 1794–96 (1980, pp. 192–193)

There is more to tragedy than its exploration of cause and perception. Fundamental to its appeal is a paradoxical effect, the heroism of defeat. As Schelling notes, a sense of defeat and its injustice is intensified by becoming a form of punishment. The unique and sublime effect of tragedy is bound to this spectacle: the punishment of an 'inevitable crime', one that heightens the confrontation between fate and free will. For psychoanalysis, trying to salvage a 'cure' from an inescapable fate, it demands consideration. This notion of 'innocent guilt' and the question of why underserved punishment should hold such deep appeal frames the second half of this chapter. In it, I extend the investigation of Lacan's relationship with tragedy to his use of Sophocles' *Antigone* and *Oedipus at Colonus*.

A concern with undeserved punishment became a staple of Romantic approaches to tragedy, from Schelling through Hölderlin onwards, but its role was recognized as far back as Aristotle's *Poetics*. Aristotle argues that the requisite 'pity or fear' he associates with tragic drama is best created by the spectacle of 'someone who is suffering undeservedly', who commits an error (*hamartia*) (*Poetics*, 53a); 'it is better if the [tragic] action is performed in ignorance' (54a). The error may be bound to an accident of birth, the pollution of a familial line, a curse (see Aeschylus, *Oresteia*). But it is not clearly the hero or heroine's fault. So what exactly is it about this guilt that is present before any crime has been committed that holds such appeal?

Once again, Lacan turns to Vernant's criticism of psychoanalysis to find a way forward. Vernant had drawn attention to Anzieu's strange claim that Oedipus recovers lost happiness when he sleeps with his mother, reminding us why this is impossible: Oedipus didn't *know* who she was. 'As Oedipus himself declares … neither his person nor his actions were to blame. In reality he has done nothing' (Vernant and Vidal-Naquet, 1981, p. 94). Lacan, characteristically, takes this criticism, acknowledges it and makes it a cornerstone of his own theory. Oedipus' ignorance is precisely why Freud chooses the hero as archetypal, Lacan (2015, p.100) argues. He is ignorant of the very fate that defines him. Indeed, it is this which makes the Oedipus myth unique amongst all the other potential tales of incest to which Freud might have turned.

This may not be entirely true regarding Freud's motives.[14] Nonetheless, it is remarkably close to the view of Oedipus Vernant himself expresses in 'Ambiguity and reversal', sounding, not for the last time, distinctly Lacanian:

> The ambiguity of what [Oedipus] says does not reflect a duplicity in his character, which is perfectly consistent, but, more profoundly, the duality of his being. Oedipus is double. He is, in himself, a riddle whose meaning he can only guess when he discovers himself to be in every respect the opposite of what he thought he was and appeared to be. Oedipus himself does not understand the secret speech that, without his realizing, lurks at the heart of what he says …
>
> (p. 90)[15]

This secret speech at the heart of us is what Lacan describes in 'Position of the Unconscious': the subject 'bears within him the worm of the cause that splits him' – 'the effect of language'. It is for this reason that the unconscious is 'this subject unknown to the self, misapprehended, misrecognized, by the ego', as heard at the end of the previous section, and why 'there's no such thing as a knowing subject' (1998, p. 126). The unknown – the unconscious – becomes identified with the symbolic order: the linguistic/cultural trap into which we are born.

Whatever the direction of influence, it would seem a 'blanket rejection of psychoanalysis' doesn't do justice to the intellectual exchange between

Vernant and Lacan. Lacan's Oedipus, like Vernant's, highlights the difference between one's destiny, written elsewhere (i.e. in the symbolic order) and one's subjective experience of life. Oedipus' life 'is guided by a problematics which is not that of his life experience, but that of his destiny – that is, what is the meaning, the significance, of his history? What does his life story mean?' (1991, p. 58). His destiny is written in the big Other, the symbolic order. Psychoanalysis enables us to perceive this. In 'The direction of treatment and the principles of its power', Lacan (2007) compares Freud's supposedly overdetermined and premature interpretations of patient's symptoms to the timid caution he ascribes to contemporary analysts, and declares that Freud's work is 'so bold that in popularizing it, we no longer recognize its import as *mantic*' (i.e. relating to divination or prophecy). In relation to Freud's case study of Ernst Lanzer, the patient known as the Rat Man, Lacan writes that,

> When Freud brings to light what can only be called the subject's lines of fate, what we ponder is Tiresias' face confronting the ambiguity where his verdict operates.
>
> For the lines that are divined here have so little to do with the subject's ego, or with anything he may make present here and now in the dyadic relation, that in the case of the Rat Man, it is by a direct hit on the pact that presided over his parents' marriage (that is, on something that occurred well before the Rat Man was born) that Freud finds several conditions intermingled in it ... and finally manages to explain the impasses in which the Rat Man's moral life and desire go astray.
>
> *(p. 499)*

Lanzer came to Freud in 1907 suffering obsessional neurosis, his obsessions centring in particular on his dead father and his fiancée. Freud traces these to guilt about marrying a woman who was poor, compared to his father who married into money. Freud is Tiresias, the prophet who understood the truth of Oedipus' fate, insofar as he traces the roots of Lanzer's illness to historic circumstances, circumstances beyond the possible content of any analytic dialogue. We share with Oedipus the fact of being determined by materials that precede us; our fate, as the order into which we are born (language, kinship, parentage) is sealed before birth:

> Oedipus' history is out there – written, and we know it, but Oedipus is ignorant of it, even as he is played out by it since the beginning ....

> Everything takes place in function of the Oracle and of the fact that Oedipus is truly other than what he realizes as his history – he is the son of Laius and Jocasta, and he starts out his life ignorant of this fact. The whole pulsation of the drama of his destiny, from the beginning to the end, hinges on the veiling of this discourse, which is his reality without his knowing it.
>
> (Lacan, 1991, p. 209)

'Pulsation', again, as in 'Position of the unconscious', describes the temporal unfolding of truths already fixed in the structure from which we arise. Oedipus is literally 'the child of *tuche*': the *tychic* is his parenthood. The crossroads where (by chance/fate) he meets and unwittingly kills his father replays the 'crossroads' where his parents met, the true 'coincidence' behind his singular existence. It is a chain of events beyond his will and his knowledge which Oedipus has obscured with the myth of his singular, heroic self, perhaps because no story of two other beings feels like it could suffice. In this sense, *Oedipus* is a 'tragedy of specificity', albeit a specificity that is universal: the tragic specificity of a name. An identity is at once unique, arbitrary and eternal. It survives biological life and death. In so doing, identity makes a myth of all of us. Names metamorphozise our living selves into immortal symbols, and it is this duality that inspires Lacan's exploration of two forms of death.

Tragedy and metamorphosis

In the midst of his reading of *Antigone*, Lacan (2008) makes an odd but apparently premeditated swerve. Having noted the comparison of Antigone's cries to those of a bird in plays by both Sophocles and Euripides, he continues:

> Let us not forget how close pagan myth is to the idea of metamorphosis .... It is the nightingale that appears in Euripides as the image of that which a human being is transformed into through his plaintive cries. The limit we have reached here is the one where the possibility of metamorphosis is located – metamorphosis that has come down through the centuries hidden in the works of Ovid.
>
> (p. 325)[16]

Lacan doesn't expand upon this observation. He certainly doesn't suggest in what ways the idea of metamorphosis may be hidden in a poem entitled the

Metamorphoses. But this Ovidian reference is not alone in the *Ethics*. It can be read alongside a small handful of allusions to metamorphosis which occur throughout the seminar, all concerned with this mysterious 'limit'. They throw light both on Lacan's exploration of tragedy's role in psychoanalysis but also Ovid's own concerns in his supremely influential poem.

In Book III of the *Metamorphoses* Ovid collates and interweaves tales associated with the tragic world of Thebes. He makes the question of innocent guilt central; the tales share a sense of inadvertent transgression, of transgressions that can only be perceived in retrospect: crimes of ignorance. These include the founder, Cadmus, accidentally killing a sacred dragon, leading to all his family's subsequent misfortune; Narcissus' doomed self-love; the hunter Actaeon stumbling upon Diana as she bathes and being turned into a stag; and Tiresias striking a pair of copulating snakes and being transformed into a woman. In the words of the classicist Micaela Janan (2007), Theban law is 'a form empty of content. It enjoins upon its subjects an absolute duty to follow its injunctions …. Yet these injunctions are unknowable except as *already* violated' (p. 15).[17] More than tragic, the world that we are presented with is Kafkaesque.

> In Thebes, the gods' implicit injunction to the artless doomed magnifies and distorts this inconsistency, so that the paradox now accrues to the command itself: 'obey a prohibition whose content you cannot know in advance' …. Before this side of the law, we are all always guilty.
>
> (p. 127)

Thebes' subsequent history 'unfolds this original flaw.' While many other characters in the *Metamorphoses* often suffer arbitrarily at the hand of the gods, this is rarely due to inadvertent *transgressions* as in Book III.[18] As Janan notes, the tales collected in Book III all echo 'the arc of unwitting transgression and iron punishment characteristic of the Theban most saliently absent from Ovid's cycle – Oedipus' (p. 126). It seems as if the absence of Oedipus is part of a game or exercise for Ovid, the object being to diffuse his 'innocent guilt' throughout the book. Equally salient, for those with psychoanalytic interests, is the figure that appears precisely where we would expect Oedipus to be: Narcissus.

Oedipus' absence and his replacement by Narcissus, discussed in chapter 2 above, has not attracted as much comment as one might expect.[19] Philip Hardie, Ingo Gildenhard and Andrew Zissos have all analysed the two tales' parallel concerns with blindness and self-knowledge (both receive prophecies from Tiresias; both are warned not to seek to know themselves. The tragedy of both is that they do). But it remains unclear why this substitution has been performed.[20]

One effect is to foreground the relationship between Narcissus and tragedy. Is Narcissus a tragic hero? He certainly fulfils some criteria: he is punished for the tragic flaw of pride (by Nemesis, who first leads him to the pool where he falls in love with his reflection). He also, like a tragic hero, embraces his death once he realizes his love can never be realised. If the tale still does not feel properly tragic this provides a foundation for looking more deeply at the complex symbolism of metamorphosis – often terrible, but not tragic.

It is Antigone, Oedipus' daughter, via whom Lacan moves towards a new theory of tragedy's aesthetic appeal, as well as a new understanding of the relationship between life and death. Antigone epitomizes not just the embrace of death but the pursuit of it. Sophocles' play devoted to her is a tale of one woman's unswerving defiance. For taking up arms against Thebes, Antigones' brother Polynices is to be punished beyond his biological death; his corpse is to be left out at the mercy of dogs and birds, unburied and unmemorialized. Antigone attempts to bury him – repeatedly – against the orders of the king and the laws of the state. For this, she is condemned to be walled up alive. In captivity, she hangs herself.

Traditional readings focused on Antigone as a rebel challenging authority: this is the tenor of a tradition stretching from Hölderlin via Hegel to Heidegger (see Steiner, 1996). Antigone's iconography was re-invigorated in twentieth-century France by Jean Anouilh, whose *Antigone* of 1944 depicted her against the backdrop of occupation. Under the threat of censorship, it is a purposefully ambiguous exploration of resistance. Lacan, in *Seminar VII*, refers to Anouilh's 'fascist Antigone' (2008, p. 308) and something of this moral ambivalence feeds into Lacan's reading. Where interpretations had historically competed over the rights and wrongs of the cause for which she dies, for Lacan it is an absence of cause, an excess of will, that defines her.

Lacan notes that she is already symbolically dead, outcast by the city, yet she still desires to die. Her brother, conversely, is physically dead but without the symbolic rites of burial that would perpetuate his memory. From these suspended states, Lacan elaborates a theory of two deaths: symbolic death and physical death. It is in the zone between them that tragedy is played out.[21]

The zone between the two deaths contains both the living dead and deathless life. As such it can be either monstrous or beautiful. Žižek associates the monstrous aspect of this limbo with the horrific, unsymbolized life substance described by Lacan in *Seminar II* with reference to Edgar Allen Poe's story, 'The Facts in the Case of M Valdemar' (1845). Valdemar is a man suspended by a hypnotist between life and death, a living corpse, becoming 'a disgusting liquefaction, something for which no language has a name' (Lacan, 1991, p. 231), 'the complete collapse of this species of swelling that is life … [into] putrid liquid' (pp. 231–232). This is the fate that threatens Polynices, left out as unmarked (unsymbolized) carrion.

But, alongside this horror, the zone between two deaths can contain beauty in so far as it borders the immortal: 'The limit involved … is something I have called the phenomenon of the beautiful, it is something I have begun to define as the limit of the second death' (Lacan, 2008, p. 320). This is an idea that emerges from Lacan's extended engagement with the *Symposium* in *Seminar VIII*. The whole discourse of Diotima, Lacan (2015) reminds us, is concerned with how 'perishable and fragile beings are sustained in their quest for permanence, which is their essential aspiration' (p. 126). Beauty leads the mortal towards the immortal. It is only through beauty that we approach 'the permanent and the eternal'; it is our precarious mode of participating in it, a 'painful escape route' out of transience. It is in this way that Socrates' Diotima helps Lacan reframe tragedy as a mediation between the contingent and the eternal.

By embracing death heroically (taking ownership of the one inevitable thing), the tragic hero achieves immortality by other means, through fame. This immortal fame is a good beyond that of justice, or even life itself, raising the individual above the human itself. Again, the power of pagan thought is bound to a vision of humanity as part of a continuum with the gods. Heroes can cross over. Yet this heroic transformation reflects the situation of every individual in so far as we combine a biological life (our mortal physical existence) and a symbolic one: a name, an identity that will not itself die. In the seminar on *Transference* Lacan argues that death as old age, as deterioration, is not to be confused

> with the one which one can define in its most general formula by saying that man aspires to annihilate himself in it in order to be inscribed in it in terms of being; if man aspires, this is obviously the hidden contradiction, the little drop you have to swallow, if man aspires to destroy himself in the very fact that he eternalizes himself.
>
> *(p. 88)*

Death, we might say, is equivalent to the mirror of the mirror stage; it grants us an image of ourselves, our lives, as whole, idealized, complete.

Alenka Zupančič (2003), in her essay 'Ethics and tragedy in Lacan', points to the moment in *Antigone* when the doomed heroine lists what she will be deprived of by death – 'no bridal bed, no bridal song hath been mine, no joy of marriage, no portion in the nurture of children' (Sophocles, *Antigone*, ll.880–83) – suggesting that, rather than manifesting a clear sense of regret, it serves to make a closed totality of her life:

> It has a very precise function of making a 'whole' out of the inconclusive metonymy of her existence and her desire …. Precisely because of its being in(de)finite, this potential can only be realized (constituted as an accomplished, 'whole' entity) *as lost*, that is, cast in the negative form.
>
> (p. 186)

This paradox is the consequence of forming something eternal (the signifier of ourselves) from the flow of existence. Lacan (1993), pondering Schreber's struggles with the idea of procreation, ascribed the difficulty to 'something radically unassimilable to the signifier. It's quite simply the subject's singular existence'. It cannot itself provide an explanation of where we've come from, what we're doing, why we're going to disappear. 'The signifier is incapable of providing him with the answer, for the good reason that it places him beyond death. The signifier already considers him dead, by nature it immortalizes him' (pp. 179–180).

The tragic hero appears to take control of the signifier of themselves; of the process of becoming a name, and immortal. The hero faces death 'in order to be remembered by posterity' (Lacan, 2015, p. 98). Lacan notes Diotima's example of Ascestis, who accepted to die in place of her husband, the king Admetus 'so that people would talk about it, so that discourse would forever immortalize her' (p. 127). In Plato's works, this theme is felt most powerfully, not in the *Symposium*, but in those dialogues concerning Socrates' calm embrace of his death, dialogues explicitly constructed to usurp tragedy.[22] In *Seminar VIII*, Lacan notes:

> This story of Achilles, who deliberately prefers death which will make him immortal to the refusal to fight which would leave him his life, is everywhere re-evoked there; in the *Apology of Socrates* itself, Socrates makes much of it to define what is going to be his own behaviour before his judges.
>
> (2015, p. 40)

As the reference to Achilles suggests, both traditions of heroic immortality, tragic and philosophical, share a source in Homer. Homer's foundational epics are prolonged meditations on the relationship between mortal beings and immortal fame – *Kleos aphthiton*, 'fame imperishable' in Lattimore's translation. Glenn Most (2005), in a consideration of this legacy, describes Achilles as 'the paradigm of a man who, given the choice, opts for a short life and eternal glory .... Homer bequeathed to Greek culture both an acute awareness of individual biological mortality and an insatiable desire for immortality in *logos*' (p. 44).[23]

Like Socrates and Achilles, Antigone embraces death. This is not without a cause – her brother – yet her very devotion reinforces a sense of something arbitrary and irrational about her will. A sense of this excess underlies the infamous speech puzzled over by Hegel and Goethe, and noted by Lacan, in which she ranks a brother's death above that of a father or husband.

> O but I would not have done the forbidden thing
> For any husband or for any son.
> For why? I could have had another husband
> And by him other sons, if one were lost;
> But, father and mother lost, where would I get
> Another brother? For thus preferring you,
> My brother, Creon condemns me and hales me away,
> Never a bride, never a mother, unfriended,
> Condemned alive to solitary death.
>
> (Sophocles, Antigone, ll. 905–12)

The lines struck Goethe as a flaw. The leading Victorian classical scholar, Richard Jebb, claimed that they were 'spurious' (see Leonard, 2005). Hegel (1977), by way of a solution, makes them central to his analysis of two competing systems of ethics in the *Phenomenology of the Spirit*: Antigone's sororial duty (reflecting divine familial duties) versus the human ethics of the state.[24] But Lacan, in *Seminar VII*, reads the passage as referring to an absolute singularity:

> 'My brother is what he is, and it is because he is what he is and only he can be what he is, that I move forward to the fatal limit.' Antigone invokes no other right than that one, a right that emerges in the language of the ineffaceable character of what is – ineffaceable, that is, from the

moment when the emergent signifier freezes it like a fixed object in spite of the flood of possible transformations. What is, is, and it is to this, to this surface, that the unshakeable, unyielding position of Antigone is fixed.

(2008, p. 343)

Tragic passion is found at this interface, what Lacan refers to often as 'this limit', a zone that marks the transformation from the undifferentiated flow of living matter to the eternal singularity of the individual that steps from it. It is the limit where the arbitrary – the chance coincidence of elements that constitutes our existence – meets the eternal symbol. Antigone is devoted to Polynices not because of a role he signifies – i.e. father, husband – but for his individuality. (This is the psychology of grief, the obverse of love, both defined by a faith in the absolutely individual.) Žižek (2001) describes Antigone's law of the pure signifier, prior to any law that judges our deeds, as 'the Law of the Name which fixes our identity beyond the eternal flow of generation and corruption' (pp. 91–92). He refers to Saul Kripke's (1980) concept of a 'rigid designator', a signifier which designates the same object 'in all possible worlds', including even one in which its properties were changed. This 'designator' fixes the kernel of the object. In Polynices' case, this is what designates him beyond any other values, including his good or evil deeds.

It is this which leads Lacan, naturally enough, from Antigone to 'the idea of metamorphosis': 'The limit … where the possibility of metamorphosis is located – metamorphosis that has come down through the centuries hidden in the works of Ovid' (Lacan, 2008).

This is an opportunity to shine some light back on the *Metamorphoses*, perhaps the most influential secular text after the epics of Homer, and key to the transmission of myths into post-classical western culture – into psychoanalysis as well as into art, music and poetry. It is Ovid's often idiosyncratic versions of the myths that survive; Ovid's delight in the use of ambivalence and paradox to unsettle readers' responses, his curious ability to transmute tragedy into something stranger. Indeed, the *Metamorphoses* has long been seen as displaying a failure of tragic effect: 'scholars are agreed that his versions of [tragic] myths hardly ever engender a "proper" Aristotelian response' (Gildenhard and Zissos, 1999, p. 163);[25] 'Ovid often dealt with tragic plots and characters, but usually in ways that transmuted them into a distinctly non-tragic form and ethos' (Tarrant, 2002, p. 18). The concerns of this chapter might help us consider the relationship between metamorphosis and tragedy a little further.

Antigone likens her own situation to that of a victim of metamorphosis. The comparison she makes is to Niobe, whose divine punishment involved seeing her husband and all 14 of her children killed before she herself was turned to stone. Lacan (2008) makes much of this comparison, returning to it three times in his discussion of the play, claiming even that 'it is around this image of the limit that the whole play turns' (p. 346):

> In effect, Antigone herself has been declaring from the beginning: 'I am dead, and I desire death.' When Antigone depicts herself as a Niobe becoming petrified, what is she identifying with, if it isn't that inanimate condition in which Freud taught us to recognize the form in which the death instinct is manifested?
>
> *(p. 346)*

Here, Lacan combines several aspects of the death drive as presented in *Beyond the Pleasure Principle*: death as stasis, as repetition, as a return to the inorganic. All are felt throughout the *Metamorphoses*. And Niobe is not the first connection Lacan has made between Ovid's poem and Freud's theory: in a similar vein, his formulation of the mirror stage draws out deathly Ovidian undertones left latent by Freud in his own appropriation of Narcissus. In Lacan's account, in so far as we are created in fascination before our reflection, the self emerges 'petrified', frozen as image, and so already bound to the 'inanimate condition' of death.[26]

The concept of narcissism has been so widely accepted by society at large that we might take it for granted. Lacan reminds us how odd it is for Freud to have positioned this figure of deathly metamorphosis at the heart of psychological development. In his 'Presentation on psychical causality' (1946), Lacan (2007) defamiliarizes narcissism, this most superficially straightforward of psychoanalytic concepts, describing it as 'obscure' but admirable that it should describe the 'essential imaginary knot in man'. And again he identifies narcissism with the death drive in its equation of 'suicide and self-love' (p. 152). For Ovid's myth is not just a drama of self-love but also of stasis, fixity, entrapment by – and in – an image. It is powerfully refigured in the mirror stage. Borch-Jacobsen (1991) locates the seeds of Lacan's narcissistic mirror stage not just in Freud's 'On narcissism' but also in his essay 'The "uncanny"', which has its own concerns with 'the mirror, the image, the double, narcissism, castration (imaginary fragmentation) and death – the frisson of things between being alive and being dead. Even the statue is there' (p. 45).

Narcissus' fate, locked into the beautiful symbol of himself, embodies his crime, but it is far from unique. Ovid's *Metamorphoses* repeatedly presents us with the image of a human transformed at the limits of his or her endurance, at once subsumed in the flux of Ovid's strange world of transformations and frozen eternally as symbols within it.[27] There is a troubling ambivalence to the fate of being metamorphosed, often presented as a combination of torture and apotheosis, life and death. The incestuous Myrrha, 'afraid of death, yet sick of life', prays to be banished from the realms of both and is transformed into a tree. As Philip Hardie (2002) notes, while Myrrha's metamorphosis responds to her specific request, it is entirely typical: 'Any and every instance of metamorphosis results in a state that is neither life nor death, but something in between' (pp. 82–83).

The scholar of Early Modern literature Colin Burrow (1988) identifies 'the full paradox of Ovid's poem' as 'how man simply does not fit in with … "this universe of fecund change"' (p. 100). The dichotomy between humans and nature reflects the unique position of humans as animals with language, including their own names. Lévi-Strauss described man divided from nature by the law of kinship, its code leaving an element of the inhuman within us. Lacan, again, develops this idea into a consideration of language more broadly. Language is itself dichotomous: like metamorphosis it both flows and arrests the flow.[28]

If Lacan finds himself drawn to images of metamorphosis it is because they express the human situation. Ovid's poem captures our dual, paradoxical nature. But Lacan finds this within tragedy also. Tragedy, for Lacan, involves a confrontation with the 'limit' where the flow of life becomes frozen and 'inhuman'. His chosen representatives of tragedy – Antigone and the dying Oedipus – exemplify this. The difference between tragedy and metamorphosis is that, where metamorphosis metaphorizes the transition between life and death, tragedy depicts the willed confrontation with it: 'man *aspires* to annihilate himself in order to have his being inscribed [in history] …. Man aspires to destroy himself in the very act of becoming immortal' (2015, p. 98). Alongside obvious discrepancies in tone, language, structure and medium, the side-stepping of mortality, it seems, distinguishes the genres. For this reason, the distance between the *Metamorphoses* and tragedy is most obvious when its characters attempt suicide. Dying, generally, is a challenge in a world of endless transformation, but the problem gains resonance when an individual attempts to take their own life: grief-stricken Aesacus dives headlong into the sea, struggling to find a way to die, but fails when he is changed into a bird; when Deadalion, having had his daughter killed by Diana, throws himself off a cliff, Apollo takes pity on him and turns him into a hawk. Ovid's Arachne is comparable to Antigone, both women in confrontation with power who choose finally to hang themselves rather than submit. But Arachne is prevented from doing so by Pallas Athena – turned, instead, into a spider.[29]

Metamorphosis makes a universal process out of the immortality that tragic heroes and heroines have to earn. The tenor of Antigone's reference to Niobe is that she *resists* this metamorphic fate; it is the king Creon who imposes the entombment that provokes her comparison. By burying Antigone with just enough food and water to keep her suspended between life and death, he hopes to obscure the tragic choice of death itself and *reduce* it to a form of metamorphosis.

The Oedipus of *Oedipus at Colonus* is important for Lacan as a figure equally residing on the border of tragedy and metamorphosis. Sophocles' play describes the end of Oedipus' life at Colonus, a village near Athens, where the hero arrives as a blinded beggar, accompanied by his daughter Antigone. Death does come to Oedipus, but it is presented as a mystical phenomenon: A messenger describes Oedipus' 'wondrous' passing, without pain, 'invisible and unknowable' (ll.1590–1650). Oedipus becomes a *daimon*, an intermediary spirit.

The ambiguity of this end feeds into Winter's (1999) criticism of psychoanalysis's appropriation of tragedy. The Lacanian reading of *Oedipus at Colonus*, she argues, 'is not an exegesis of the play but a creative adaptation that is not interested in Colonus as a place except insofar as it represents finality or death' (p. 115). And even this reductionism is misleading because Sophocles' late play is different: 'For Oedipus, the end of his life is not death but transformation into another kind of being' (p. 115). In fact, the play's mystical conclusion serves 'to suspend the automatic association of the authority of tragedy itself with the authority of death' (pp. 113–114), an association which defined its value to psychoanalysis.

> The end of *Oedipus at Colonus* suggests the possibility that death may not always be the ultimate metaphor for the authority or authenticity of human experience …. If a man does not end up dying, but rather becomes a *daimon*, then his mortality no longer works to put all of life into perspective for him.
>
> (p. 113)

Yet, as we've seen, it is precisely this redefinition of death that appeals to Lacan. In his theory no one 'ends up' dying; they begin by dying. This is precisely what his exploration of Sophocles has been intended to demonstrate. Like Oedipus in his final days, we are suspended between mortal and immortal realms, mutable life and immutable symbol.

Conclusion: tragedy as cure

If we start with a universal tragedy at the root of our psyche, what is left of the concept of cure? What could it mean? Freud, in his *New Introductory Lectures* (1933), produces one suggestion cryptic enough to be, as Lacan (1977) says, 'worthy of the pre-Socratics' (p. 44): '*Wo Es war, soll Ich werden.*' James Strachey translated this as 'Where Id was, there Ego shall be'. Strachey's version suggests that the daemonic Id, with its ancestry of fate and determinism, might simply be displaced by the autonomous ego. The once intractable conflict of free will and determinism is simply won by free will.

When Lacan translates Freud's maxim, it is as '*Là où c'était là comme sujet dois-je advenir*': there where it was, there must I, as subject, come to happen (Nobus and Quinn, 2005, p. 55). As well as rescuing back some cryptic opacity from Strachey's optimistic lucidity, Lacan draws out an obligation buried within this maxim: 'I *must*' rather than the passive 'Ego shall be.' With this, he says, Freud 'brings forth the paradox of an imperative that presses me to assume my own causality' (Lacan, 2007, p. 734).

What could this mean? 'There where it was' – where *what* was? One answer is: all the things that are not the 'I'; everything imposing on our existence (like fate or a daemon) that is not the subject itself. Where fate was, there shall I, as subject, come to happen. To delve further into this odd proposition, it is helpful to look at the word 'assume' in the imperative to 'assume my own causality'. The translator of the *Écrits* notes the semantic complexity of Lacan's 'assume', incorporating, in the French: 'adopting', 'owning', 'dealing with', 'coming to terms with'. In English there is also clearly a sense of presumption as well. But what could it mean to assume a responsibility for my causality?

Miller (1999) states that 'The primacy of the o/Other entails that the subject is caused' (p. 7): we are caused by language, by our culture. This is why, in his words, Lacan is led from theorizing the *speaking* subject to the *spoken* subject. As we heard earlier in this chapter, 'The effect of language is to introduce the cause into the subject. Through this effect, he is not the cause of himself.' Hence the imperative to assume one's own causality is 'paradoxical'. But paradoxical is not worthless; in Lacanian theory it more often signals the direction we should pursue. The potential fruitfulness of this paradox becomes clearer if we turn the concerns of this chapter on their head and see how, rather than trying to avoid fate, we seek it out. It makes us special, as indeed does guilt. We *want* a sense of our past as fixed and prophetic and determining, no matter how ominous. We *seek* the analyst as oracle to explain us to ourselves, to mythologise us. 'Fate pulls unfolding time back into the past and precedent. It drives out chance from a reign of law' (Smith and Kerrigan, 1984, p. xiii). But this can be desirable. What we flee is chaos and a sense of insignificance.

Freud recognized the extent to which guilt could provide a solution to psychological needs. In his analysis of trauma, an irrational sense of retroactive guilt was a means whereby we make sense of what was, at the time, an experience of randomness and incomprehensibility. And even apparently rational guilt can be used in the same way – it is through our morality, as the moral philosopher Bernard Williams has suggested, that we often try to make our lives 'immune from luck' (in Phillips, 1995, p. 21). Morality establishes an order to things. Better to be determined by a past curse or transgression than by sheer chance and contingency. In this, psychoanalysis becomes our co-conspirator. This is the concern of Adam Phillips in his essay 'Contingency for beginners' (1995): Freud's translation of accidental events into unconsciously determined ones; his campaign against chance and coincidence (in this sense Phillips continues the line of enquiry initiated by Derrida). The analyst, if they are not careful, can end up overplaying the role of oracle, the one who sees the whole of a life as one, past, present and future, who can interpret the real meaning of the analysand's speech, including significations of which the speaker remains unaware. Freud was far from unaware of the analyst's potential complicity, but it is Lacan who mines the issue for what it might tell us about the object and end of analysis. For Lacan, the end of analysis comes when the analysand de-supposes the analyst of knowledge, so that the analyst falls from position of 'subject supposed to know'. In so far as a 'cure' is ever achieved, it is when we move from assuming someone else has knowledge about what causes us (a resituating of the big Other, God, Fate, etc.) to assuming responsibility for the cause within us. This is nothing more or less than the cause introduced into the subject by the symbolic order. The illusion is that someone or something can read it for us and may, thereby, sufficiently account for our origins.

This is a dark twist on the theories of self-determination and freedom associated with Sartrean existentialism. Sartre's redefinition of freedom also involves a conscious act, an originary choice of consciousness independent of any extraneous determination (see Roudinesco, 2014).[30] Lacan, unlike

Sartre, places huge emphasis on the *inescapability* of extraneous determination – the symbolic order/Other – but identifies freedom with a paradoxical act of recognition and responsibility nonetheless. This is the paradox of the imperative, 'there where it was, there must I, as subject, come to happen'; it demands a paradoxical freedom analogous to that identified with tragic heroism: 'to prove one's freedom by the very loss of this freedom, and to go down with a declaration of free will'.

It is as such that Lacanian theory arrives at a surprising optimism compared to Freud. 'It is always a question of the subject qua indeterminate', Lacan (1977, p. 26) writes. Don't fall for Fate as absolute. Structural linguistics shows us that meaning is relative, words derive their meaning in relation to other words. Even if the unconscious works like a language, that does not fix its contents in place. There is no Other of the Other, no godlike metalanguage to interpret significance once and for all (see Lacan, 2007). No God, no Master and no 'analyst', if by that we mean someone who can tell us our truth, who has access to our fate.

Miller (1999) considers the impact this had on the end of analysis, which becomes 'unthinkable in terms of liberation; it is thought of, rather, in terms of *assumption*' (p. 7). And Žižek (1996) describes the end of the psychoanalytic cure as follows: 'in fully assuming the uttermost contingency of its being, the subject becomes the "cause of itself" in the sense of no longer looking for a guarantee of his or her existence in another's desire' (p. 3). Tragedy, the *Metamorphoses* and the *Symposium* all showed us the conversion of accidental existence into eternal forms. Lacan demonstrates that this is something we all do to ourselves. But it does not need to be the final word, or something to which we are blind.

Hence the importance of *Oedipus at Colonus* in *Seminar II*, a seminar ostensibly on 'the ego in Freud's theory and the technique of psychoanalysis'. Refracted through *Beyond the Pleasure Principle*, this is an ego caught in the structure that speaks it, a life eclipsed by its myth. The aim of analysis is not to liberate us into the freedom and happiness born of a healthy ego. 'What is healing?' Lacan (1991) asks, and replies: 'The realisation of the subject through a speech which comes from elsewhere, traversing it' (p. 233). The virtue of the later Oedipus is not that he confronts death but that he confronts identity. 'That is the end of Oedipus's psychoanalysis – the psychoanalysis of Oedipus is only completed at Colonus, when he tears his face apart' (p. 214). Lacan draws attention repeatedly to Oedipus' line, 'Am I made man in the hour I cease to be?' (p. 214), for Oedipus is considering his cessation as a *myth*. In Storr's (1912) translation, the line reads, 'So, when I cease to be, my worth begins.'

Lacan depicts Oedipus' tearing apart as a self-induced *sparagmos*. And, relishing the perversity, declares this a cure. It inspires a new take on the *corps morcelé* in Lacan's teaching. The primal chaos, the sense of fragmentation that haunts the synthetic ego, gains potentially positive connotations when Lacan (1953) notes in the same year as *Seminar II* that images of violence and destruction typically appear in analysand's dreams and associations at a phase in treatment when aggressivity enters the transference. It is a sign that treatment is progressing in the right direction, towards the disintegration of the rigid unity of the ego – a loss of faith in the Oracle, in the book that contains our fate.

Notes

1. 'The respect ancient peoples paid to dreams is a tribute ... to the untamed, indestructible elements in the human soul, the *daemonic* powers that produce the dream-wish and that we rediscover in our Unconscious' (p. 406).
2. The concept of the 'tragic' is not expressed in any language not derived from the Greek; see Kauffman (1992) and Storm (1998).
3. Winter also discusses the status of Sophocles in the context of a nineteenth-century revival of Greek literature, with Athens as a unique and privileged reference point. Sophoclean tragedy gains its high status and reputation for formal perfection from the studies made by Friedrich and August Wilhelm Schlegel.
4. Interestingly, Anzieu was an attendee at Lacan's *Seminar II* and perhaps recalled Lacan's own comment: 'all the heroes of Greek mythology have some sort of connection with [the Oedipus] myth' (Lacan 1991, p. 229).
5. On Lacan and *tuche*, see Forrester (1990).
6. Aristotle discusses *endoxa* in *Posterior Analytics: Topica* and *The Art of Rhetoric*.
7. For extended consideration of the connection, see Easterling (1997).
8. David Tracy (2005) sees the concept of sin in Augustine's thought, both individual and original, eclipsing the space of tragedy.
9. See Chaucer's Troilus in the deeply Boethian *Troilus and Criseyde* (1382–86) raised up to a God's eye view at the poem's conclusion, a gesture that appears to undo in one stroke its superficial, pagan theme of tragic fortune.
10. Lacan's first intellectual hero, Spinoza, wrestles with immanent cause – a species of Aristotelian efficient cause – now allied with God/Nature in *Ethics* (1674).
11. It is of note that *Beyond the Pleasure Principle* (1920) appeared the year after Freud's essay 'The "uncanny"' (1919), with its interest in states between life and death.
12. See Freud (1900) on the atemporal unconscious.
13. See also 'Subversion of the subject', where Lacan (2007, p. 687) argues that the 'somatic *ananke*' of being born prematurely, helpless and dependent, is maintained in the language that appears to give form to need. 'Fate' moves from the body to language to desire; Žižek (2005, p. 32) associates this with Lacan's obsession with topological models of 'curved' space in the 1960s and 1970s, seeing a connection between the collapsing of diachrony, paradox, retroaction and curved space.
14. See Freud (1900, p. 263) where his point is that Oedipus is ignorant of his *wishes*.
15. The relationship between Vernant and Lacan is complex, with mutual influence of Lévi-Strauss; Vernant admits huge influence of Lévi-Strauss (Detienne and Vernant, 1991). See Leonard (2005) on Lacan meeting Vernant at a conference entitled 'The

158 Exploiting tragedy

Languages of Criticism and the Sciences of Man', held at Johns Hopkins in 1966; see also Dosse (1997).

Hal Foster (2003) speculates that Vernant was influenced by Lacan (in general); see also Benvenuto and Vernant (1996).

16 The plays concerned are Euripides' *Phoenissae* and Sophocles' *Antigone*.
17 Janan pursues the law back to Agenor, Cadmus' father, whose irrational anger forces his son to flee 'his father's country and his wrath'.
18 Janan finds only two examples outside the Theban cycle: Dryope transformed into a tree after plucking a flower that hides the nymph Lotus (*Metamorphoses*, 9.326–93) and Ocyrhoe became a horse after prophesying Achilles' future (2.635–75).
19 'The absence of any extended reference to Oedipus in Ovid's otherwise rather comprehensive mythological compendium is a remarkable silence and one that demands investigation' (Gildenhard and Zissos, 2000, p. 130).
20 See Philip Hardie (1998) on Narcissus as a substitute drama 'of blindness, sight and insight'; Gildenhard and Zissos (2000) note 'structural and thematic parallels' centred on the trope of paradox.
21 Lacan retrieves the concept originally from the Marquis de Sade's novel *Juliette* (1801), which describes the desire to wipe an individual entirely from existence.
22 See Socrates' desire for death in the *Phaedo*. For two views on Plato's appropriation and subversion of the characteristics of tragic drama, see Nussbaum (1986) and Beck (2006).
23 There is also a clue regarding the poetic comparison of Antigone's cries to a bird: 'In early Greek lyric poetry, the temporal immortality of the beloved or of the lover is celebrated in the image of a bird, which is unencumbered by spatial limitations. Theogonis furnishes his beloved Kyrnos with wings that allow him to fly out over the sea; Pindar pays tribute in the image of the royal eagle as much to himself as to the victor whom he is paid to immortalize .... In this light, the Platonic theory of eros can be understood as the translation of a topos from love poetry into philosophy: eros bestows immortality in *logos*' (Most, 2005, p. 44).
24 'The loss of the brother is therefore irreparable to the sister and her duty towards him is highest. The brother is the member of the Family in whom Spirit had become an individuality which turns towards another sphere, and passes over into the consciousness of universality ... He passes from the divine law, in which he lived, over to the human law. But the sister becomes, or the wife remains, the guardian of the divine law. In this way the two sexes overcome their (merely) natural being and appear in ethical significance, as diverse beings who share between two distinctions belonging to ethical substance' (Hegel, 1977, p. 275).
25 Aristotle *(Poetics*, 1449b24–8) suggested that a tragic plot should elicit emotions of pity and fear in the audience.
26 The signifier by which we are manifested only serves 'to petrify the subject in question' (Lacan, 2008, p. 346).
27 A significant exception in the poem are the incidents of *sparagmos*, ritual tearing apart – Actaeon, Pentheus, Orpheus – which express something of the violence of the 'second death' that wipes an individual symbolically from existence into the pure nothing on the other side of the signifier. As such, these moments stand as the opposite of metamorphosis, and connect to fantasies of mutilation, castration – nothingness manifested. Actaeon, not even recognized by his own hounds, provides the ultimate example of a symbolic death preceding the biological.
28 This is what Žižek (1997) describes as the 'parasitical symbolic machine' colonizing living matter: language as a dead entity, yet one which 'behaves as if it possesses a life of its own' (p. 89). A sense of language as a substance beyond meaning, with an abundant, undead life of its own (comparable to the Lacanian drive) is present in

the *Metamorphoses*: it is felt in the reduction of human speech to animal cries (Actaeon, Io, Procne or the Cercopes), or into the literal spinning of webs (Arachne); perhaps the most vivid example of this insistent, disembodied life can be found in the spectacle of Philomela's detached *lingua* 'pulsing and murmuring incoherently to the dark earth' (*Metamorphosis* VI, 557–60).

29 On suicide and tragedy, see Champagne (1992), Leonard (2005), Loraux (1987), and Garrison (1995); Garrison looks at the prevalence of female suicide in tragedy.

30 Miller (1999) also finds an echo of Sartrean originary choice in '*Psychique causalite*', regarded by him as Lacan's entry into psychoanalysis. After the Second World War, Sartre's biography of Baudelaire popularized the notion of originary choice of consciousness independent of any extraneous determination.

References

Aeschylus, *Oresteia*, trans. R. Fagles (1977), London, Penguin Classics.
Anzieu, D. (1966) 'Métamorphose d'Oedipe: Un conflit d'interprétations', *Les Temps Modernes*, no. 245, pp. 675–715.
Aristotle, *Metaphysics*, trans. Hugh Lawson-Tancred (1998), London, Penguin Classics.
Aristotle, *Nicomachean Ethics*, trans. J. A. K. Thompson (2004), London, Penguin Classics.
Aristotle, *Physics*, trans. R. Waterfield (2008), Oxford, Oxford World Classics.
Aristotle, *Poetics*, trans M. Heath (2006), London, Penguin Classics.
Aristotle, *Posterior Analytics. Topica*, trans. H. Tredennick and E. S. Forster (1960), Cambridge, MA, Harvard University Press.
Aristotle, *The Art of Rhetoric*, trans. J. H. Freese (1926), Cambridge, MA, Harvard University Press.
Beck, M. C. (2006) *Tragedy and the Philosophical Life: A Response to Martha Nussbaum*, Lewiston, E. Mellen Press.
Benvenuto, S. and Vernant, J.-P. (1996) 'Oedipus without Freud: A conversation', *European Journal of Psychoanalysis*, no. 3/4. Available at www.psychomedia.it/jep/pages/number3-4.htm (accessed 4/4/2014).
Boethius, *The Consolation of Philosophy*, trans. Victor Watts (1999), London, Penguin Classics.
Borch-Jacobsen, M. (1991) *Lacan: The Absolute Master*, Stanford, Stanford University Press.
Burrow, C. (1988) 'Original fictions: Metamorphoses in the *Faerie Queene*', in Martindale, C. (ed.) *Ovid Renewed: Ovidian Influences on Literature and Art from the Middle Ages to the Twentieth Century*, Cambridge, Cambridge University Press, pp. 99–119.
Champagne, R. (1992) *The Structuralists on Myth*, New York, Garland.
Chaucer, G. (1382–86) *Troilus and Criseyde*, Oxford, Oxford World Classics.
Detienne, Marcel and Vernant, Jean-Pierre (1991) *Cunning Intelligence in Greek Culture and Society* (trans. Janet Lloyd), Chicago, University of Chicago Press.
Dosse, F. (1997) *The History of Structuralism*, vol. 1 (trans. D. Glassman), Minneapolis, University of Minnesota Press.
Easterling, P. E. (1997) 'A show for Dionysus', in Easterling, P. E. (ed.) *The Cambridge Companion to Greek Tragedy*, Cambridge, Cambridge University Press, pp. 36–53.
Encyclopedia Britannica (2008) *The Britannica Guide to the 100 Most Influential Scientists*, London, Running Press.
Fink, B. (1995) 'Science and psychoanalysis', in Fink, B., Feldstein, R. and Jaanus, M. (eds) *Reading Seminar XI: Lacan's Four Fundamental Concepts of Psychoanalysis*, Albany, SUNY Press, pp. 55–64.

Forrester, J. (1990) *The Seductions of Psychoanalysis: Freud, Lacan and Derrida*, Cambridge, Cambridge University Press.
Foster, H. (2003) 'Medusa and the real', *Anthropology and Aesthetics*, no. 44, pp. 181–190.
Freud, E. (ed.) (1960) *Letters of Sigmund Freud* (trans. Tania and James Stern), New York, Basic Books.
Freud, S. (1894) 'The neuro-psychoses of defense', in Strachey, J. (ed.) *The Standard Edition of the Complete Psychological Works of Sigmund Freud*, vol. 3, London, Hogarth Press, pp. 43–70.
Freud, S. (1900) *The Interpretation of Dreams*, in Strachey, J. (ed.) *The Standard Edition of the Complete Psychological Works of Sigmund Freud*, vols 4–5-, London, Hogarth Press, pp. 1–627.
Freud, S. (1914) *On Narcissism: An Introduction*, in Strachey, J. (ed.) *The Standard Edition of the Complete Psychological Works of Sigmund Freud*, vol. 14, London, Hogarth Press, pp. 67–101.
Freud, S. (1919) 'The "uncanny"', in Strachey, J. (ed.) *The Standard Edition of the Complete Psychological Works of Sigmund Freud*, vol. 17, London, Hogarth Press, pp. 217–256.
Freud, S. (1920) *Beyond the Pleasure Principle*, in Strachey, J. (ed.) *The Standard Edition of the Complete Psychological Works of Sigmund Freud*, vol. 17, London, Hogarth Press, pp. 1–63.
Freud, S. (1933) *New Introductory Lectures*, in Strachey, J. (ed.) *The Standard Edition of the Complete Psychological Works of Sigmund Freud*, vol. 22, London, Hogarth Press, pp. 1–183.
Garrison, E. (1995) *Groaning Tears: Ethical and Dramatic Aspects of Suicide in Greek Tragedy*, Amsterdam, E. J. Brill.
Gildenhard, I. and Zissos, A. (1999) '"Somatic economies": Tragic bodies and poetic design in Ovid's Metamorphoses', in Hardie, P., Barchiesi, A. and Hinds, S. (eds), *Ovidian Transformations: Essays on Ovid's Metamorphoses and its Reception*, Cambridge, Cambridge Philological Society, pp. 162–181.
Gildenhard, I. and Zissos, A. (2000) 'Ovid's Narcissus (MET. 3.339–510): Echoes of Oedipus', *American Journal of Philology*, vol. 121, pp. 129–147.
Hall, E. (1997) 'The sociology of Greek Tragedy', in Easterling, P. E. (ed.) *The Cambridge Companion to Greek Tragedy*, Cambridge, Cambridge University Press, pp. 93–126.
Hankinson, R. J. (1995) 'Science', in Barnes, J. (ed.) *The Cambridge Companion to Aristotle*, Cambridge, Cambridge University Press, pp. 140–167.
Hardie, P. (1998) 'Lucretius and the delusions of Narcissus', *Materiali e Discussioni*, no. 20/21, pp. 71–89.
Hardie, P. (2002) *Ovid's Poetics of Illusion*, Cambridge, Cambridge University Press.
Hegel, G. W. F. (1977) *Phenomenology of the Spirit* (trans. A. V. Miller), Oxford, Oxford University Press.
Heidegger, M. (1998) 'Plato's doctrine of truth', in McNeill, W. (ed.) *Pathmarks*, Cambridge, Cambridge University Press, pp. 155–182.
Janan, M. (2007) '"In the name of the father": Ovid's Theban law', in Lamour, D. H. J. and Spencer, D. (eds) *Sites of Rome*, Oxford, Oxford University Press, pp. 102–137.
Kauffman, W. (1992) *Tragedy and Philosophy*, Princeton, Princeton University Press.
Kripke, S. (1980) *Naming and Necessity*, Cambridge, Harvard University Press.
Lacan, J. (1953) 'Some reflections on the ego', *International Journal of Psychoanalysis*, vol. 34, pp. 11–17.
Lacan, J. (1977) *Seminar XI: The Four Fundamental Concepts of Psychoanalysis* (ed. J.-A. Miller, trans. A. Sheridan), London, Penguin.
Lacan, J. (1990) *Television* (ed. J. Copjec, trans. D. Hollier, R. Krauss and A. Michelson), New York, Norton.

Lacan, J. (1991) *Seminar II: The Ego in Freud's Theory and in the Technique of Psychoanalysis* (ed. J.-A. Miller, trans. J. Forrester), New York, Norton.
Lacan, J. (1993) *Seminar III: The Psychoses* (ed. J.-A. Miller, trans. R. Grigg), London, Routledge.
Lacan, J. (1998) *Seminar XX: Encore – On Feminine Sexuality: The Limits of Love and Knowledge* (ed. J.-A. Miller, trans. B. Fink), New York, Norton.
Lacan, J. (2007) *Écrits: The First Complete Edition in English* (trans. B. Fink), New York, Norton.
Lacan, J. (2008) *Seminar VII: The Ethics of Psychoanalysis* (ed. J.-A. Miller, trans. D. Porter), London, Routledge.
Lacan, J. (2014) *Seminar X: Anxiety* (ed. J.-A. Miller, trans. A. R. Price), London, Polity Press.
Lacan, Jacques (2015) *Seminar VIII: Transference* (ed. J.-A. Miller, trans. Bruce Fink), London, Polity Press.
Leonard, M. (2005) *Athens in Paris: Ancient Greece and the Political in Post-War French Thought*, Oxford, Oxford University Press.
Loraux, N. (1987) *Tragic Ways of Killing a Woman* (trans. A. Forster), Cambridge, Harvard University Press.
Masson, J. M. (1985) *The Complete Letters of Sigmund Freud to Wilhelm Fliess, 1887–1904*, Cambridge, Harvard University Press.
Miller, J.-A. (1999) *Shifting Paradigms in Lacan* (unpublished) [Lecture to American Lacanian Link, University of California, Los Angeles], 7 March.
Most, G. W. (2005) 'Six remarks on Platonic Eros', in Bartsch, S. and Bartscherer, T. (eds) *Erotikon: Essays on Eros, Ancient and Modern*, Chicago, Chicago University Press, pp. 33–47.
Nobus, D. and Quinn, M. (2005) *Knowing Nothing, Staying Stupid*, London, Routledge.
Nussbaum, N. (1986) *The Fragility of Goodness: Luck and Ethics in Greek Tragedy and Philosophy*, Cambridge, Cambridge University Press.
Ovid, *Metamorphoses*, trans. Mary Innes (1955), London, Penguin Classics.
Padel, R. (1992) *In and Out of the Mind: Greek Images of the Tragic Self*, Princeton, Princeton University Press.
Phillips, A. (1995) *On Flirtation*, London, Faber.
Roudinesco, E. (2014), *Lacan: In Spite of Everything* (trans. Gregory Elliott), London, Verso.
Schelling, F. W. J. (1980) *The Unconditional in Human Knowledge: Four Early Essays 1794–6* (trans. F. Marti), Lewisburg, Bucknell University Press.
Shew, M. (2008) 'The phenomenon of chance in Ancient Greek thought', unpublished PhD thesis, University of Oregon, Eugene.
Smith, J. H. and Kerrigan, W. (eds) (1984) *Taking Chances: Derrida, Psychoanalysis and Literature*, Baltimore, Johns Hopkins University Press.
Sophocles, *The Theban Plays*, trans. E. F. Watling (1947) London, Penguin.
Spinoza, B. (1674) *Ethics*, The Hague, n.p.
Steiner, G. (1996) *Antigones*, New Haven, Yale University Press.
Storm, W. (1998) *After Dionysus: A Theory of the Tragic*, Ithaca, Cornell University Press.
Storr, F. (1912) *Sophocles, with an English Translation*, London, Heinemann.
Tarrant, R. (2002) 'Ovid and ancient literary history', in Hardie, P. (ed.) *The Cambridge Companion to Ovid*, Cambridge, Cambridge University Press, pp. 13–33.
Tracy, D. (2005) 'The divided consciousness of Augustine on Eros', in Bartsch, S. and Bartscherer, T. (eds) *Erotikon: Essays on Eros, Ancient and Modern*, Chicago, Chicago University Press, pp. 91–106.
Verhaeghe, P. (2002) 'Causality in science and psychoanalysis', in Glynos, J. and Stavrakakis, Y. (eds) *Lacan and Science*, London, Karnac, pp. 119–145.

Vernant, J.-P. and Vidal-Naquet, P. (1981) *Myth and Tragedy in Ancient Greece* (trans. J. Lloyd), Sussex, Harvester Press.
Winslow, R. (2007) *Aristotle and Rational Discovery*, New York, Continuum.
Winter, S. (1999) *Freud and the Institution of Psychoanalytic Knowledge*, Stanford, Stanford University Press.
Žižek, S. (1996) 'From desire to drive: Why Lacan is not Lacaniano', *Atlántica de Las Artes*, vol. 14 [online]. Available at http://Žižek.livejournal.com/2266.html (accessed 1/12/2015).
Žižek, S. (1997) *The Plague of Fantasies*, London, Verso.
Žižek, S. (2001) *Enjoy Your Symptom*, London, Routledge.
Zupančič, A. (2003) 'Ethics and tragedy in Lacan', in Rabaté, J.-M. (ed.) *The Cambridge Companion to Lacan*, Cambridge, Cambridge University Press, pp. 173–190.
Žižek, S. (2005) *The Metastases of Enjoyment: On Women and Causality*, London, Verso.

5

UNKNOWN PLEASURES

Orgasms and epistemology

Introduction: Tiresias, the seer

Tiresias, the blind prophet of Thebes, appears at several points in Lacan's work. Sometimes it is in reference to his general powers of divination, or in relation to the story of Oedipus in which he plays a leading role (see Lacan, 2007). Most often, it is in connection with a curious episode recounted in Ovid's *Metamorphoses*, in which he is called upon to settle an argument between Jupiter and Juno over who enjoys sex more: men or women.[1] Tiresias pays a heavy price for getting involved. The following is the account of this episode given by Lacan in his tenth seminar:

> Tiresias, the seer, who ought to be the patron of psychoanalysts, was blinded by an act of vengeance of the supreme goddess, Juno, the jealous one – and, as Ovid explains very well to us in the third book of the *Metamorphoses*, from verse 316 to verse 338, if Tiresias offended Juno, it is because he is consulted for a joke – the Gods do not always measure the consequences of their acts – by Jupiter who for once was having a relaxed relationship with his wife and teasing her about the fact that undoubtedly 'the pleasure that you experience is greater' – he is the one who is speaking – 'than that experienced by the man'. But then he says: 'But, by the way, what am I thinking of? Tiresias was a woman for seven years ....'
>
> This is why he can testify before Jupiter and Juno. Whatever might be the consequences he must testify to the truth and corroborate what

> Jupiter says: It is women who enjoy (*jouissent*). Their *jouissance* is greater, whether it is a quarter or a tenth more than that of the man – there are more precise versions.
>
> (Lacan, 2014, p. 169)

Jupiter makes his claim that women experience greater sexual pleasure than men and, understandably, falls into a dispute with his wife. Tiresias is called upon as an expert witness because he was changed into a woman for seven years after striking a pair of copulating snakes on Mount Cyllene. He confirms Jupiter's suspicion. Then, Ovid says, if rumours are to be believed, Juno was 'more indignant than she had any right to be, more so than the case demanded' (*Metamorphoses*, III, 333–335), and she condemns Tiresias to eternal blindness. Jupiter, by way of consolation, grants Tiresias the power to see into the future.

Tiresias is 'consulted for a joke', but the joke turns sour. Besides his more famous prophetic abilities, Tiresias' transexual knowledge has an element of bathos, but the episode is too provocative to be dismissed as merely a comic fable. Lacan returns to it throughout his seminars, going so far as to say that Tiresias should be the 'patron saint of psychoanalysts'. Because of his insight? This seems an ambitious comparison. Perhaps it is because of the anger he inspires. Like psychoanalysis generally, he can't win once he begins to speculate about gendered pleasure.

The female orgasm is central to the controversies of psychoanalysis. Freud's (1905) positing of a superior vaginal (as oppose to clitoral) orgasm is presented as evidence of how little he understood the 'dark continent' of female sexuality (see Koedt, 1970). More than just anatomical wrongheadedness, it betrays fantasies, male fantasies about women. As does Jupiter – and this is surely part of the reason for Juno's anger. Juno herself doesn't speak in response to Tiresias, but she is clearly peeved, 'More indignant than she had any right to be'. In no version is it suggested exactly why she should react this way – Ovid, in time-honoured fashion, implies the reaction is excessive and irrational – but it is the start of an indignation that will reverberate down the millennia, felt when men use supposed authority to pronounce on female experience (even when, as here, it is men collaborating on a fantasy of a female pleasure that renders their own inadequate). While the question of Juno's anger is made explicit, the issue of why Jupiter was speculating in the first place is passed over. This chapter asks that question, via an examination of the myth's recurrence in Lacan's thoughts about the epistemological quest of psychoanalysis. When it comes to other people's pleasure, the desire to know is entwined with the desire to possess; a theory can be a fantasy also, and a fantasy can be a provocative weapon. But fantasizing about someone else's pleasure complicates oppositions – subject and object, male and female – and, as this phenomenon assumes greater prominence in Lacan's theory, it allows him to restructure psychoanalytic models of gender and sexuality.

These psychological themes are strikingly present in the Ovidian source for the myth. Alongside a further interrogation of psychoanalysis, this chapter explores the astonishing way in which Ovid communicates questions and ideas through his presentation and sequencing of tales. Lacan himself ties his interest in Tiresias to the Ovidian context explicitly on several occasions.[2] The Ovidian source is important because Ovid is also concerned with a relationship between gender, fantasy, transgression and anger. The tale of Tiresias' ill-judged judgment feeds in and out of adjacent myths, usually involving forbidden sights, experiences or knowledge, most often associated with the feminine. After Cadmus has founded Thebes, we read the story of one of his grandsons, Actaeon. Actaeon trespasses on the goddess Diana bathing. She turns him into a stag, and he is torn apart by his own hounds. In the next tale, Semele demands to experience her lover, Jupiter, in all his divine potency ('show yourself to me as you appear to Juno', *Metamorphoses*, III, 293–295) and is consequently burned to ashes ('her mortal frame could not endure the exaltation', III, 310–312). Jupiter and Juno's debate over sexual pleasure follows; Tiresias is called upon. As proof of his powers, we are given the story of Narcissus, forbidden to know himself (advice from Tiresias in prophet mode). Book III ends by recounting the death of Pentheus; Pentheus spies on the female followers of Bacchus (Dionysus) as they practise their secret rites, but he is discovered and, like Actaeon, torn apart (this time by maenads, followers of Dionysus). As I explore the role that several of these tales play in psychoanalysis, it is also an opportunity to consider the motivations behind Ovid's uniquely influential poetry.

Whose *jouissance* is it anyway?

Lacan knows that this myth of Jupiter, Juno and Tiresias touches upon a foundational problem for psychoanalysis. It appears again in his 'Guiding remarks for a convention on female sexuality': a provocative, potentially patronizing scenario, the male analyst making this address to the convention. Tread carefully, one might think. Lacan doesn't. In a section entitled 'The darkness cast upon the vaginal organ', Lacan (2007) describes what seems

166 Unknown pleasures

to him a prohibition regarding the understanding of female sexual pleasure. In fact, so difficult is this issue that, he declares, 'a convention on female sexuality is not about to cause to weigh upon us the threat of Tiresias' fate':

> The apperception of a prohibition … may serve us as a prelude.
>
> Is it confirmed by the fact that our discipline – which, justifying its field in terms of sexuality, seemed to promise to bring the whole secret of sexuality to light – has left what is recognized about feminine *jouissance* at the exact point at which a hardly zealous physiology threw in the towel?
>
> The rather trivial opposition between clitoral *jouissance* and vaginal satisfaction has been so greatly reinforced by the theory that it has worried many subjects, and the theory has even taken up this worry as a theme, if not as a demand – though we cannot say, for all that, that the opposition between them has been elucidated any more correctly.
>
> This is true because the nature of vaginal orgasm has kept its obscurity inviolate.
>
> (p. 612)

Lacan identifies Freud's opposing of clitoral and vaginal orgasm as a source of anxieties: anxiety about the 'wrong' and 'right' sorts of pleasure, as well as anxiety about the patriarchal assumptions of psychoanalysis itself. This is true even if he dismisses the opposition itself as 'rather trivial'. There is something more going on beneath the surface here, Lacan suggests. And psychoanalysis is not the only field to find itself on a quest, pursuing the inviolate 'nature of vaginal orgasm', coming up against a 'prohibition' apparently inherent to it. When Lacan refers to a 'hardly zealous physiology' pursuing its own investigations, he has in mind William Masters and Virginia Johnson (1966), pioneers of research into sexual response in the late 1950s and 1960s. He mentions them by name, along with the inadequacy of their approach, in *Seminar XVII* (1991):

> These studies by a certain Masters and Johnson are not, frankly, lacking in interest. Nevertheless, when … on the basis of certain quotations, I see it appear there that the greater orgasm, which is apparently the woman's orgasm, emanates from the total personality, I do wonder how a movie camera that takes images in colour, placed inside an appendage representing the penis, recording from the inside what takes

place on the lining of what, on its being inserted, surrounds it, is capable of grasping the said total personality.

(pp. 71–72)

In Lacan's account, the narrowly empirical methodology of Masters and Johnson misses the point. A camera will not capture the 'totality' they have identified with female orgasm. It is a totality he refers to as *jouissance*, and the impossibility of 'capturing' it, in language, in thought, will become part of its identity. It will also be one of several components that means it exacerbates psychoanalysis's fraught relationship with feminine sexuality.

Jouissance is a French term for enjoyment, with connotations of orgasm. It proves valuable for Lacan as a term to describe an excess of pleasure, one that is almost unbearable. By tradition, *jouissance* is left untranslated in his work, lending it a mystique for the English reader, but masking some other associations in the original French (Forrester, 1990). Grammatical nuances push the concept into the realm of abstraction: *jouissance* is always used in the singular, accompanied by the definite article (Gallop, 1984; Macey, 1988). There is an ambiguity in the phrase *la jouissance de la femme*, connoting both female orgasm and enjoyment of women. There is also an element of legality in the term: it is used in the sense of 'to enjoy *possession*'.[3] But it was not originally so strictly gendered (Macey, 1988; Miller, 1999). It first appears in the seminar of March 5, 1958, simply as 'a notion … that has always been implied in our reflections on desire but that deserves to be distinguished from it' (Braunstein, 2003, p. 102). By 'Subversion of the Subject' (1960), it more clearly has connotations of orgasm, but Lacan soon identifies it with all extremities of sensation, including pain. It lies beyond the pleasure principle. And, at the same time, it is beyond speech and thought. It is in these later formulations that it is most identified with the feminine.

Hence Lacan's provocative claim, repeated on several occasions: if we do not understand *jouissance* it is because women themselves fail to speak of it. In his 'Guiding remarks for a convention', he complains: 'Representatives of the fairer sex, however loud their voices among analysts, do not seem to have given their all to remove the seal of secrecy' (2007, p. 613). What's more, in Lacan's most damning kind of assessment, they have instead confined themselves 'to metaphors whose loftiness in the ideal signifies nothing preferable to what the hoi polloi give us by way of a less intentional poetry' (p. 613).[4] They mask the mystery with clichés, including those pertaining to vaginal orgasm introduced by Freud.

It is in *Seminar XX* that Lacan (1998) pursues the reason for this at greatest length. Having complained that women analysts 'haven't contributed one iota to the question of feminine sexuality', he adds: 'There must be an internal reason for that, related to the structure of the apparatus of *jouissance*' (pp. 57–58). Lacan's play on 'apparatus' is bawdy, but his point is precisely that neither the anatomical speculations of Freud or Masters and Johnson will locate the 'structure' of *jouissance*: it is necessarily beyond the limited, finite pleasures of language, beyond the symbolic order. As such, *won't speak* becomes *can't speak*.

> The plausibility of what I am claiming here – namely, that woman knows nothing of this *jouissance* – is underscored by the fact that in all the time people have been begging them, begging them on their hands and knees – I spoke last time of women analysts – to try to tell us, not a word! We've never been able to get anything out of them. So we call this *jouissance* by whatever name we come up with, 'vaginal' …
>
> (p. 75)

As in the case of Jupiter and Juno, we see a relationship between an idea of immense pleasure and the silence imposed on those supposed to experience it. In *Seminar XX*, Lacan conflates the silence and the immensity to derive a *jouissance* that is profoundly mystical. But the result is still, inevitably, anger on the part of those who have been dispossessed of their own orgasm. This arises famously when Lacan draws on the example of two female Christian mystics apparently rendered oblivious by their own bliss, Hadewijch of Antwerp and Saint Teresa:

> For the Hadewijch in question, it's like for Saint Teresa – you need but go to Rome and see the statue by Bernini to immediately understand that she's coming. There's no doubt about it. What is she getting off on? It is clear that the essential testimony of the mystics consists in saying that they experience it, but know nothing about it.
>
> (p. 76)[5]

Lacan is not the first to light upon Teresa as exemplary of mystical feminine ecstasy, and on Bernini's statue, *The Ecstasy of St Teresa* (1645–52), in particular. Joseph Breuer had dubbed Teresa 'the patron saint of hysteria' in *Studies in Hysteria* (Macey, 1988, p. 205). And she had been popular with the surrealists, a photograph of Bernini's statue appearing in Dali's 1933 photo montage, *The Phenomenon of Ecstasy*. It is this image that graces the cover of the illustrated edition of Bataille's *L'Erotisme* in 1965. Teresa is an icon of convulsive beauty, of religio-erotic transgression. But, as Luce Irigaray (1985) points out, in one of the most famous criticisms of Lacan, she is defined by a statue made by a man and shaped by 'the phallic gaze' (p. 47). It is a male fantasy.

Tom Hayes explores the provocative nature of fantasy in 'A Jouissance Beyond the Phallus: Juno, Saint Teresa, Bernini, Lacan' (1999). The source of Juno's anger is not difficult to figure out, he says: Juno did not want to acknowledge that she experienced greater pleasure in lovemaking because to do so would require her to 'validate' her husband's fantasy, 'to acknowledge that the picture she knew Jupiter had in his mind of her in a state of uncontrolled self-shattering ecstasy was accurate' (p. 331). There are two interrelated forms of 'self-shattering' in the myth, two losses of autonomy: one in which she is lost to pleasure itself, the other to someone else's fantasy of that pleasure – a violation of the imagination.[6] But this violation, and the shame it causes, is a curious phenomenon, one rich with complex intersubjectivity. The disordering of subject and other it implies will become central to the effects (and theoretical value) of *jouissance*. It is worth looking closer at the *Ethics* seminar, because it is here that Lacan expands the concept's potential, and does so with several references to Ovid's myths.

It is in *Seminar VII*, on *The Ethics of Psychoanalysis* (2008), that *jouissance* becomes 'impossible' or, at least, forbidden, identified with the primal, forbidden object, situated in the real, beyond what might be symbolized (see Miller, 1999). Lacan takes *Beyond the Pleasure Principle* to what he presents as a natural conclusion. Noting that the 'pleasure' of the pleasure principle depends upon moderation, he situates 'beyond' it any excess of sensation – pain or pleasure – that we find unendurable. It is confrontation with this excess that our moderate, pleasure-seeking consciousness defends against. He then identifies this excessive pleasure within us with *Das Ding* – the beyond of the signified, the unimaginable 'thing-in-itself'.

This odd imposition is a phenomenon that Miller describes using the term *extimacy*: the sense that pleasure can be experienced as a foreign presence within us, and a threatening one. At its extreme it is intrusive, and experienced as other. In *Seminar VII*, Lacan turns to another Ovidian myth to illustrate his point: the tale of Apollo and Daphne. Normally, he argues, when we are faced with an invasion of excess stimulation, the flight instinct intervenes. We flee it. This is the neurological model Freud presents in *Project for a Scientific Psychology* (1895). Pain in this account, Lacan (2008) points out, only 'derives from the fact that the motor reaction, the flight reaction, is impossible … it opens precisely onto that limit where a living being has no possibility of escape' (pp. 72–73). And there is no escape because the stimulation comes from *within*. Lacan turns to Daphne as an example: 'Isn't something of this suggested by the insight of the poets in that myth of Daphne transformed into a tree under the pressure of a pain from which she cannot flee?' (p. 73).

Ovid's *Metamorphoses* is again mined for images of confinement, extremity of emotion and, most significantly, an element of paradox. Yet Lacan's account of the myth is not an entirely fair one. In Ovid's version, it is clearly the lustful Apollo himself that she cannot flee. Being unable to outrun the god, Daphne prays to her father, Peneus, begging for her beauty to be taken away (I, 518–557). Peneus transforms her into a laurel tree. It is the very first metamorphosis after Ovid's account of creation and introduces a theme that will define the poem: the sexual desire of gods for humans.

Lacan's morally dubious misreading supports a dangerous blurring of lines. It belongs in a long line of male ideas about female will that is itself revealing. The idea that Daphne's excitation comes from within has echoes of a tradition at its height in the middle ages, whereby Ovid's tales are upturned to serve Christian morals. In this tradition, the cruel edges of Ovid's own poetry are reborn as a highly charged misogyny. Chaste female victims of rape become symbols of lust.[7] Meanwhile, the amorous pursuits of the classical gods become the divine love of the Christian God, and assault is read as annunciation. It is a travesty of Ovid's pagan poem yet draws on carefully crafted ambivalence within the *Metamorphoses* itself. The final response of Daphne, now Laurel, inclining her new-made branches and seeming, finally, to submit to Apollo's appeals is a powerful example in itself ('the laurel tree inclined her newmade branches, and seemed to nod her leafy top, as if it were a head, in consent' (I, 566–7). Seemed to who, we might ask? Indeed, the whole tale is unsettled by Daphne's impassioned commitment to chastity in the first place: long before Apollo appears, she is blushing at the thought of marriage, 'as if it were some crime' (I, 484).

Metamorphosis, in Ovid's poem, is always into the realm of speechlessness. Its victims lose control over expression. Instead, at the inexpressible limit of their experiences, they are frozen as symbols subject to others' readings; their interiority, at the moment of its greatest intensity, can only be revealed outside (like a blush, but on a larger scale). As we've seen, *jouissance* becomes increasingly associated with a failure of speech that arises simultaneously with exposure to others' readings (partners, prophets, psychoanalysts): silence and shame belong together, it seems.

There is plenty that is ugly and unjust about this. But a consideration of the phenomenon of dispossession can lead to more than just misogyny. And, as we've glimpsed, fantasy can complicate received ideas about gender as well as reinforcing them. In the following section, I explore this further via a figure whose own Ovidian erotica had a profound influence on Lacan: Pierre Klossowski.

Klossowski with Actaeon: 'the itch to be seen'

Klossowski was born in 1905, brother of the artist Balthus, and central to the Parisian intellectual scene of the 1950s and 1960s in his own right. A writer, translator and artist, he wrote full-length volumes on Sade and Nietzsche, five novels of his own, and translated works by Virgil, Heidegger, Kafka, Nietzsche and Walter Benjamin. He collaborated with Bataille on the review *Acéphale* in the late 1930s, part of a close-knit circle that included Lacan. His influence on Lacan is deep but, in the words of Mikkel Borch-Jacobsen (1991), 'encrypted' (p. 279).

The Ovidian myth that bridges their work is that of Actaeon and Diana, the episode directly preceding the dispute between Jupiter and Juno in Book III of the *Metamorphoses* and echoing its themes. Both men's interest in the myth appears to have been stimulated by the publication of the first French translation of Giordano Bruno's *Heroic Frenzies (De gl' Heroici Fuori)* in 1954, a Neoplatonic treatise, dating from 1585, containing an extended allegorical revisioning of Actaeon (Bruno is referred to specifically by Lacan in 'The Freudian thing').[8,9] In 1956, Klossowski published *Le bain de Diane* (1998), an erotic novella based on the Actaeon myth, written in a distinctive poetic-philosophical style, exploring guilt, voyeurism, exhibitionism and desire. But, before turning to Klossowski's novella, it is worth recognizing the psychological and ethical complexity of the myth as told by Ovid.

Actaeon's tale is the gateway through which we enter the sexual and epistemological transgressions of Book III of the *Metamorphoses*, for which Tiresias's odd judgment serves as a fulcrum. In Ovid's version of the myth, Actaeon is out hunting when he stumbles upon Diana bathing in a secluded grotto. Her nymphs try to cover her but are too short. Instead, she splashes water into Actaeon's face and declares, furiously: 'Now you may say that I have been seen by you with my clothes off – if you can say it' (III, 192–193). Actaeon is transformed into a stag, and his hunting dogs, not recognizing him, tear him apart. As in the Juno episode, Ovid explicitly problematizes this conclusion, acknowledging the debate provoked by Diana's action: 'When the story was told, opinions were divided: some thought that the goddess had been too cruel, others praised her, and declared her act in keeping with her strict chastity. Both sides could justify their views' (III, 253–255).

Klossowski's (1998) novella explores this double-edged, self-conscious chastity, its relationship to both cruelty and seduction. His starting point inverts Ovid's own and shifts the entire tale onto the ground of fantasy: 'Diana, invisible, observes Actaeon in the thicket from which he imagines he can spy on her …' (pp. 32–33). From this – the desire inflaming the mind of a mortal – Diana experiences 'the desire to see her own body' (p. 33). But for this she has to adopt physical form. This is supplied by an intermediary daemon, which 'becomes the fantasy of Actaeon and the mirror of Diana' (p. 51). From being a feminine deity expressing herself in the 'singleness of a *closed* nature, sufficient unto herself, finding in chastity the fullness of her essence' (p. 12), she is transformed.

> When Diana holds [Actaeon] in her gaze …. She understands the trick of this mediation that so exposes her, that introduces in her the itch to *be seen* … and while the defilement of a mortal man's gaze succeeds in molding her nakedness to the now visible contours that she can no longer disavow, she savors the wicked breach opened in this body's closed being.
>
> *(p. 60)*

Desire defeats our self-coherence: Diana, subject to the emotions of a body inside of which she knows she is desired, exposes herself to the shame of offering unutterable charms …. Diana blushes in Actaeon's eyes, *blushes in her chastity* (p. 61).

Klossowski plays with the tension between blushing and chastity. Chastity is private, enclosed, self-sufficient. The blush is a public betrayal of interiority. This is true to Ovid's account: we are given no physical description of Diana (perhaps prompting Klossowski's invisible deity), but we know she blushes, 'red as the clouds which flash beneath the sun's slant rays, red as the rosy dawn were the cheeks of Diana as she stood there in view without her robes' (*Metamorphoses*, III, 183–185). It arises out of shame. But the logic of a shame that can arise from someone else's actions is odd, unless we read it as an indication that we are already split, possessed internally by the other's enjoyment, divided by *jouissance* (see Copjec, 2006).

We have already witnessed the conjunction of chastity and blush in the case of Daphne. Chastity is dangerously paradoxical. It acknowledges the very desires it forswears and achieves a seduction by its prohibition. This complexity is felt in the story of Callisto, one of Diana's attendant nymphs, who is seduced by Jupiter. When she becomes visibly pregnant, she is exposed and cast out by Diana herself. Moralizing interpretations of the *Metamorphoses* such as the *Ovide Moralisé* take this judgment further and determine that Callisto's very *chastity* was only for show. Throughout the *Metamorphoses*, Jupiter pursues chaste mortal women, until this installs a tension deep within the luxuriant pastoral setting itself. Pastoral in Ovid's *Metamorphoses* becomes associated with violation, and sight with lust. Eventually it, too, seems morally ambivalent, artful, never more clearly than with regards to Diana's bathing pool: buried in the depths of a 'lush valley ... by a murmuring spring', a woodland cave 'which no hand of man had ever wrought: but nature by her own devices had imitated art ... had carved a natural arch from the living stone' (III, 155–165). Even nature, it seems, can be accused of complicity, of seeking attention, the accusation hinging on whether it's *meant* to be seen and who it thinks might be looking.[10]

Desire is desire of the other (Lacan, 1977). This describes a desire for reciprocation, to be desired by the other, but also the extent to which our very desires are borrowed, thereby echoing the other's desire. It suggests a logic that turns identity inside out, and installs within us someone else's fantasy. *Jouissance* is the means by which this inversion is carried out. The joint interest of Lacan and Klossowski in this phenomenon – the problematizing of self, and autonomy, by pleasure – finds another outlet when they turn to a figure who foregrounds the issue in stark terms: the Marquis de Sade.

The first Klossowskian text to assist Lacan in his exploration of *jouissance* and the Other is his study of the Marquis de Sade, *Sade, mon prochain* (1947). Borch-Jacobsen cites developments in Lacan's seventh seminar – on Sade, courtly love and the Gnostic tradition – as all directly inspired by this work, but it is in his paper 'Kant with Sade' that Lacan (2007) makes an explicit acknowledgment of his contemporary: 'We are now finally enjoined to examine *Sade, My Neighbor*, the invocation of which we owe to the perspicacity of Pierre Klossowski' (p. 666).[11] And it is in this paper that Lacan's thoughts on a self-splitting *jouissance* crystallize. It hinges on the historical conjunction of Immanuel Kant and the Marquis de Sade. Sade published *Philosophy in the Bedroom* (1795) seven years after Kant's *Critique of*

Practical Reason (1788), and Lacan sets out to demonstrate that Sade's work 'completes' Kant's philosophy.

Kant's ethical philosophy centres on the Categorical Imperative: act only according to that maxim whereby you can, at the same time, will that it should become a universal law.[12] Freud himself, in 'The economic problem of masochism' (1924), had identified the Categorical Imperative as 'the direct heir of the Oedipus complex' in its installation of guilt, of a means of self-surveillance: the formulation of what Freud came to term the superego (p. 167).[13] This sometimes 'harsh, cruel' superego retains the parents' strength, severity and inclination 'to supervise and to punish' as the original libidinous relationship to parents becomes desexualized.

For Lacan (2007), Sade dramatizes the *jouissance* lurking behind the superego's severity as it polices us from within. Diana's chastity, we've seen, is threatened by 'a wicked breach in the body's closed being': so, in a similar breaching of boundaries, *jouissance* instates itself 'at the most inmost core of the subject', whom it then provokes by offending their sense of modesty (p. 651). The word Lacan uses for modesty is *pudeur*, which can also refer to chastity (and has its etymological roots in the Latin *pudor*, shame). The ambivalent, blushing Daphne, subject to Apollo's uninvited attentions, reflects this self-division. Our modesty can only be offended when the other's will, their *jouissance*, has crossed into us. We sense the law within us by means of *jouissance*, but both *jouissance* and the law that regulates it separate us from ourselves.

In 'Kant with Sade', Lacan finds a medical term to express the same collapsing of oppositions: 'For modesty is an amboceptor with respect to the circumstances of being … the one's immodesty by itself violating the other's modesty' (p. 651). An amboceptor (from the Latin *ambo*, meaning 'both') is a receptor on the surface of a cell with two groups of atoms, allowing it to unite the immunizing body with the 'complement'. Lacan (2014) uses the same biological metaphor in *Seminar X* (the year of 'Kant with Sade') in the course of his extended obstetric meditations: It is the placenta that makes a parasite of the child inside the body of the mother, a privileging of 'elements that we could qualify as amboceptors'. The imagery of amboceptors helps Lacan underline 'that it is as necessary to articulate the relationship of the maternal subject to the breast as that of the suckling to the breast' (p. 215). An intersubjective drama, involving the mother's desire as much as her milk, is found at the very start of infantile development. The purpose of Lacan's references to amboceptors is to indicate that the subjective relationship of desire is always, necessarily, two-way.

This accounts for the slipperiness of Lacan's grammar. *De* (in *le désir de l'Autre*) can function as subjective genitive (the other's desire) or objective genitive (a desire for the other) and is intentionally designed by Lacan to suggest both. Bruce Fink describes *De* as the most difficult word to translate in the *Écrits*, and Lacan's use as highly unusual (see Lacan, 2007). Obviously, the same applies to *la jouissance de l'Autre*: is it the *jouissance* the other has or the subject's *jouissance* of the other? Grammar reflects the inherently reciprocal nature of possession.

Sadomasochistic scenarios highlight the curious pact involved in desire. Alongside Sade, an invaluable text for Lacan is Freud's own study of sadomasochistic fantasies, '"A child is being beaten": a contribution to the study of the origin of sexual perversions' (1919). The essay explores a fantasy Freud reports as common among patients: the beating of a child. As Freud's title indicates, and Lacan (1991) points out, it is a fantasy 'made up of a proposition' ('a child is being beaten') (p. 65). And what is striking in the essay is the degree to which the subject fantasizing has a shifting, ambiguous position in relation to the fantasy itself: the obsession develops through phases, from a voyeuristic scenario in which the beating is observed, to a sadistic one, to a masochistic one in which the patient is receiving the beating, to one in which they do not personally appear in it at all. The subject is secondary, circulating the proposition itself, changing roles.[14]

> If this proposition has the effect of being sustained by a subject, it's undoubtedly a subject, as Freud immediately analyses, *divided by jouissance* .... The 'You are beating me' is this half of the subject whose formula constitutes his liaison with *jouissance*. He receives, to be sure, his own message in inverted form – here this means his own *jouissance* in the form of the Other's *jouissance*.
>
> (p. 65)

What is truly Other for the subject is *jouissance*; thus, in the words of Jacques-Alain Miller (1994), 'it is in relation to *jouissance* that the Other is really Other' (p. 79). And, as Miller observes, the very difficulty of defining the 'Other' is because it stands for every field in which the subject is defined (see Miller, 1999); it evolves from being synonymous with the symbolic order, with language and the law, to representing a force at once more abstract and more personal (like a god) (Miller, 1994). An Other defined by jouissance allows Lacan to distinguish the 'big A', God of the philosophers, repository of knowledge, and barred A, God of Abraham, a God with desire.

The Actaeon myth can be seen as a competition over the role of Other, one made pointed by Diana's own status as a god. The asymmetry of goddess and mortal is highlighted by Klossowski. Hence Diana's anger is in part at Actaeon's reversal of roles: a mortal spying on a goddess. The amboceptive nature of sight gives it power; it imposes roles and can reverse them. But Diana's divine status is part of Klossowski's *defence* of Actaeon. Klossowski, drawing on Augustine's response to Greek myth, uses Diana's divinity to turn the tables on her, on this story that turns the tables on voyeuristic males. Klossowski (1998) cites Augustine's mock indignation: 'So the gods are permitted to join in union with mortal women, and men are forbidden to possess goddesses? What a harsh, indeed incredible condition!' (p. 12). Klossowski, apparently Actaeon's defence counsel, questions why Diana is visible in the first place. He calls upon Augustine as an expert witness, partly due to their shared concern with the pagan gods' perversions. For Augustine, the Greek gods are shameless egotists and exhibitionists. 'These gods bear witness to a contradictory exigency: they want to be worshipped in their most immoral, most shameful behaviour. These gods take pleasure in their own shame' (p. 82). To him, 'it is no surprise that the gods themselves introduced stage shows to the world of men' (p. 33). Augustine cites the Roman tradition whereby it was the gods who ordered the institution of stage shows in Rome, having been called upon for mercy during the ravages of the plague. 'The plague subsided, but then a new, almost incurable plague began to rage: the corruption of morals by the theatre' (p. 82).[15] 'Thus did the gods teach men to contemplate themselves in the spectacle,' Klossowski writes, 'just as the gods contemplate themselves in the imaginations of men' (p. 33).

This voyeuristic scenario helps Lacan develop the other into the Other, the abstract gaze explored in chapter 4 above. The few critics who have sought the influence of Klossowski's *Le bain de Diane* in Lacan's work tend to concentrate on explicit references to Actaeon in *Seminar XI* and 'The Freudian thing' (written up the year *Le bain de Diane* was published, from a paper delivered in 1955). But, such is the nature of this encrypted relationship, much of Klossowski's influence arises elsewhere in *Seminar XI* where Lacan explores the voyeur's gaze. Klossowski's presence shadows Lacan's explicit reference point: Sartre's discussion of an 'Actaeon Complex' in L'être et le néant [*Being and Nothingness*] (1943). The passage highlights the value of the Actaeon myth to Lacan, but also helps us clarify one of the most carelessly used aspects of Lacanian theory: the gaze.

In his discussion of the gaze as the 'underside of consciousness', the implicit, God-like vision necessary for existence to cohere, Lacan (1977,

p. 83) refers to Sartre's phenomenological exploration of shame. In what Lacan describes as 'one of the most brilliant passages' of *Being and Nothingness*, Sartre describes a man caught spying at a keyhole, transformed suddenly from gazer to gazed-at, subject to object. As such, 'the gaze that surprises me and reduces me to shame, since this is the feeling he regards as the most dominant' describes more than just the vision of another human being. The gaze 'is not a seen gaze, but a gaze imagined by me in the field of the Other' (p. 84). Lacan points out that Sartre 'does not refer to the organ of sight but to rustling leaves, suddenly heard while out hunting, to a footstep heard in a corridor' (p. 84). Indeed, Sartre's recognition that the gaze relates to more than the literal presence of someone's eyes receives Lacan's praise as early as *Seminar I*: it is 'magisterial', 'essential reading for an analyst' (1988, p. 215). For the man at the keyhole, the gaze 'surprises him in the function of voyeur, disturbs him, overwhelms him and reduces him to a feeling of shame' (1977, p. 84). The voyeur had thought he was the one wielding vision as power, but there is always another gaze (an Other gaze) exposing us as subjects of desire, not objectivity (marked by lack, not plenitude). 'I see only from one point, but in my existence I am looked at from all sides' (p. 72).

Miller (1999) notes, with understatement, that the big Other carries some of the characteristics that philosophers and theologians have ascribed to God. In *Seminar X*, Lacan (2014) outlines 'the correlation between this omnipotence and something which is, as I might say all seeingness': 'the God that everybody or almost everybody in our cultural arena, I mean in the God that everybody believes in without believing in him, namely this universal eye that is brought to bear on all our actions' (pp. 284–285).

The psychological necessity of faith in this universal eye provides Lacan with a logic of perversions. On some level, the voyeur and the exhibitionist know that God's gaze is lacking – and seek to mend this absence in their own way. In Miller's (1989)[16] account of Lacan's theory, the voyeur

> brings in the gaze itself to obstruct the hole in the Other – he brings in the gaze to make the Other whole; the voyeur needs to make the Other exist to be an instrument of his [or her] *jouissance*.

Once again, an interplay of roles is predicated on the idea of *jouissance* in the other. We don't need other humans with whom to form amboceptive relationships; God will do. Voyeurs enjoy on behalf of the gods. The reverse of this voyeurism is exhibitionism. The classicist N. J. Richardson (1974) records a common folk belief amongst the ancient Greeks that indecent exposure may amuse and please a god. The gods are always watching, with various possible demands implied: that we behave, seduce, entertain. There is the idea of tragedy as the 'show for Dionysus' and the tradition, noted by Augustine, that all theatre might be for the amusement of the gods. And God's sight, of course, is not a purely pagan concern. It is not long after the Judaeo-Christian story of creation that God is peeping into Eden, disappointed with what he finds.

Genesis is different to the *Metamorphoses*, however. Judeo-Christianity is defined by a gaze that judges rather than lusts. The effect is to provoke both guilt and shame: 'They eat of the tree of knowledge and cover themselves with fig leaves, before trying to hide themselves when they hear the voice of God, fearful because they were naked' (Genesis 3: 7–11). As in Sartre's example, it is a sound that announces a gaze; this establishes its threatening omniscience, the impossibility of restricting it to a particular individual and therefore a fixed point. We ought to be more struck by this shame than we are, Russell Grigg (2005) suggests: 'One can understand that guilt and remorse follow from Adam and Eve's transgression in Paradise, but the reason for the appearance of shame is less obvious.' It is not simply explained by the sudden introduction of sin and lust into the world. Shame is not guilt. Grigg points out the very different tenor of their antonyms: guilt/guiltless, shame/shameless.

It is Miller (2006), again, who draws from Lacan's theory a means of distinguishing the terms according to their relation to the Other: 'Guilt is the effect on the subject of an Other that judges, thus of an Other that contains the values that the subject has supposedly transgressed.' Shame is related 'to an Other prior to the Other that judges, that it is a primordial Other, not one that judges but instead one that only sees or lets be seen' (p. 15). Shame is a 'primary affect'. This is why nudity, while shameful, can be solved simply by covering up. On the down side, in so far as it 'is independent of anything of the order of misdeed, harm, or transgression that might give rise to it' (p. 15), control can easily slip from our grasp. Someone's gaze can make us ashamed in a way it can't make us guilty.

Ovid suggests that Actaeon is not guilty of any wrongdoing: 'calm reflection will show that destiny was to blame for Actaeon's misfortunes, not any guilt on his own part,' Ovid writes, 'for there is nothing sinful in losing one's way' (*Metamorphosis*, III, 142). Twice he states that there is no crime (*scelus*). Actaeon has wandered unwittingly into the scene. But Diana's shame does not depend on his intent, and so this excuse would prove unpersuasive. Fittingly, Actaeon's punishment imposes shame on him: once transformed into a stag, he has too much shame (*pudor*) to return home to the royal palace. Indeed, in another inversion of the appropriate hierarchy of sight, he becomes subject to the hungry gaze of his own hounds, much as Diana has been subject to Actaeon's unintentionally impudent gaze. Even hunting dogs can serve as the Other by whom we are judged.

So we've seen some of the ways in which *jouissance* confuses distinctions of subject and other generally, and male and female specifically. It grounds the fundamentally amboceptive nature of our selfhood, reinforced, at the deepest level, by the gaze. Indeed, this gaze is such a primary, constitutive element of consciousness that the issue moves from the realm of gender to that of the gods. But gender is not shaken off so easily. For all the slipperiness of subjectivity, and reciprocity of desire, we maintain gendered identity. Or at least try. Which leads us back to the question of what exactly it is we're ashamed about when seen naked.

Shame and castration: veiling absence

There is one more possible clue to the puzzle of Diana's anger. In an apocryphal variant of the Actaeon myth, recorded by the second-century Assyrian writer Lucian, a spiteful Juno suggests that Diana turned him into a stag because she was worried he would spread an *unfavourable* judgment on her looks. It is true that it is Actaeon's speech – identified by Miller with judgment – that Diana first mocks him for losing. I mention this predictable, misogynist spin on the tale because it is actually most true to Lacan's own theory: shame veils and reveals a will to exhibit, but it is a will to exhibit what is not there.

Bice Benvenuto (1994) makes a further distinction, this time between shame and embarrassment. Benvenuto notes Freud's use of both terms (*Scham* and *Verlegenheit*) in his analysis of dreams of appearing naked. These, Freud claims, mask exhibitionist desires. Benvenuto suggests we distinguish shame and embarrassment accordingly: embarrassment is 'the conscious feeling of having been found out by the other, whereas shame is the encounter of the subject with the veil which covers and points out his/her nakedness as well as his/her will to exhibit' (p. 132).

A veil becomes central to visual depictions of the Actaeon myth: a piece of fabric, a curtain of some kind, usually red, drawn back by the hunter to 'reveal' Diana, is a visual trope repeated across innumerable depictions.[17] It is a symbol of discovery and transgression, but so inadequate one might wonder what it was doing there in the first place.

The veil is also a constant presence in Lacan's seminars and lectures. 'If one wants to deceive a man, what one presents to him is the painting of a veil, that is to say, something that incites him to ask what is behind it' (1977, p. 112).[18] The veil tantalizes but, here, it tantalizes to distract from an absence. Six years after *Seminar XI*, Lacan will elaborate on this image: 'What is the love of truth? The love of truth is the love of this weakness whose veil we have lifted, it's the love of what truth hides, which is called castration' (1991, p. 58).

Behind the veil is a threatening lack, and it is Truth's job to disguise it. As ever in Lacan's thinking, sexuality is bound up with epistemology. Lacan's use of the veil stands in conscious opposition to a well-established tradition of sexual allegory, that of truth as a woman in need of hunting down and stripping. This informs the tradition from which Giordano Bruno's neo-Platonic account emerges: Actaeon as a hunter in pursuit of truth. The broad sense of Bruno's allegory survives in Sartre's (1943) own, brief delineation of the 'Actaeon Complex', by which 'one pulls off the veils of nature'; research 'always involves the idea of a nudity that one exposes by putting aside the obstacles that cover it, as Actaeon pushes aside the branches the better to see Diana at her bath' (p. 667; see also Bowie, 1988). Here, nakedness equals truth. It is in this sense that Peter Brooks sees the Actaeon myth as relating to Freud's conjecture in his *Three Essays on the Theory of Infantile Sexuality* (1905), that the 'desire to know' (*der Wisstrieb*) develops from the 'urge to see' (*der Schautrieb*) (see Brooks, 1993).

Sight has been a central metaphor for the search for truth since Ancient Greece. But, as is clear here, there is a gendering at work, of truth and he who hunts her.[19] This gendered tradition even weaves together the myth of Actaeon and differing traditions as to Tiresias' blindness. Callimachus, in his *Bath of Pallas*, describes Tiresias coming to a fountain with unbearable thirst; he sees Athena naked and is blinded (Heath, 1993). While this provides an alternative to the story of Juno blinding him, the classicist Eric Csapo (1997), in a structural analysis, sees the tales as equivalent: in each version, Tiresias learns sexual secrets and is punished with symbolic castration.

Lacan's theory suggests that castration may be what he finds in the first place: the sense of lack that persists when the last veil is lifted. For Lacan, sexual and epistemological investigations are indeed foundational, but arrive at a threatening absence. And this is in line with Freud's work. In his essay on Leonardo da Vinci, Freud (1910) suggests that the investigatory gaze becomes fixated on the quest for a body that has no real existence: the phallic woman. The child begins to display an intense desire to look, a desire to see other people's genitals, and the mother's most of all. But this instinct turns to disgust and horror upon discovering that she doesn't have the expected male organ. Lacan, to put his entire theory in a nutshell, simply renders this castration general: no one possesses the phallus, in so far as it is a fantasy, as we shall see in the next section.[20]

Lacan (2007) does appropriate Giordano Bruno's Neoplatonic Actaeon in 'The Freudian thing', Actaeon representing the intellect intent on capturing divine wisdom, but Lacan's hunter arrives at anything but the 'emblematic abode of truth' that we might expect, in spite of the 'damp shade' and its naked occupant (p. 343). 'For truth proves to be complex in essence, humble in its office and alien to reality … rather inhuman, Diana perhaps' (p 362). This is Diana as a cold fantasy, a refusal, one that reaches for the veil and so preserves our desire.

The well-established identification of scopophilia with patriarchal power contributes to confusion regarding Lacan's own theory of the gaze.[21] Lacan's gaze is rarely an instrument of Foucauldian oppression, rather he emphasizes its *failure*. The true consequence of drawing back the veil is that the veil is promptly restored, for it keeps desire in place. And it is not just women who have to veil themselves. As Benvenuto (1994) puts it, both men and women have to get dressed to disguise their lack. Shame is concerned with 'an acknowledged cover-up'. The cover-up concerns the absence of an object of desire in reality (it can be contrasted with the logic of perversion, which displaces desire onto an object that *can* be found).[22] This is the burden of that ultimate veil: the phallus.

A phallus amongst the Bacchae

> The phallus is not a fantasy, if what is understood by that is an imaginary effect. Nor is it as such an object (part, internal, good, bad, etc. …) in so far as this term tends to accentuate the reality involved in a relationship. It is even less the organ, penis or clitoris, which it symbolizes. And it is not incidental that Freud took his reference for it from the simulacrum which it represented for the Ancients.
>
> For the phallus is a signifier, a signifier whose function in the intra-subjective economy of analysis might lift the veil from that which it served in the mysteries.
>
> *Jacques Lacan (2007, p. 579)*

In Lacan's paper, 'The signification of the phallus', we are introduced to the phallus in the context of ritual, specifically 'the mysteries', ancient religious cults that required initiation into secret doctrines. If the phallus is not a fantasy in any conventional sense, nor an organ, these rituals might help us understand its odd status. The festivals of Dionysus involved huge model *phalloi* carried in procession by the god's worshippers.[23] In Greek mythology, these worshippers were known as maenads (or Bacchae/Bacchantes in Roman mythology, after Bacchus, the Roman name for Dionysus); their name literally translates as 'raving ones'. Lacan makes a point of associating his concept of the phallus with these cult rituals. His language suggests that they are in some way necessary for understanding the concept itself – and even that a reinterpretation of the mysteries might be a consequence of his theory. But why?

To understand their presence here, we need to turn to Klossowski again. Borch-Jacobsen (1991) describes it as striking that the concept of the phallus, while present in Lacan's 1938 encyclopedia article on Family Complexes, was 'almost completely eclipsed' (p. 279) in his work until the appearance of Klossowski's *Le bain de Diane* (1998) in 1956. Following publication of *Le bain de Diane*, Lacan delivers his seminar of 1955/6 on the psychoses where the concept of the phallus returns in force. It then takes a central place in the following two seminars ('The object relation' and 'Formation of the unconscious'). And Lacan scatters several clues to its Klossowskian inheritance. One is his use of the term 'simulacrum'. This is a favourite term of Klossowski's; see the chapter 'Simulacra and the theatrical nature of gods and goddesses' in *Sacred and Mythic Origins of Certain Practices of the Women of Rome* (published as part of *Le bain de Diane*, pp. 123–125). John Taylor (2009) discusses the centrality of the concept to Klossowski's *oeuvre*. Klossowski claimed to 'fabricate simulacra'. Taylor notes that while the word *simulacrum* is restricted by English usage to 'a representation', an 'imitation' or 'a superficial likeness', contemporary French maintains traces of more concrete Latin meanings: 'statue (of a pagan god)', and 'phantom'.[24]

So the French and Latin terms convey something subtly different from the English, with its sense of cold artifice or copy. They describe something more pagan and more ghostly. When Lacan (2007) borrows the term, he elides simulacrum and signifier: the signifier becomes a veil for the absent object:

> The phallus can only play its role as veiled, that is, as in itself the sign of the latency with which everything signifiable is struck as soon as it is raised (*aufgehoben*) to the function of signifier.
>
> The phallus is the signifier of this *Aufhebung* itself which it inaugurates (initiates) by its own disappearance. This is why the demon of *Aidos*

(*Scham*/shame) in the ancient mysteries rises up exactly at the moment when the phallus is unveiled (cf the famous painting of the Villa of Pompeii).

(p. 581)

Like all signifiers, the phallus involves a simultaneous process of appearance and disappearance: the symbol marks the absence of the thing itself. Lacan asserts that the phallus holds pride of place as the 'empty signifier' signifying the very difference by which meaning can happen: not division between the sexes but a more primary division between the One and the not-one. As the 'empty signifier' it also represents the impossibility of coinciding with what it is meant to signify: a signifier of signification's inherent failure (see Barnard, 2005). And ancient worship supports this privileged place in Lacan's theory. 'The demon of *Aidos*/shame (p. 210)' is rightly heard by Borch-Jacobsen (1991) as a distinctly Klossowskian note.[25] We have encountered both daemons and shame in Klossowski's version of the Actaeon myth: shame as the paradoxical need to hide what is not there. There is also a large dose of Hegel here: *Aufgehoben* is used by Hegel to describe the interaction of thesis and antithesis, with a range of sometimes paradoxical connotations: superseded, raised up, abolished, reversed, sublated – most of all, preserved by alteration: by moving into fantasy. The signifier of the phallus preserves the fantasy of the phallus. It allows us to maintain our belief in it. Hence Lacan's swerve to a curiously specific reference, 'the famous painting of the Villa of Pompeii'. This, in fact, is the direct source for the image of shame at unveiling, as Lacan himself notes. The Villa of Pompeii is a well-preserved ruin of a Roman villa half a kilometre north of Pompeii, and its 'painting' is part of a room of frescos depicting what appears to be an initiation ritual, the initiation of a young woman into the cult of Dionysus. The frescoes depict a series of interlinked scenes, a woman on a throne, a scroll being read, a lyre played – followed by the initiate's apparent panic at something, her whipping by a winged female figure, and the appearance of a gowned figure with a thyrsus, long stalks with a pine cone on top connected to the fertility *phalloi* of the Greek cults.

One explanation for the room of frescoes is that rituals were carried out here in secret. The mysteries, imported from Greek cults, gained huge popularity in Rome, eventually being banned in 186 BC as they were seen to be incompatible with the austerity of Rome's own customs. The practice went underground, preserved for women. The frescoes in the Villa of Mysteries present the smoke and mirrors of ritual, the conscious manipulation of veils that belongs to a mystery cult (including the veil of secrecy itself). If they represent an initiation, Lacan suggests, it is an initiation into a fantasy – a fantasy of what the opposite sex might symbolize. They provide a quieter version of the Bacchic frenzy but no less centred on a phallic symbol.

Recent scholarship has questioned the extent to which these frenzied maenads reflect historical reality or are themselves a fantasy.[26] Given the concerns of this chapter, the fantasy element itself is thought-provoking. An interesting modern parallel to Bacchic frenzy is analysed by Linda Williams (1990) in her seminal study of pornography, *Hard Core*, felicitously subtitled *Power, Pleasure and the 'Frenzy of the Visible.'* Williams discusses pornography's reinforcement of the phallic signifier by way of its performance of feminine pleasure. It reduces women to maenads, dispossessed by ecstasy. But there is a twist. Given that the majority of the audience for the films themselves is male, the male gaze is focused, at least in part, on the phallus. The viewer joins the performers in this ritual of worship. In a Lacanian analysis of pornography, Mark Bracher (1993) asks whether porn allows men clandestine expression of non-phallic desires and *jouissances*, bypassing normative repression. It is a psychological insight to which Ovid, Freud and Lacan are alert, as they are alert to its threatening nature.

Ovid concludes Book III of the *Metamorphoses* with the story of Pentheus (Actaeon's cousin), rendered most vividly in Euripides' *The Bacchae*. The play weaves together all the themes under discussion here: sight, gender transgression, epistemological transgression, *jouissance*, desire and anger. It has long been recognized as exceptionally concerned with the hunger to see and to know, bound to gendered mystery, with a sustained emphasis on the visual (see Winnington-Ingram, 1948). In it, the women of Thebes have fled to the wild to worship Dionysus in Bacchic revelry. Pentheus, the king's son (and grandson of the founder Cadmus), refuses to worship this new god. He has many of the women arrested. Looking for Dionysus himself, he comes across Tiresias and Cadmus in Bacchic garb. It turns out that even they have become followers. Eventually, Pentheus decides to disguise himself in order to watch the rituals. Dionysus, in disguise, helps Pentheus dress as a woman. Pentheus goes to the sacred grove and is able to see the forbidden sights of the ritual, but he is discovered. The Bacchantes, crazed, tear him limb from limb, chief among them his own mother.[27]

As the only surviving tragedy with Dionysus, god of tragedy, as its subject the *Bacchae* has a particularly intimate relation to the genre itself (see Arvanitakis, 2007). The origins of tragedy have been traced to the Dionysiac satyr chorus and associated hymns in honour of the god since the writings of Herodotus and Aristotle. The association is supported by the god's association with invasive passions. Traditionally, Dionysus was identified with a pre-rational state before Reason or Mind (*Nous*) imposed order. Homer refers to Dionysus as *mainomenos*, the mad god (*Iliad*, 4, 130–140). He was Lysios, the loosener (Arvanitakis, 2007). The most extreme manifestation of this side of the god's character involves the actual tearing apart of the human body, a constant theme in myths related to Dionysus. His mother is Semele, the mortal consumed in the flames of Zeus' passion, burned up in the most vivid mythical representation of *jouissance*. Dionysus is born of this ecstasy, and tragedy is concerned with its dangerous proximity. Klossowski (1998) discovers it throughout Thebes: 'Semele, Agave [mother of Pentheus] and Actaeon were all troubled by the same passion: *ecstasy*' (p. 25). The root meaning of the term in Greek is 'standing outside of' or 'standing apart from' something. Heidegger plays with this term in *Being and Time*. And, of course, it is echoed in Lacanian *extimacy*. It is an inherited illness of Cadmus' troubled line, men and women possessed, with the gods in their blood. Dodds (1960), in an influential reading of the tragedy informed by the psychoanalysis of his time, sees resistance to Dionysus as resistance to 'the elemental in one's own nature' (p. xiv), moving the emphasis from myth to individual psychology.

But, as Euripides' play makes clear, it is both more and less than 'elemental'; it is a form of pleasure with specific, entrenched gender associations. It is the female Bacchae, Dionysus' female followers, who make a *ritual* of ecstasy.[28] Tragedy, likewise, is not just concerned with 'madness' or 'possession' but with the dangers of the feminine in particular. Edith Hall (1997) has studied the prominent role of women in Athenian tragedy, a curious phenomenon given their exclusion from public life.[29] Female tragic choruses in the surviving plays outnumber male choruses by 21–10. Hall provides two possible explanations: one is that this is connected to women's prominent role in Ancient Greek religion, especially funerary lamentation and sacrifices, thereby becoming associated with death and killing. The second explanation involves the Dionysiac origin of tragedy, an ancestry that remains evident in the frequent references to Bacchic frenzy in relation to the killing of family members, in addition to the threatening motif by which the departure of women from the household gives rise to its destruction. 'Moreover, women were regarded as more susceptible to invasive passions than men, especially the invasion of eros and daemonic possession' (Padel, 1983, p. 161). And the daemons that possess them are female too. Ruth Padel (1992), in *In and*

Out of the Mind, notes that inner violence in Greek culture is generally personified as female: the personifications of madness, Ate and Lyssa, are both feminine, both daemonic. Finally, Froma Zeitlin (1990) makes the connection between Dionysus, frenzied loss of control and cultural notions of feminine sexuality:

> The fact that women are far more closely connected to his rites, his *orgia*, leads me to speculate that these Dionysiac gestures reflect more closely a cultural notion of female orgasmic activity. These symptoms, we might say, diffuse over the entire body as a form of wild kinetic agitation or an intense trance-like state and include the two divergent extremes of feelings of fusion and fragmentation.
>
> (p. 148)

We are back at the exceptionalism of the female orgasm, and at the *jouissance* we have seen described, an experience of both inexpressible totality and fragmentation. Tragedy confirms the association of this sexual-mystical state with violence: female pleasure is not just a mystery, but a threat. Its *victims* tend to be men. The description of Pentheus torn apart by the maenads in a grotesque take on ritual *sparagmos*, the tearing apart of a sacrificial victim, is amongst the most graphically violent in Greek literature. Dionysus himself as a child was torn to pieces by the Titans at the command of Juno. According to some myths, Orpheus died when he was dismembered by maenads furious at him for not honouring Dionysus, or, in Ovid's account, because he transferred his erotic attention to young boys.

It is this threatening side of the Bacchae that inspires Lacan's first published classical reference. It occurs in the conclusion to an article that he wrote for the Surrealist journal *Minotaure* in 1933 on the Papin sisters, who he describes as 'castrating Bacchantes'.[30] The sisters, Christine and Lea Papin, were maids who had killed and mutilated their employer's wife and daughter. The case had fascinated commentators of the day, read mostly through the lens of class war; it inspired, at least in part, Sartre's *Le Mur* (1939), Simone de Beauvoir's *La force de l'âge* (1960) and the play *The Maids* by Jean Genet (1947). Lacan, as ever, goes against the grain. The art dealer Daniel-Henry Kahnweiler (Ricci, 2012), in a tantalizing glimpse of the times, describes Picasso returning from visiting Lacan, angry that the analyst thought the Papin sisters were insane rather than revolutionaries. But, for Lacan, psychosis is more than a dismissive label. It is understandable that he turns his attention to the case when people are encroaching on his territory, the psychoses; and when the case is so rich with timeless symbolism as well as reflections of its time.

Lacan moves the debate regarding the sisters' motives away from the political and sociological readings that had been popular to one that casts the event as a ritual: 'the drama unfolded rapidly ... each of them seized an opponent, tore out her eyes, while she was still alive ... and battered her to death' (Crichton and Cordess, 1995, p. 567). Having stripped and mutilated the bodies, the sisters 'then washed the instruments of these horrifying rites, cleaned themselves down and lay together in the same bed', concluding 'their bloody orgy' (p. 567). As if these were not enough classical echoes, in the course of a further crisis, Christine attempted to tear out her own eyes. Lacan refers to emotions evoked by the 'symbolism of the crime', the aspect of Oedipal riddle.

> *They had to try to solve the enigma of sex with nothing but the help of their closed world* .... One must have listened attentively to the strange declarations of such patients to know the madness that their restricted conscience erects on the riddle of the phallus and around female castration.
>
> (p. 572)

'One must have listened' – ie. this demands the interpretation of an analyst. Already, three years before his first analytic presentation, and 25 years before delivering 'The signification of the phallus', Lacan is working with a cluster of associated ideas, circling the riddle of gender.

Lacan makes his Bacchic reference explicit at the end of the paper, portraying the twins as a failed mystery cult:

> They tore out their [victims'] eyes, like castrating Bacchantes. It is the sacrilegious curiosity, which has troubled man since the beginning of time, which inspired them when they tore their victims to pieces, when they hunted in their gaping wounds for what Christine in her innocence was later to call before the judge 'the mystery of life'.
>
> (p. 573)

The modern-day Bacchantes manifest an epistemological desire, looking for truth, the true phallus, finding nothing. While Lacan's interest in Bacchic imagery evolves from the *grand guignol* of the Papin sisters, already it is bound to both a quest for knowledge and the threat of female desire experienced as violence.

The threat of female jouissance inspires Lacan to recast the prohibitive law instilled within us by the mythical, primal father. He turns to the version of the myth delivered by Freud in *Moses and Monotheism* (1939), a revised version of the horde myth in which it is the youngest son who elevates the (murdered) primal father to divine proportions in the face of matriarchy.[31] With this in mind, Lacan develops the concept of a symbolic Father (*Nom du Père*) whose task is to pin down the symbolic order and fit potentially threatening (potentially feminine) pleasure to it so that it does not overwhelm us.

It is the 'dominance of the woman as mother' that initially establishes female desire as threatening: 'The mother's desire is not something that is bearable just like that, that you are indifferent to. It will always wreak havoc' (Lacan, 1991, p. 78). This threatening maternal *jouissance*, and the paternal law it necessitates, underwrite an asymmetry. We elevate the father, writes Vehaeghe (2006), 'to combat a danger we locate in the woman/mother, a danger that, in one way or another, always has to do with *jouissance* and our fear of becoming its victim' (p. 43). This is the logic of the prohibition that defines male desire. For men 'the means of *jouissance* are open on the principle that he has renounced this closed, foreign *jouissance*, renounced the mother' (Lacan, 1991, p. 78).

Yet if this *jouissance* was foreign in any absolute sense, there would be no need to renounce it. Clearly, it is fundamental. A man's very masculinity is only established 'through being what he renounces by way of jouissance'; 'Henceforth the male is and is not what he is with respect to jouissance' (p. 78). It is foreign in the sense of being *extimate*. The fear of contamination unsettles gender demarcation as it underlines it. This is precisely the aspect of psychology that gives *The Bacchae* its unsettling power. Pentheus is fascinated by the all-female rituals surrounding the worship of Dionysus and seeks to know them; to achieve this, Dionysus dresses him as a woman. This is the focus of Froma Zeitlin (1990) in 'Playing the other': she argues that transvestism in Dionysus' cult and symbolic gender inversions in Greek ritual generally explain the role of women as the 'other' of the masculine identity defined in Greek tragedy. But they also attest to the effort involved in sustaining that opposition.

> If the Dionysiac tends in the myths to destroy men more often than women, and if the male approach to the god, as in the case of Pentheus, may be made through feminine disguise, then we might understand better how the other side of male sexual desire may also entail a fear of

contamination with the feminine that will transform the male into a *maenad*.

(p. 148)

The ritual simulacrum of the phallus can be seen as a lightning rod for these anxieties, a pact of fantasy by which our roles in relationship to *jouissance* are assigned. It underlies what Lacan (2007) describes as *mascarade*: It is *mascarade* 'that the presence of the Other liberates in the sexual role' (p. 616), the means by which we manipulate the veil and play the Other. This is a realm opened up by the absence of innate sexuation in Lacanian theory. Certainly, as critics have long noted, the phallus and castration are not gender-neutral symbols.[32] But Lacan argues against essentialist models of gender. Having asserted that castration 'presupposes the subjectivity of the Other as the locus of its law', ie. places the burden on fantasy, he concludes 'the difference between the sexes [*altérité*] is denatured by this alienation' (p. 616). *Mascarade* holds it together; *Jouissance* is the glue, the substance with which these intermediary fantasies operate (a sense of this is felt in Lacan's formulation of the pseudo-physical lamella: attaching to things, turning itself inside out, etc.). It is the circulation of maenadic *jouissance* around the *phalloi* that allows the symbol to signify. This gives the Bacchic context in which Lacan (2007) presents the phallus its importance. The phallus only exists in the Other's fantasy, as a locus for their desire. Benvenuto (1994) presents beauty itself as the feminine version of this *mascarade*: 'beauty is the feminine phallus – as well as the dress of feminine modesty' (p. 87). Beauty is the phallus as veil behind which the feminine hides its lack. And, having seen the function of the veil of chastity, we can conclude that the phallus and modesty itself perform equivalent functions.

Masochism is another veil that has been confused with the truth, another fantasy that serves to conceal an enduring impasse. Perceptible 'in the male myth of her alleged masochism' is 'a trace of the *unbroached* realm of woman's *jouissance*' (p. 86), Lacan (1990) writes in *Television*. It is not just a male concept but a male *myth*, with the function we've seen myth serve of providing a resolution for the irresolvable. For Lacan, a theory centred on *jouissance* allows us to *correct* lazy psychoanalytic concepts of innate female passivity and masochism.

> The supposed value ... of *feminine masochism*, as it is called, should be subjected, parenthetically, to serious scrutiny. It belongs to a dialogue that may be defined, in many respects, as a masculine phantasy. There is

every reason to believe that to sustain this phantasy would be an act of complicity on our part.

(p. 193)

In the 'Guiding remarks for a convention', Lacan (2007) refers to Freud's own caution regarding binary models of gender: 'Do we recall Freud's oft-repeated advice not to reduce the supplement of the feminine with respect to the masculine to the complement of the passive with respect to the active?' (p. 615). The reference is to Freud's 'Instincts and their vicissitudes' (1915), in which Freud emphasizes that every drive is, by definition, active. The paper is a key point of reference for Lacan in his reformulation of the *Trieb* but also, as here, reforming lazy assumptions about masculine and feminine psychology. In *Seminar XI*'s chapter, 'From love to the libido', this fantasy of complimentary pairs is part of the means by which our 'traditional' poles of sexuation and their attendant fantasies provide succour in response to the underlying impossible (real) division, that resulting from the subject's entry into mortal existence as conveyed by the lamella myth. Lacan (1977) promises that 'scattered throughout' Freud's work we find his assertion 'that the polar reference activity/passivity is there in order to name, to cover, to metaphorize that which remains unfathomable in sexual difference' (p. 192).

Hence, 'to sustain this phantasy would be an act of complicity on our part' (p. 193). Complicity by analysts because, even though 'there is a certain amount of consent on the part of women' to this fantasy, this 'means nothing' – or, at least, does not mean it is more than a fantasy. The veil of fantasy appears again:

> It is quite striking to see that the representatives of this sex in the analytic circle are particularly disposed to maintain the fundamental belief in feminine masochism. It may be that there is a veil here, concerning the interests of the sex, that should not be lifted too quickly.
>
> (p. 193)

Lacan's final argument gives with one hand and takes away with the other. Women, here, are still robbed of speech, dispossessed of their own sexuality, but in the cause of avoiding easy answers. Against the supposedly 'fundamental' nature of masochism, Lacan (2007) locates the roots of the fantasy in 'male invention': 'Can we rely on what masochistic perversion owes to male invention and conclude that female masochism is a fantasy of male desire?' (again, *de* – fantasy *of* male desire – places the fantasy beyond any one subject) (p. 615). It is a somewhat suspect claim but, again, true to aspects of Freud's own struggles passed over in seeking to make his theory fit cultural commonplaces. In his essay 'Rape, seduction, psychoanalysis', John Forrester (1990) notes that critics who see Freud imposing masochistic desire on women are misunderstanding Freud, 'whose discussion of feminine masochism is entirely based, as he, perhaps ironically, notes, on work with male patients' (p. 65). These masochistic fantasies, Freud (1924) writes, 'place the subject in a characteristically female situation; they signify, that is, being castrated (i.e. 'the wish to have a passive (feminine) sexual relation with the father'), or copulated with, or giving birth to a baby' (p. 162). The most significant evidence in this respect is provided by the diary of President Schreber. Schreber's psychosis involved fantasies that God was turning him into a woman so as to enjoy him sexually. He becomes, in Lacan's (1991) reading, a tool of God's *jouissance*. As Eric Laurent (2007) describes, Schreber's text could be seen as a lengthy consideration of 'the enigma of the *jouissance* of God':

> What is enigmatic for Schreber is that God or the Other should enjoy his passive being and that he should support this .... He experiences himself as an isolated subject, One, in relation with a *jouissance* full to the point of becoming the point of *jouissance* of the universe.
>
> (p. 124)

We are moving back towards that aspect of *jouissance* which makes it ineffable. We are back to the One, the mystical *jouissance* of divine totality, a fantasy that is as religious as it is sexual. We've considered the differences between being loved by Zeus and by a Christian God, but clearly divine lust is not entirely limited to pagans. In their ecstasies, Christian mystics – Teresa, Hadewijch – revive the Dionysiac. Indeed, the Christian God, via the Dionysiac Christ, makes possible again a divine-erotic encounter lost in the more urbane, less reverential Roman era (one in which the mystical Dionysus becomes transformed into the drunken Bacchus). Christianity appropriates the mystical and, with it, the possibility of this encounter and fusion with God (Benvenuto, 1994, pp. 16–17). But this allows the return of an anxiety. Ascribing *jouissance* to the other sex was a way of disavowing it, accepting gender limits. Now we are confronted, once again, with human limits. With not being gods.

Insufficient pleasures

Ovid derives humour from having his gods behave like humans. Yet the tantalizing fantasy of their power remains, the power to have what you want and enjoy it. Lacan (2014) returns to the myth of Apollo and Daphne in the seminar on *Anxiety*, three years after employing it in the *Ethics*. Again, he presents himself as concerned with something apparently 'hidden' in Ovid's poem, but this time he gives an entirely different interpretation of metamorphosis. Now metamorphosis demonstrates the satisfaction of the gods: 'the relationship of the god is very different from ours to the object of his desire .... Apollo is not castrated either before or afterwards'; in fact, 'After the transformation the laurel is not Daphne but Apollo. What's specific to a god is that, once satisfied, he transforms himself into the object of his desire, even if he must thereby be petrified therein' (p. 307).

This is metamorphosis as complete satisfaction, a plenitude to set beside mortal lack ('Apollo is not castrated either before or afterwards').[33] Lacan develops ideas from *Seminar VIII*, in which he contrasts the love of gods with human love, in which we can only ever *have* the object of our desire in fantasy: 'Nothing is further from the trembling one feels in one's being when in love than a god's desire', Lacan (2015) writes. 'You have to see what happens when they take it into their heads to love a mortal woman, for example. Nothing will stop them until the mortal, out of desperation, turns into a laurel or a frog' (p. 161).

Anxiety, it turns out, centres on not being able to enjoy like a god. But this is based on a belief that we *should*. This sense of pressure becomes a striking aspect of Lacan's thoughts on man and gods from *Seminar X* onwards. It is a pressure only enhanced by the Judeo-Christian God (see Harari, 2001).

> God commands me to jouir, to enjoy – it's in the text .... Recall the difference that lies between Aristotle's universal mover God, the God of the sovereign good God, Plato's delusional conception, and the God of the Jews, who's a God one speaks to, a God who asks something of you, and who, in Ecclesiastes, gives you the order *Jouis* – which really crowns it all.
>
> To *jouir* on order is all the same something about which each of us can sense that, if there's a wellspring, an origin, of anxiety, then it must be found somewhere there. To the imperative *Jouis*, I can only reply one thing, which is *J'ouis*, *I hear*, but naturally I don't *jouir* so easily for all that.
>
> (pp. 79–80)

The biblical source Lacan refers to is Ecclesiastes 8: 15: 'So I commend the enjoyment of life, because there is nothing better for a person under the sun than to eat and drink and be glad.' The God of the Israelites is puzzling: less easily satisfied than Zeus, more complex than an abstract Platonic Good. Yahweh has given us the world, and this imposes obligations, one of which is to enjoy it (in *Seminar XX* Lacan will ascribe this imperative to the super-ego itself – 'The superego is the imperative of *jouissance* – Enjoy!' (1998, p. 3)). It in this way that the godlike Other creates a sense of anxiety. Anxiety is bound to a deficiency of *jouissance* and to this Other who enjoys themselves fully. This dual sense of inadequacy before the gods is heard in *Television*: this time, Lacan (1990) turns to Dante's Beatrice experiencing her own paroxysms of ecstasy, eyelids fluttering …

> and there emerges that Other whom we can identify only through her *jouissance*: her whom he, Dante, cannot satisfy, because from her, he can have only this look, only this object, but of whom he tells us that God fulfils her utterly; it is precisely by receiving the assurance of that from her own mouth that he arouses us.
>
> To which something in us replies: annoyance [*ennui*]. A word from which … I've composed the term: 'oneyance' [*unien*]. By which I designate the identification of the Other with the One. I would say: the mystical One.
>
> (p. 23)

The One as complete, offering complete satisfaction, is a provocation. It is a satisfaction we cannot deliver or receive, even if our own myths and fantasies portray it. It is here that Lacan turns to an old favourite: 'the mystical One whose crude equivalent is given to us through its comical other – Aristophanes … presenting the beast-with-two-backs' (p. 23). It is a bitter degradation of the mystical One, aligning it with Aristophanes' 'clowning' and Iago's venomous depiction of sex. Later in the same volume, Lacan again turns his sights on myths of post-coital 'fusion'. Here, counter to all romantic myth, orgasm is identified with division rather than unification:

> Orgasm is in itself anxiety, to the extent that forever, by dint of a central fault, desire is separated from fulfilment.
>
> Let no one offer as an objection those moments of peace, of fusion of the couple, in which each can view him or herself truly happy with the other … It was in order to demonstrate this to you that I commented at length on Ovid's fable based on the myth of Tiresias.
>
> (p. 86)

Tiresias is now identified with a fundamental frustration, and orgasm with an impossible totality. Tiresias's knowledge of bliss, therefore, points towards an experience that never arrives. But we keep trying, and this is the burden of the dialectic Lacan sets up between the finite individual and the infinite Other associated with *jouissance*. It is productive in its own way. First, it produces psychoanalysis, thanks to the figure of the hysteric and a clinical focus on sexually dysfunctional female patients that Freud inherited from the famed neurologist Jean-Martin Charcot. The mysterious, disrupted workings of these neurotic women propped up Freud's medical-intellectual quest. Macey (1988) puts it succinctly: 'Psychoanalysis and hysteria are historically and epistemologically inseparable .... The riddle of femininity is therefore not simply coeval with psychoanalysis; it is a constituent element thereof, and the entire edifice of psychoanalysis rests upon a question it cannot answer' (p. 200).

And must not answer? As Lacan (2007) says to the convention: if this state of affairs betrays an impasse in their investigations, 'the least one can nevertheless expect from psychoanalysts, meeting at a convention, is that they not forget that their method was born of a similar impasse' (p. 613). Indeed, psychoanalysis should distinguish itself by holding on to the difficulty, the paradox, unlike all those other commentators who believe they have solved them. The impasse of gender keeps the veil in place. In *Seminar XVII*, having begun by pointing out how few species rely on any form of *sexual* reproduction in order to demonstrate 'how little it is part of nature's intentions that [sex] form a whole, a sphere', Lacan (1991) concedes that one thing is certain: 'If for man it works out more or less okay, it's due to a trick that makes it possible, by first of all making it *insoluble*' (p. 34). So long as it is insoluble, the veil remains in place. The animation of desire is the crowning achievement in itself, and no desire is more effective at maintaining the play of veils than the desire for knowledge.

It is telling that much of this line of thought originates in *Seminar XVII*, one of the most explicitly political seminars, in which psychoanalysis, as an institution, is in question. To the students who query its authority, and have reservations about the institution of Lacan himself, now a 68-year-old legend, Lacan (1991) demonstrates that no one has the means of pulling apart psychoanalysis as he does. It is here that he introduces his contention that it is the discourse of the hysteric herself which provokes the emergence of psychoanalytic discourse: 'What hysterics ultimately want one to know is that language runs off the rails concerning the magnitude of what she as woman is capable of revealing concerning *jouissance*' (p. 34).

The hysteric fabricates 'a man as best she can, a man who would be animated by the desire to know' (p. 36). A man who is willing to take on the challenge of Tiresias. It is a fantasy that underlies the analytic experience. Lacan is fully aware of how psychoanalysis is involved in the masked drama. The knowledge it implies is seductive; it offers the patient an amboceptive relationship with the subject-supposed-to-know. Ultimately, the universality of this occurrence undermines the attribution of gender roles. 'In saying "she" we are making the hysteric a woman, but this is not her privilege alone. Many men get themselves analysed who, by this fact alone, are obliged to pass through the hysteric's discourse' (p. 33). Indeed, by 1970, Socrates himself has become a hysteric – the greatest hysteric of all – his protestations of ignorance provoking in others the desire for knowledge.

The confrontation of the finite individual with the infinite promise of *jouissance* does not just produce psychoanalysis, but all philosophy. The subtitle of *Seminar XX, Encore*, is 'The limits of love and knowledge'. The message of the seminar, put simply, is that we want it *encore* because there is a limit to how much we will ever fulfil our dreams of love and knowledge, dreams defined by a fantasy of totality and completion that is necessarily infinite. The pre-Socratics once again come to Lacan's aid. Parmenides had asserted that 'where there is being, infinity is required', and Lacan weaves this philosophy into his own theory that 'this requirement of the One … stems from the Other' (Lacan, 1998, p. 10).[34] This infinitude is now where we find the mystical *jouissance* (the godlike orgasm), and therefore why it cannot be expressed. It would take a totality of language: 'Saying it all is literally impossible: words fail' – even if it is through this very impossibility 'that the truth holds onto the real' (1990, p. 7). Again, the model is that of repetition around an inexpressible trauma, this time the trauma of impossible truth/*jouissance*. Impasses are where we hold on. Truth is ineffable but knowledge continues its labour of achieving it, driven by its very deficiency of *jouissance*. This is the engine of philosophy:

> What I am calling the hysteria of this discourse stems precisely from the fact that if this historical machine, which is in fact only the progress of the schools and nothing more, ever did culminate in absolute knowledge, it would only be to mark the annulment, the failure, the disappearance at the conclusion of the only thing that motivates the function of knowledge – its dialectic with *jouissance*.
>
> *(Lacan, 1991, p. 36)*

The figure of Tiresias has led Lacan from enquiries regarding a specifically feminine pleasure to speculations regarding the deficiency of human experience, to a consideration of the provocative stand-off of psychoanalysis itself. Lacan is profoundly aware of the discomfiting power dynamics on which his discipline is built: patients seeking answers that analysts don't possess, seeking attention, authority, desire; analysts colluding in this by assuming a position of knowledge; men fantasizing about women's sexuality, installing myth and mystery in place of conceptual deadlock; both women and men taking the fantasies imposed on them and using them as a mask. Lacan sets out to disturb psychoanalytic complacencies, and to unsettle assumptions about gender in particular. The genders need mystery to keep themselves discrete, he argues, a mystery preserved through interdictions. Yet, if this is not the reputation that sticks, it is due to Lacan's own, stubborn adherence to the poles of masculine and feminine in his terminology. The non-negotiable centrality of the phallus means he will never escape the bind in which Tiresias finds himself. In his last, unpublished seminar, Lacan describes our self-definition according to the phallus as an 'initiation' and psychoanalysis as an 'anti-initiation'. But he also states: 'It is necessary that in the absence of initiation one is either man or woman … as a third sex cannot subsist in the presence of the other two' (in Benvenuto, 1994, p. 150). The transsexual Tiresias may be patron saint of psychoanalysis, but he remains a fantasy.

Notes

1 The episode is mentioned in *Seminar X* (1962–3), *Seminar XIII* (1965–6), *L'Étourdit* (1973), *Seminar XV* (1967–8), *Seminar XIX* (1971–2).
2 *Seminar X* (2014) is where Lacan makes most obvious his proximity to the Ovidian source for Tiresias, although in *Seminar XIII* (1965–6) he again says 'read the myth of Tiresias' and refers to 'twenty verses of Ovid': 'Read the myth of Tiresias, there are here twenty verses of Ovid that I put in my first report, that of Rome, because it is an essential point and one that I tried to get across again since, when people were speaking about feminine sexuality in Amsterdam' (p. 258 1/6/1966, XX). In *Seminar X*, Lacan (2014) also mentions T. S. Eliot's reference to Tiresias in *The Wasteland*: 'this text regarding which Mr. T. S. Eliot in a note to *The Wasteland* underlines what he calls the very great anthropological interest' (p. 169). In his footnotes to *The Wasteland*, Eliot describes Tiresias as 'the most important personage in the poem, uniting all the rest …. What Tiresias *sees*, in fact, is the substance of the poem.'
3 See Lacan (1998), where he discusses the concept of 'usufruct', the juridical sense of 'the right to enjoy', in the process playing with the fact that he is now teaching in a faculty of law.
4 The comment is sandwiched between references to Lou Andreas-Salomé and Melanie Klein. Elsewhere, Helene Deutsch and Karen Horney come in for Lacan's (1973) criticism.

5 The ecstasy of Christian Teresa connects to classical myth: 'The earliest example I have seen of the pose Bernini chose for Teresa is an ancient Roman cameo of a hermaphrodite. Lavin suggests Bernini had seen Corregio's *Danae*. Perhaps he had also seen Titian's Farnese nude or his *Rape of Europa*' (Hayes, 1999, p. 332).
6 The literary theorist Leo Bersani (1987), exploring the relationship between sex and a fragmentation of self, renders *jouissance* itself as 'shattering'.
7 Io and Syrinx, Callisto, Proserpine, even Procne and Philomela receive this treatment (see Dimmick, 1992).
8 See Bowie (1988) and Logan (2002). Logan also notes Actaeon in Dali's *Echo and Narcissus* (1937) and Coctaeu's *Testament of Orpheus* (1949); there are also powerful Renaissance precedents in Boccaccio's *The Hunt of Diana* (1334) and Petrarch's versions (see Canzoniere 23 and 52).
9 In 'The Freudian thing' it is Freud himself who is cast as Actaeon, 'according to the signification Giordano Bruno drew from his myth in the *Heroic Frenzies* … [Actaeon as] the prey of the dogs of his own thoughts' (Lacan, 2007 p. 343); Borch-Jacobsen (1991) claims: 'it would not be hard to show that Lacan's "prosopoeia" consciously takes up [Klossowski's] writing strategy' (p. 260).
10 See Heath (1993, pp. 55 and 64) and also Hinds (2002) who describes 'a characteristic tension in the landscapes of the *Metamorphoses* between the beautiful setting and the sufferings which befall most of the characters who inhabit or enter it' (p. 130).
11 The text was to have served as preface to *Philosophy in the Bedroom*. It appeared in *Critique* (Lacan, 1963) as a review of the edition for which it was intended. The first to read Kant and Sade together were Horkheimer and Adorno in *Dialectic of Enlightenment* (1947).

Lacan's only other explicit mention of Klossowski is in *Seminar IX* (1961–2) in relation to the theory of fantasy: 'I would have no trouble reminding you that on other paths, the works and then the reflections on the works by himself of Pierre Klossowski converge with this path of research into phantasy as we have elaborated it this year' (p. 310).
12 This is its first formulation (Kant, 1993).
13 See Freud (1923a) on identifying the super-ego with the father: 'the source of the general character of harshness and cruelty exhibited by the ideal – its dictatorial "Thou shalt"' (pp. 54–55).
14 A similar phenomenon is described in 'Hysterical phantasies, bisexuality and the question of bad faith' (Freud, 1908).
15 See also Augustine's *Confessions*. Book III of *Metamorphoses* is self-consciously theatrical. Ovid forges connections to the theatre in a number of ways, placing the reader in the position of a theatrical spectator with intense visual description. Also, his allusions to Sophocles and Euripides themselves make Book III theatrical, as does 'the tree-girt plain' where Pentheus encounters the Bacchic orgies, explicitly configured as a site for spectatorship from every side. In a grisly twist, the story of Actaeon was apparently popular in the Roman gladiatorial circus and would be acted out with real deaths (Hinds, 2002).
16 From 'Jacques-Alain Miller's perversion', an online account of Miller's paper delivered at the Paris/New York Psychoanalytic Workshop, 2 April 1989, transcribed by Josefina Ayerza (www.lacan.com/frameI1.htm).
17 As well as in Titian's *Death of Actaeon* (1652), it occurs in works by Charles Joseph Natoire, Breughel, van Balen, Vernoese, Joseph Heintz.
18 Lacan connects this to the tale of Zeuxis and Parrhasios: in a contest, Zeuxis makes artificial grapes so realistic they attract the birds, then Parrhasios paints a veil on the wall so realistic that Zeuxis asks what is behind it.

198 Unknown pleasures

19 See Brooks (1993) on psychoanalysis's repetition of the phallic gaze implicit in philosophy; Irigaray (1985) notes and deplores that Freud's scenarios of sexual difference are invariably visual: little boy looking at female genitals.
20 As well as having real and symbolic roles (Lacan, 1994).
21 See Laura Mulvey's seminal essay, 'Visual pleasure and narrative cinema' (1975), on this active/passive dichotomy of male gaze and female object.
22 See Freud's (1923b) introduction of *Verleugnung* (disavowal) on refusal to recognize the absent penis.
23 See Cole (1993), Csapo (1997) and Easterling (1997). Freud (1910) himself draws on Bacchic tradition, referring to Richard Payne Knight's *A Discourse on the Worship of Priapus* (1786): In early days, 'the genitals were the pride and hope of human beings. The existence of phallic cults are seen as evidence of the child's obsession with genitals' (p. 97); see also Armstrong (2005).
24 '[Klossowski's] intimacy with Latin, and with Latin literature, cannot be over-emphasized …. Klossowski's style disorients readers unaware of this linguistic background (which includes, moreover, his consorting with liturgical and biblical Latin during his World War II years spent as a Dominican novitiate)' (Taylor, 2009, p. 245).
25 Lacan will refer to this demon of *Aidos*/shame two years later in his seminar on transference. Shame, again, is associated with the lure of something projected behind a veil: this time the veil is Socrates himself, and it is Alcibiades imagining his object of desire to be concealed within the philosopher. Shame arises alongside Alcibiades' failure to discover it. See Lacan (2015, p. 176).
26 For a comprehensive assessment, see Dillon (2002).
27 Pentheus' fate is linked to Actaeon's by both Euripides and Ovid: in a failed attempt to avoid his own death by dismemberment, Pentheus calls out: 'Help me, aunt Autonoe, let the ghost of your Actaeon move you to pity me!' (*Metamorphoses*, III, 720).
28 Dodds (1951) insists that the Bacchants were not mere revelers – the corresponding verb *bakkheuein* is not to have a good time, but to share in a particular religious rite and (or) have a particular religious experience – the experience of communion with a god which transformed a human being into a *bakkhos* or a *bakkhe*. The three Attic tragedians associate Bacchic madness with the plots and the tragic characters of the majority of their extant plays (see Schlesier, 1993).
29 'In the second century AD, the satirist Lucian remarked that "there are more females than males in these plays" (*De Saltione* 28); a character in a novel of similar date also comments on the large number of plots which women have contributed to the stage (Achilles Tatius, *Leucippe and Clitophon* 1.8). Only one extant tragedy, Sophocles' *Philoctetes*, contains no women' (Hall, 1997, pp. 105–106).
30 Borch-Jacobsen (1991) describes Lacan writing on the Papin sisters while discovering psychoanalysis under treatment by Rudolf Loewenstein.
31 See Armstrong (2005) on Freud's ambivalence towards maternal power.
32 In *Gender Trouble* (1990), Judith Butler explores Freud's and Lacan's discussions of the symbolic phallus by pointing out the connection between the phallus and the penis. She writes, 'The law requires conformity to its own notion of "nature." It gains its legitimacy through the binary and asymmetrical naturalization of bodies in which the phallus, though clearly not identical to the penis, deploys the penis as its naturalized instrument and sign' (p. 135). In *Bodies that Matter* (1993), she further explores the possibilities for the phallus in her discussion of the lesbian phallus. If, as she notes, Freud enumerates a set of analogies and substitutions that rhetorically affirm the fundamental transferability of the phallus from the penis elsewhere, then any number of other things might come to stand in for the phallus.

33 Additionally, Vernant (Vernant and Vidal-Naquet, 1981) notes that amongst the gods incest is not forbidden.
34 Lacan's Parmenides is largely the figure of Plato's dialogue, *Parmenides*. These concerns loom large in *Ou pire* (1971–2) and *Y a de l'Un*, a brief summary of which was first published in *Scilicet* in 1975. Dolar (2004) notes an early reference to Parmenides in the 'Presentation on psychical causality' (1946); there is also one in *Seminar II*. In the midst of clarifying the big Other, Lacan mentions *Parmenides*, 'where the question of the one and the other was addressed in the most vigorous and single-minded way' (p. 236).

References

Armstrong, R. (2005) *A Compulsion for Antiquity: Freud and the Ancient World*, Ithaca, Cornell University Press.
Arvanitakis, K. I. (2007) 'Some thoughts on the essence of the tragic', in Williams, P. and Gabbard, G. O. (eds) *Key Papers in Literature and Psychoanalysis*, London, Karnac, pp. 125–140
Augustine, *Confessions*, trans. R. S. Pine-Coffin (2002), London, Penguin Classics.
Barnard, S. (2005) 'Introduction', in Barnard, S. and Fink, B. (eds) *Reading Seminar XX*, Albany, State University of New York Press, pp. 1–20.
Benvenuto, B. (1994) *Concerning the Rites of Psychoanalysis: or The Villa of the Mysteries*, Cambridge, Polity Press.
Bersani, L. (1987) 'Is the rectum a grave?', *AIDS: Cultural Analysis/Cultural Activism*, vol. 43 (October), pp. 197–222.
Borch-Jacobsen, M. (1991) *Lacan: The Absolute Master*, Stanford, Stanford University Press.
Bowie, M. (1988) *Freud, Proust and Lacan: Theory as Fiction*, Cambridge, Cambridge University Press.
Bracher, M. (1993) *Lacan, Discourse and Social Change*, Ithaca, Cornell University Press.
Braunstein, N. (2003) 'Desire and jouissance in the teachings of Lacan', in Rabaté, J.-M. (ed.) *The Cambridge Companion to Lacan*, Cambridge, Cambridge University Press, pp. 102–115
Brooks, P. (1993) *Body Work: Objects of Desire in Modern Narrative*, Cambridge, MA, Harvard University Press.
Bruno, G. (1954) *Des Fureurs Héroiques* (ed. and trans. P.-H. Michel), Paris, Les Belles Lattree.
Butler, J. (1990) *Gender Trouble*, London, Routledge.
Butler, J. (1993) *Bodies That Matter*, London, Routledge.
Cole, S. G. (1993) 'Procession and celebration at the Dionysia', in Scodel, R. (ed.) *Theatre and Society in the Classical World*, Ann Arbor, Michigan University Press, pp. 25–38.
Copjec, J. (2006) 'May '68, the emotional month', *Silent Partners*, vol. 112, no. 3, pp. 90–114.
Crichton, P. and Cordess, C. (1995) 'Motives of paranoid crime: The crime of the Papin sisters', *Journal of Forensic Psychiatry*, vol. 6, no. 3, pp. 564–575.
Csapo, E. (1997) 'Riding the phallus for Dionysus: iconology, ritual and gender-role de/construction', *Phoenix*, vol. 51, pp. 253–295.
Dillon, M. (2002), *Girls and Women in Classical Greek Religion*, London, Routledge.
Dimmick, J. (1992), 'Ovid in the middle ages: authority and poetry', in Hardie, P. (ed.) *The Cambridge Companion to Ovid*, Cambridge, Cambridge University Press, pp. 264–287.

Dodds, E. R. (1951) *The Greeks and the Irrational*, Sacramento, California University Press.
Dodds, E. R. (1960) *Euripides' Bacchae*, Oxford, Clarendon.
Dolar, M. (2004) 'In Parmenidem parvi comentarii', *Helios*, vol. 31, no. 1/2, pp. 63–98.
Easterling, P. E. (1997) 'A show for Dionysus', in Easterling, P. E. (ed.) *The Cambridge Companion to Greek Tragedy*, Cambridge, Cambridge University Press, pp. 36–53.
Ecclesiastes 8: 15, *The Bible, King James Version with Apocrypha*, ed. D. Norton (2006), London, Penguin Classics.
Forrester, J. (1990) *The Seductions of Psychoanalysis: Freud, Lacan and Derrida*, Cambridge, Cambridge University Press.
Freud, S. (1895) *Project for a Scientific Psychology*, in Strachey, J. (ed.) *The Standard Edition of the Complete Psychological Works of Sigmund Freud*, vol. 1, London, Hogarth Press, pp. 283–411.
Freud, S. (1905) *Three Essays on the Theory of Sexuality*, in Strachey, J. (ed.) *The Standard Edition of the Complete Psychological Works of Sigmund Freud*, vol. 7, London, Hogarth Press, pp. 125–323.
Freud, S. (1908), Hysterical phantasies, bisexuality and the question of bad faith', in Strachey, J. (ed.) *The Standard Edition of the Complete Psychological Works of Sigmund Freud*, vol. 9, London, Hogarth Press, pp. 155–166.
Freud, S. (1910) 'Leonardo da Vinci and a memory of his childhood', in Strachey, J. (ed.) *The Standard Edition of the Complete Psychological Works of Sigmund Freud*, vol. 11, London, Hogarth Press, pp. 59–137.
Freud, S. (1915) 'Instincts and their vicissitudes', in Strachey, J. (ed.) *The Standard Edition of the Complete Psychological Works of Sigmund Freud*, vol. 14, London, Hogarth Press, pp. 109–139.
Freud, S. (1919) '"A child is being beaten": A contribution to the study of the origin of sexual perversions', in Strachey, J. (ed.) *The Standard Edition of the Complete Psychological Works of Sigmund Freud*, vol. 17, London, Hogarth Press, pp. 175–204.
Freud, S. (1923a) *The Ego and the Id*, in Strachey, J. (ed.) *The Standard Edition of the Complete Psychological Works of Sigmund Freud*, vol. 19, London, Hogarth Press, pp. 3–67.
Freud, S. (1923b) 'Infantile genital organization', in Strachey, J. (ed.) *The Standard Edition of the Complete Psychological Works of Sigmund Freud*, vol. 19, London, Hogarth Press, pp. 141–147.
Freud, S. (1924) 'Economic problem of masochism', in Strachey, J. (ed.) *The Standard Edition of the Complete Psychological Works of Sigmund Freud*, vol. 19, London, Hogarth Press, pp. 157–171.
Freud, S. (1939) 'Moses and monotheism', in Strachey, J. (ed.) *The Standard Edition of the Complete Psychological Works of Sigmund Freud*, vol. 23, London, Hogarth Press, pp. 1–139.
Gallop, J. (1984) *The Daughter's Seduction: Feminism and Psychoanalysis*, Ithaca, Cornell University Press.
Genesis 3: 7–11, *The Bible, King James Version with Apocrypha*, ed. D. Norton (2006), London, Penguin Classics.
Grigg, R. (2005) 'Shame and guilt', *Afreudite: Portuguese Review of Pure and Applied Psychoanalysis*, vol. 1, no. 1, pp. 1–9.
Hall, E. (1997) 'The sociology of Athenian tragedy', in Easterling, P. E. (ed.) *The Cambridge Companion to Greek Tragedy*, Cambridge, Cambridge University Press, pp. 93–126.
Harari, R. (2001) *Lacan's Seminar on Anxiety*, New York, Other Press.
Hayes, T. (1999) 'A jouissance beyond the phallus: Juno, Saint Teresa, Bernini, Lacan', *American Imago*, vol. 56, no. 4, pp. xx–xx.
Heath, J. (1993) *Actaeon, the Unmannerly Intruder*, New York and Bern, Peter Lang.

Hinds, S. (2002) 'Landscape with figures: aesthetics of place in the Metamorphoses and its tradition', in Hardie, P. (ed.) *The Cambridge Companion to Ovid*, Cambridge, Cambridge University Press, pp. 122–149.
Homer, *The Iliad*, trans. R. Lattimore (1975), New York, Harper Collins.
Horkheimer, M. and Adorno, T. W. (1947) *Dialektik der Aufklärung*, Amsterdam, Querido Verlag.
Kant, I. (1993) *Grounding for the Metaphysics of Morals* (trans. J. W. Ellington), London, Hackett.
Klossowski, P. (1947) *Sade, mon prochain*, Paris, Seuil.
Klossowski, P. (1998) *Le Bain de Diane* (trans. S. Hawkes and S. Sartarelli), New York, Marsilio.
Koedt, A. (1970) *The Myth of the Vaginal Orgasm*, Boston, New England Free Press.
Irigaray, L. (1985) *The Sex Which Is Not One*, Ithaca, Cornell University Press.
Lacan, J. (1933) 'Motives of paranoid crime: the crime of the Papin sisters', *Le Minotaure*, no. 3/4, pp. 25–28.
Lacan, J. (1963) 'Kant avec Sade', *Critique*, vol. 191 (April), pp. 297–299.
Lacan, J. (1973) 'L'Étourdit', *Scilicet*, vol. 4, pp. 5–52.
Lacan, J. (1977) *Seminar XI: The Four Fundamental Concepts of Psychoanalysis* (ed. J.-A. Miller, trans. A. Sheridan), London, Penguin.
Lacan, J. (1988) *Seminar I: Freud's Papers on Technique (1953–1954)* (ed. J.-A. Miller, trans. J. Forrester), Cambridge, Cambridge University Press.
Lacan, J. (1990) *Television* (ed. J. Copjec, trans. D. Hollier, R. Krauss and A. Michelson), New York, Norton.
Lacan, J. (1991) *Seminar XVII: The Other Side of Psychoanalysis* (ed. J.-A. Miller, trans. R. Grigg), New York, Norton.
Lacan, J. (1994) *Le Séminaire IV: La relation d'objet, 1956–57* (ed. J.-A. Miller), Paris, Seuil.
Lacan, J. (1998) *Seminar XX: Encore – On Feminine Sexuality: The Limits of Love and Knowledge* (ed. J.-A. Miller, trans. B. Fink), New York, Norton.
Lacan, J. (2007) *Écrits: The First Complete Edition in English* (trans. B. Fink), New York, Norton.
Lacan, J. (2008) *Seminar VII: The Ethics of Psychoanalysis* (ed. J.-A. Miller, trans. D. Porter), London, Routledge.
Lacan, J. (2014) *Seminar X: Anxiety* (ed. J.-A. Miller, trans. A. R. Price), London, Polity Press.
Lacan, J. (1961–2) *Seminar IX: L'Identification*, trans. C. Gallagher (unpublished).
Lacan, J. (1965–6) *Seminar XIII: The Object of Psychoanalysis*, trans. C. Gallagher (unpublished).
Lacan, J. (1967–8) *Seminar XV: The Psychoanalytic Act*, trans. C. Gallagher (unpublished).
Lacan, J. (1971–2) *Seminar XIX: Or Worse …*, trans. C. Gallagher (unpublished).
Lacan, Jacques (2015), *Seminar VIII: Transference* (ed. J.-A. Miller, trans. B. Fink), London, Polity Press.
Laurent, E. (2007) 'Three enigmas: meaning, signification, jouissance', in Voruz, V. (ed.) *The Later Lacan: An Introduction*, Albany, State University of New York Press, pp. 116–127.
Logan, M.-R. (2002) 'Antique myth and modern mind: Jacques Lacan's version of Actaeon and the fictions of surrealism', *Journal of Modern Literature*, vol. 25, no. 3/4, pp. 90–100.
Lucian, *Selected Dialogues*, trans. C. D. N. Costa (2009), Oxford, Oxford World Classics.
Macey, D. (1988) *Lacan in Contexts*, London, Verso.
Masters, W. and Johnson, V. (1966) *Human Sexual Response*, New York, Bantam.
Miller, J.-A. (1989) *Perversion* [Lecture to the Paris-New York Psychoanalysis Workshop], 2 April.

Miller, J.-A. (1994) 'Extimité', in Bracher, M., Alcorn, M. W., Corthell, R. J. and Massardier-Kenney, F. (eds) *Lacanian Theory of Discourse: Subject, Structure and Society*, New York, New York University Press, pp. 74–87.

Miller, J.-A. (1999) *Shifting Paradigms in Lacan* [Lecture to American Lacanian Link, University of California at Los Angeles], 7 March.

Miller, J.-A. (2006) 'On shame', in Clemens, J. and Grigg, R. (eds) *Jacques Lacan and the Other Side of Psychoanalysis: Reflections on Seminar XVII*, Chapel Hill, Duke University Press, pp. 11–28.

Mulvey, L. (1975) 'Visual pleasure and narrative cinema', *Screen*, vol. 16, no. 3, pp. 6–18.

Ovid, *Metamorphoses*, trans. Mary Innes (1955), London, Penguin Classics.

Padel, R. (1983) 'Women: Model for possession by Greek daemons', in Cameron, A. and Kuhrt, A. (eds) *Images of Women in Antiquity*, Detroit: Wayne State University Press, pp. 3–19.

Padel, R. (1992) *In and Out of the Mind: Greek Images of the Tragic Self*, Princeton, Princeton University Press.

Ricci, G. (2012) 'Picasso e Lacan' [online]. Available at http://milanoartexpo.com/2012/12/16/picasso-e-lacan-di-giancarlo-ricci-milano-arte-expo-per-la-mostra-a-palazzo-reale/ (accessed 24/08/2015).

Richardson, N. J. (1974) *The Homeric Hymn to Demeter*, Oxford, Oxford University Press.

Sartre, J.-P. (1943) *L'être et le néant*, Paris, Gallimard.

Schlesier, R. (1993) 'Mixtures of masks: Maenads as tragic models', in Carpenter, T. H. and Faraone, C. A. (eds) *Masks of Dionysus*, Ithaca, Cornell University Press, pp. 89–114.

Taylor, J. (2009) 'Meta-eroticism and simulacra (Pierre Klossowski)', in Taylor, J. (ed.) *Paths to Contemporary French Literature*, vol. 2, New Brunswick, Transaction Publishers, pp. 245–250.

Verhaeghe, P. (2006) 'Enjoyment and impossibility: Lacan's revision of the Oedipus complex', in Clemens, J. and Grigg, R. (eds) *Jacques Lacan and the Other Side of Psychoanalysis: Reflections on Seminar XVII*, Chapel Hill, Duke University Press, pp. 29–49.

Vernant, J.-P. and Vidal-Naquet, P. (1981) *Myth and Tragedy in Ancient Greece* (trans. J. Lloyd), Sussex, Harvester Press.

Williams, L. (1999) *Hard Core: Power, Pleasure and the 'Frenzy of the Visible'*, Sacramento, California University Press.

Winnington-Ingram, R. P. (1948) *Euripides and Dionysus: An Interpretation of the Bacchae*, Cambridge, Cambridge University Press.

Zeitlin, F. I. (1990) 'Playing the other', in Winkler, J. J. and Zeitlin, F. I. (eds) *Nothing to Do with Dionysos? Athenian Drama in Its Social Context*, Princeton, Princeton University Press, pp. 63–96.

INDEX

A Compulsion for Antiquity: Freud and the Ancient World (Armstrong) 3
absence: cause and 137; Eros and 69; signifier and 99–100, 183; *tuche* and 116; of universal eye 177; veiling of 179–81
Academy, Platonic 10, 11, 13, 45
accidental universe 114–18
Achilles 148–9
Actaeon: and competition over role of Other 176; and ecstasy 185; as hunter in pursuit of truth 180, 181; innocence of 178; and shame 178–9, 183; and *sparagmos* 158n27; story of 145, 165, 171–2
activity 190
Adam and Eve 178
Admetus 148
Adonis 92
Aesacus 152
agalma 26
Agathon 31, 69
Agave 185
Alcibiades 26–7
Althusser, Louis 31
amboceptor 174, 176
Ammon 32
anamnesis 15
Anaxagoras 104
Anaximander 107
Androgyne 55–6, 58, 61, 85n4, 86n10; *see also* 'circle-people'
anger: in *The Bacchae* 184; of Diana toward Actaeon 176, 179; of Juno toward Tiresias 164, 168, 169

Anouilh, Jean 146
Anthropic Principle 103, 119–20nn15–16
anthropomorphism 101–2, 104–5
Antigone: and death as signifier 148; embrace of death by 149–51; and metamorphosis 144, 152, 153; and repetition 80; symbolic death of 146–7
Antigone (Anouilh) 146
Antigone (Sophocles) 144, 146, 148
Anu 92
anxiety 192, 193
Anytos 16
Anzieu, Didier 128–9, 142, 157n4
Apollo 153, 169–70, 174, 192
Apollodorus 40
aporia 28, 38, 42, 136
appearances 105, 130–1
Arachne 153
archetypes 97–8, 101
areté 14–16, 19, 24
Aristodemus 40
Aristophanes, sexual reproduction myth of 52–90, 193
Aristophanes's myth of Eros 7, 52–3, 86n13, 91; and flawed universe 110, 114; Freud's use of 53–67, 95; Lacan's use of 67–78; and the One 193; and truth of myths 79, 84, 85
Aristotle: on cause 7, 115, 116, 137; on chance 129, 130; on creation 104; on form and function 24; on 'good' 104; on Plato's dialogues 38; against science

129–32; on sexual reproduction 62; on undeserved punishment 141–2
Armstrong, Richard 3, 79
Ascestis 148
Asdiwal 87n22
asexual reproduction 53, 87n16
Association psychoanalytique internationale 34, 48n27
asymmetry 113–14
Ate 186
Athena 180
Atlantis 45
atopia 20, 27, 30, 42, 43–6
Attis 92
Augustine (Saint) 135, 157n8, 176, 178
autochthony 53, 65, 80–1
autoeroticism 59, 95–6
automaton 116, 117, 130, 140

Baader, Franz von 56
Bacchae 181–91, 198n28
The Bacchae 184–6
Bacchantes 181–91, 198n28
Bacchus 165, 182
Badiou, Alain 42
Baer, Karl Ernest von 86n8
Baldwin, James 97
Barthes, Roland 5
Bataille, Georges 87n16
Bath of Pallas (Callimachus) 180
Beatrice 193
beauty 147, 189
Being and Nothingness (Sartre) 113, 177
Being-toward-death 99–100
Benvenuto, Bice 179, 181, 189
Bernini, Gian Lorenzo 168–9, 197n5
Beyond the Pleasure Principle (Freud): and creation 95, 100; death drive in 62, 65, 74, 151; and lamella 74, 78, 84; publication of 47n16; repetition in 78, 119n7, 139; sexual reproduction myth in 53, 60, 61–7, 71, 87n16; teaching of 21–32
Bios 86n11
bird imagery 158n23
Black Skin, White Masks (Fanon) 31
blinding and blindness: of Oedipus 133, 134, 135, 145–6; of Tiresias 163–4, 180
blushing 172–3
Boehme, Jakob 56
Boothby, Richard 75
Bosch, Hieronymus 111
Bracher, Mark 184
breast: loss of 74; suckling of 174
Breuer, Joseph 168

Brooks, Peter 180
Brücke, Ernst 17, 57, 62
Bruno, Giordano 171, 180, 181, 197n9
Buhler, Charlotte 96
Bull, Malcolm 110–11
Burckhardt, Jacob 108
Burkert, Walter 126
Burrow, Colin 152
Butler, Judith 198n32

Cadmus 80, 145, 165, 184, 185
Callimachus 180
Callisto 173
castration: and absence 99; and fragmentation 111, 138, 151, 158n27; and lamella 69; and phallus 187, 189; phantasies of 99; shame and 179–81; symbolic 180–1
castration anxiety 69, 71, 99–106
castration myths 91–2, 108, 128
Categorical Imperative 174
causality 7, 115–16, 136–8, 140–1, 154–5, 157n10
cell division 63
chance 115–17; cause and 136–7, 155; as subjective vs objective 131; tragedy and 125–6, 129, 130, 144
Charcot, Jean-Martin 194
chastity 170, 172–3, 174
childhood abuse 93
Chloe 84
Christ 107, 191
Christianity 105–6, 135
chronology: and creation myths 96–9; structuralism and 97–8, 119n10
Cinyras 92
'circle-people' 69–70, 114; *see also* Androgyne
circumcision 75
Claus, Carl 62
clinamen 115–16, 120n25
cogito 26
coherence: and creation 106, 138; fantasies of 138; knowledge and 15; self- 172
collective unconscious 101
comedy 78
correct behaviour 24–5
cosmic dualism 109–11
creation: out of nothingness 99–106; Plato and Aristotle on 104; signifiers and 100; and thought 103
creationism: and God 104–5; of Lacan 92–3, 98, 99–106; in Neoplatonic thought 109
creation myths 7, 91–124; and accidental universe 114–18; early 92; and flawed

universe 106–14; and Lacan's creation *ex nihilo* 99–106; problem of chronology in 96–9; and spontaneous universe 93–6; value of 91–3
Creon 149, 153
Crews, Frederick 3
Critias 45
Csapo, Eric 180
curiosity 9, 28
curriculum 13, 47n8

daimon 126, 132–3
Dali, Salvador 168–9
Dante 193
Daphne 169–70, 173, 174, 192
Daphnis 84
Darwin, Charles: and creation 92–3, 95, 97, 102–3, 119n14; and sexual reproduction 62, 65–6
Davies, Paul 119n15
da Vinci, Leonardo 59, 180–1
'*de*' 175
Deadalion 152–3
death: fated 108; and nothingness 100; symbolic vs physical 146–51, 158n24, 158n27
death drive 62–5; and creation out of nothingness 100, 114; vs drive 74; formulation of 21, 22, 29, 85; and irrational repetition 139; and mythology 77; narcissism and 151–2; as negative libido 111–12
de Beauvoir, Simone 31, 186
decentring 24
deferred action 95
De Freud à Platon (Georgiades) 47n7
dehiscence 111
Democritus 115, 116
De Rerum Natura (Lucretius) 115, 120n26
Derrida, J. 117–18, 155
Descartes, René 26
desire: of Actaeon for Diana 172; in *The Bacchae* 184; and death drive 22; gendered 92; of gods for humans 170; having object of 191–2; immortal 67–78, 149; for knowledge 7, 26, 27, 67, 130, 180, 194–5; to look 177, 180–1; and loss 84; love and 66; masochistic 190–1; object of 27; of other 173, 175; and phallus 188, 189; porn and 184; to possess 165; reciprocity of 174–5; repetitive 25; same-sex 55; sexual 53, 59–60, 84–5; source of 84; threat of female 187; for truth 26, 106, 187; for unity 26, 137; of whole vs part object 83

destiny 143
development 102
dialectical technique 9, 11–14, 38, 41–2, 46–7n7
Diana: chastity of 174; and competition over role of Other 176; and Deadalion 152, 165; and desire for knowledge 180, 181; myth of Actaeon and 145, 171–3; shame of 178–9
Dionysus: mirror of 109, 133; and theatre 135; worship of 182–6, 188, 191
Dionysus Lysis 61
Dionysus-Zagreus 107, 110
Diotima 71–3, 86n14, 147, 148
Discord 111
Discovering Plato (Koyré) 39
The Discovery of the Unconscious (Ellenberger) 3
dismemberment myths 107–8, 111, 184–6
double-entendres 134
doxa 16, 18
dragon 80
drive 67, 74, 76, 77–8, 84
dualism 109–11, 112
Du Bois-Reymond, Emil 57

Easterling, Patricia 134–5
École Freudienne de Paris 10, 46n2
École Pratiques des Hautes Études 13, 32
Écrits (Lacan) 12, 33; Miller and 36; Plato and Aristotle in 4; and seminars 45; source material for 39; and tragedy as cure 154; translation of '*de*' in 175
ecstasy 168–9, 184, 185, 193
The Ecstasy of St. Teresa (sculpture) 168–9, 197n5
eels, sexual reproduction of 62
ego 23–4; development of 95, 96; and tragedy 135, 154, 156; and tragic violence 111
ego-libido 59–60
ego psychology 23–5, 75–6
Ego Psychology and the Problem of Adaptation (Hartmann) 23
elementary structures 98
Eliot, T. S. 196n2
elitism 19–20, 31–2, 39
Ellenberger, Henri 3, 55–6
embarrassment 179
Empedocles 12, 112, 120n24
energy 57, 85n5
Ephialtes 86n13
Epicurus 115, 116
episteme 15–16, 20, 27, 82
epistemological transgression 184

epistemology: and creation 105; orgasms and 163–202; of psychoanalysis 7, 11–21, 22, 25; and sexuality 180; sexuality and 67, 180
eros 21
Eros: creation of 92, 118n1; and myth of sexual reproduction 7, 58–61, 62, 66, 70, 82, 86nn6–7; and Thanatos 86n11, 114
Erotism (Bataille) 87n16
ethology 24, 47n18
ethos 132
Euripides 144, 184–6
Eve, Adam and 178
evolutionism 102–3, 104
exhibitionism 177–8, 179
existentialism 112–13
'Existential Psychoanalysis' 113
exogamy 95, 119n7
extimacy 169, 185, 188
eye(s): and gaze 137–8; universal 138–41

Fanon, Franz 31
fantasy(ies): analysis and 18; of coherence 138; of complementary pairs 190; of creation 93, 94; and desire 73, 173; of detachable penis 71; of having object of desire 192; of knowledge 26; and love 82; male 164, 169, 190; masochistic 191; and mirror stage 111; Oedipus complex as 81; origin of 94; of other people's pleasure 7, 165, 196; phallus as 181–2, 183, 184, 189; and 'phantasy' 118–19n4; retroactive 108; sadomasochistic 175; of totality and completion 195
Faraday, Michael 57
fate 7, 125–9, 143–4, 155
fated death 108
Father, symbolic 187
fault (*faute*) 29
female desire as threatening 188
female orgasm 7; and Dionysus 184, 186; and men's fantasies about women 164–5, 169; mythologizing of 7; in story of Jupiter and Juno 163–4; totality of 166–7; vaginal vs. clitoral 164, 166
female pole 84
Ficino, Marsilio 110
Final Cause 137
Fink, Bruce 34, 39, 175
first causes 93–6, 104–6
flawed universe 106–14
Flemming, Walther 63
Fliess, Wilhelm 126
Forrester, John 114, 191
Foucault, Michel 5

fragmented body 111
frame narratives 40
Frankland, Graham 3, 58–9, 86n7
Frazer, James 92, 107
freedom: paradoxical 155–6; and tragedy 127, 141
Freud: Biologist of the Mind (Sulloway) 3
Freud, Sigmund: on accidental universe 114, 115, 117–18; atopic 30; on binary models of gender 190; and chronology 96, 139; classicism of 1–2, 3, 4; Darwinism of 92–3, 95, 102–3; on death drive 21–2, 29; on decentring 24; and Eros 58–9; on fate and chance 126, 127–8, 129; on fear of castration 71; on female orgasm 164, 166, 167; on flawed universe 107–8, 109, 112–14; hostility to ideas of 10, 46n1; on incest 98; and lamella 74; on libido 74, 76–7; on masochism 174, 191; mythic-molecular vision of 61–7; on narcissism 60, 96, 151; on *Naturphilosophie* 60–1; on Oedipus myth 92, 126–7, 142; on phallus 180, 181; and Plato 12, 58, 72, 73; on pleasure 169; projected Institute of psychoanalytical education of 13, 47n8; as prophet 143; on psychoanalysis as science 17, 28; on repetition 80; on sadomasochistic fantasies 175; on sexual reproduction 76; on shame 179; and spontaneous universe 93–6; studies of 3, 5; on superego 174; on threat of female *jouissance* 188; on tragedy 127, 128, 154, 155; on trauma and repression 78; on truth of myths 78; on urge to see and desire to know 180; use of Aristophanes' sexual reproduction myth by 53–67; writing style of 4
Freud's Literary Culture (Frankland) 3
Furness, Raymond 56, 85n4
Future of an Illusion (Freud) 86n9

Gadamer, Hans 97
Gaia 92
Gavarni, Paul 101
the gaze 137, 138, 140, 176–9; phallic 169, 181, 184, 198n19, 198n21
gender: binary models of 190; and castration 189; and *jouissance* 188, 191; and phallus 187, 189; reproduction and 84, 194
gender demarcation 188–9
gendered desire 92
gendered identity 179
gendered pleasure 164
gendering of truth 180
gender transgression 184

Genesis 178
Genet, Jean 186
Georgiades, Patrice 47n7
germ plasm theory 63–4
Gestalt psychology 102, 119n13
Gildenhard, Ingo 145
Gill, Christopher 78
Gilson, Etienne 120n20
global mirror-stage 103
God: all-seeing 135, 138–41, 177–8; creationism and 104–5; and *jouissance* 191, 192–3; in Neoplatonism 109, 110
gods: and causality 120n6; desire to compete with 69–70; and good 108; humans vs 132, 191–2; love of human vs 192; point of view of 134, 139; sexual desire of humans by 170, 176; in tragedy 133, 145
god's eye standpoint 132, 138–41
Goethe, Johann Wolfgang von 86n7, 149
The Golden Bough (Frazer) 92, 107
'good' 104, 108
Gorgias 14, 47n11
Grigg, Russell 178
Grote, George 46–7n7
Group Psychology and the Analysis of the Ego (Freud) 58
guilt: and creation 107; in Genesis 178; innocent 141–54; Oedipal 95, 127, 174; and tragedy 132; and trauma 155
Guthrie, W. K. C. 27, 38

Hadewijch of Antwerp 168, 191
Haeckel, Ernst 95, 119n5
Hall, Edith 139, 185
hamartia / hamarton 132
Hankinson, R. J. 62
Hard Core (Williams) 184
Hardie, Philip 145, 152
Hartmann, Heinz 23, 24
Hartmann, Max 64
Hayes, Tom 169
Hegel, Georg Wilhelm Friedrich 20, 31–2, 113, 149, 183
Heidegger, Martin 99–100, 113, 131, 185
Hera 109
Heraclitus 106, 111–12, 113, 132–3
Hermetica 109, 110
Heroic Frenzies (Bruno) 171, 197n9
heroic immortality 146–50
Hesiod 61, 91, 108, 118n1
heterosexuality and sexual reproduction myth 54–6
History of Animals (Aristotle) 62
History of Greek Civilization (Burckhardt) 108
Homer 149, 185

hommelette 75–6, 87n18
homosexuality 54–5, 59, 85n3
homunculus 75–6
horde myth 95, 115, 188
humanism 113
humans vs gods 132, 191–2
humour in Plato's dialogues 40–2
Hyppolite, Jean 32, 112
hysteria 35, 42, 93, 168, 194–5

Iago 193
imaginary 78
immortal desire 67–78
immortality: of germ plasm 63, 75; of gods vs. humans 69–70; heroic 146–50, 153; and mirror of Dionysus 109; and myth of Narcissus 110; primal loss of 73–4; and self-reproduction 65; and sexual reproduction 61–7, 72–3, 85; and tragedy 152
immortal life force 67
immortal parts 63–4
impasse(s): of Freud 7, 68, 143; of gender 194; of *jouissance* 195; of masochism 189; in Plato 28; response to 30, 33, 46
incest 108, 128, 199n33
incest taboo 95, 98
individual agency 132
individuality 149–50; love as expression of 73, 86n15
initiating event 93–6
innocent guilt 141–54; and metamorphosis 144–54; and secret speech 141–4
The Interpretation of Dreams (Freud) 126
Irigaray, Luce 169

Jacques Lacan (Roudinesco) 5
Janan, Micaela 145
The Jealous Potter (Lévi-Strauss) 87n22
Jebb, Richard 149
Jocasta 133, 144
Johnson, Virginia 166–7, 168
Jones, Ernest 3, 95
jouissance 7, 74; definition and use of term 167; and desire of other 173, 175; and Dionysus 184, 186; and female masochism 189–91; God and 192–3; maternal 188; and men's fantasies about women 164–5, 169; mystical 168–9, 191, 195, 197n5; of Other 193–4; pornography and 184; prohibition regarding understanding of 165–71; self-splitting 173–4; of Semele with Zeus 185; and shame 172–3; in story of Jupiter and Juno 163–4; as threatening 188–9

judgment 178, 179
Juliet 126
Jung, Carl: on archetypes 97–8, 101; and
    Beyond the Pleasure Principle 62; Freud's
    split from 112; on hysteria 93; Lacan and
    119n12; on libido 60–1, 92
Juno 163–4, 165, 168, 179, 180, 186
Jupiter 163–4, 165, 168, 173

Kahnweiler, Daniel-Henry 186
Kama 61
Kant, Immanuel 104, 113, 119–20n16, 136,
    173–4, 197n11
Kerrigan, William 125–6
Khaos 92
Kirk, G. S. 79
Klein, Melanie 74
Klossowski, Pierre 171–9, 182–3, 185,
    197n11, 198n24
knowing subject 140–1, 142
knowledge: constitution by language of 18;
    distaste for 29; myth of psychological
    origin of 105; nature of 28;
    psychoanalysis as kind of 11–21; as
    recollection 15, 47n10; and truth 16,
    18, 26
Kojève, Alexandre 12, 31–2, 34–5,
    40–1, 113
Koyré, Alexandre 12–13, 16, 39
Kripke, Saul 150
Kronos 92, 108
Kumarbi 92
Kyrnos 158n23

Lacan: In Spite of Everything (Roudinesco) 5
Lacan, Jacques: biographical sources on 4–5;
    on Platonic dialogue 9; published
    teachings of 4; studies of 4–6; use of
    Aristophanes' sexual reproduction myth
    by 67–85
Lacanian seminars *see* seminar(s)
lack 68–71
Lacoue-Labarthe, Philippe 86n9
La force de l'âge (de Beauvoir) 186
Laius 144
Lamarck, Jean-Baptiste 64
lamella 67–78, 87n19
language: and causality 140–1, 154–5;
    constitution of knowledge by 18; effect
    on subject of 30; and incest 98; and
    metamorphosis 152, 158–9n28; and
    truth 25
Lanzer, Ernst 143
Laurent, Eric 191
law 136

The Laws (Plato) 104
Leader, Darian 48n23, 75
Le bain de Diane (Klossowski) 171, 172,
    176, 182
Leçons d'introduction à la lecture de Hegel
    (Kojève) 35
Le Gaufey, Guy 48n22
Lemaire, Anika 35
Le Mur (Sartre) 186
Leonard, Miriam 42, 128, 129
lesbianism and sexual reproduction myth
    54–5, 85n2
lesbian phallus 198n32
L'étourdit (Lacan) 34–5
Lévi-Strauss, Claude 7, 80–1, 87n22,
    97–8, 152
libido: and dangers of Eros 58–61; death
    drive as negative 111–12; Freud's concept
    of 54, 56, 85n1; Lacan on
    76–7, 84
The Life and Work of Sigmund Freud (Jones) 3
linguisterie 33–4
linguistic ambiguity 134
Lipschütz, Alexander 86n12
'Little Hans' 71
Loewenstein, Rudolf 23, 36
Logos 86n9
longing 69
Longus 84
loss, primal 73–4, 84
lost object 75, 76, 77, 84
love, myth of 82–3
Lucian 179
Lucretius 115–16, 120n26
Ludwig 70
Lyssa 186

Macey, David 36
madness 185–6, 187, 198n28
maenads 182, 184, 186
The Maids (Genet) 186
maieutics 13, 25, 31
male pole 84
Mannoni, Octave 13–14, 16, 19–20, 102
mascarade 189
masochism 174, 189–91
Masters, William 166–7, 168
mastery 20
maternal power 187, 198n31
Maupas, Émile 86n12
meiosis 63
Meno (Plato) 13, 14–16, 26, 27, 43–4
Merope 133
Metamorphoses (Ovid): Actaeon and Diana in
    171–3, 178; Apollo and Daphne in 170;

metamorphosis in 144–5, 150–3; Narcissus and Oedipus in 60; Pentheus in 184; Tiresias and Juno in 163–5
metamorphosis 144–54, 170, 192
Mill, John Stuart 12, 46–7n7
Miller, Jacques-Alain 4, 5, 9, 10, 35–6, 37, 45–6
Miller, Paul Allen 75
mirror of Dionysus 109, 133
mirror phase/stage: and castration 99; and chronology 96–7, 98; creation myth and 109, 118; death and 147–8; first report on 31; global 103; and Narcissus 151–2; and Neoplatonism 109, 110; vs reflection 114; reformulations of 48n23; and reunification 111; split born of 106, 110–11; terminology for 98–9
Mithras 107
modesty 174
Moll, Albert 85n1
Monism 58
mortality 61–7
Most, Glenn 149
mother, loss of 74
music 25, 47n19
Musil, Robert 56
Muthos 79
Myrrha 92, 152
mystery cults 181–2, 183–5, 198n23
mysticism 58
myth(s): castration 91–2, 108, 128; creation 91–124; dismemberment 107–8, 111, 184–6; horde 95, 115, 188; as hypothesis 52, 66; of love 82–3; of pleasure 163–5; redefinition of 77–8; truth of 78–85; *see also* sexual reproduction myth

Nachmansohn, Max 12, 58, 86n6
Nachträglichkeit 95, 119n8
nakedness: and shame 172, 178–9; and truth 180
narcissism 59–60; and death drive 151–2; primary 96
Narcissus: vs Dionysus 109–10; and dualism 110, 120n23; and mirror stage 151; and Oedipus 60, 66, 145–6; and self-knowledge 165; and self-love 59; and tragedy 146
nature, psychoanalysis against 21–6
Naturphilosophie 55, 56, 60, 61, 112
navel 70
Neikos 12, 86n11
Nemesis 146
Neoplatonism 109, 110, 171, 180, 181
nerve-force 57

New Introductory Lectures (Freud) 77, 154
Nichomachean Ethics (Aristotle) 104, 130
Nichtigkeit 69
Nietzsche, Friedrich 20–1, 42, 48n30
Nilus (Saint) 107
Niobe 151, 153
non-relation 113
nothingness: creation out of 99–106; death and 100; signifier and 100
Nous 104
Nussbaum, Martha 38, 73, 130, 131–2

object of desire 27, 48n22
object-relations school 74
objet petit a 27, 48n22
Oedipal guilt 95
Oedipus: and creation myths 92; in eyes of God 139; and fate 125–9; and humans vs gods 132–5; and innocent guilt 142–4; Levi-Strauss on 80–1; and metamorphosis 146, 152, 153–4; and Narcissus 60, 66, 145–6; and science 86n9; and tragedy as cure 156–7; and universal truth 12
Oedipus (Sophocles) 127
Oedipus at Colonus (Sophocles) 153–4, 156
Oedipus complex 60, 81, 93, 108, 126
Oedipus Tyrannos (Sophocles) 132, 133, 134
the One 109, 114, 193
On Nature (Parmenides) 105
ontology 99, 114
oracle 125–6, 127, 144, 155, 157
orgasm: as anxiety 193; *see also* female orgasm
origin 120n26
original fantasy 94
original sin 107–9
Orpheus 107, 158n27, 186
orthe doxa 16–17, 20
Osiris 92
the Other: competition over role of 176; desire of 173, 175; gaze of 176–7; in gender demarcation 188–9; *jouissance of* 193–4; judgment by 178, 179; playing 188–9; in sexual reproduction 73, 84; and tragedy 132, 156
Otus 86n13
Ouranos 92, 108
Ovid: on Actaeon and Diana 171–3, 178; on Apollo and Daphne 169–70, 191–2; on metamorphosis 144–5, 150–3, 171; on Narcissus and Oedipus 60; on Orpheus 186; on Pentheus 184; on Tiresias and Juno 163–5, 193–4

Padel, Ruth 133, 185–6
Pallas Athena 153

Pankejeff, Sergei 94
Papin, Christine and Lea 186–7
Paracelsus 56
Parmenides 28, 105, 112, 113, 195, 199n34
Parrhasios 197n18
part-objects 74
passivity 190
patient presentation 47n9
Pausanius 41, 80, 92
pederasty 85n3
Peneus 170
Penia 82
penis, phallus and 198n32
Pentheus 158n27, 165, 184, 186, 188, 198n27
Pericles 19
Pfister, Oskar 12
Phaedrus 92
phainomena 130
phallic gaze 169, 181, 184, 198n19, 198n21
phallic woman 180–1
phallus 181–91; feminine 189; lesbian 198n32; in mystery cults 181–2, 183–4, 198n23; and penis 198n32; as signifier 181–4, 189
Phanes 61
'phantasy' 94, 108, 118–19n4
The Phenomenology of Spirit (Hegel) 32
The Phenomenon of Ecstasy (photo montage) 168–9
Philia 12
Phillips, Adam 125, 155
phylogenesis 94–5
Physics (Aristotle) 7, 115, 116, 129
Picasso, Pablo 186
Pindar 158n23
placenta 74, 76, 174
Plato: aloof 10; on atopic conditions 20–1; on creation 104; curriculum of 13, 47n8; on death 148–9; and ego psychology 24–5; and Freud 12; on knowledge 10–11, 13, 14–17; literary style of 38; myriad faces of 9–10; and original sin 108–9; *Schwärmerei* of 103–4; and science 27; and teaching 22–3, 28; and truth 25–6
Plato, and the Other Companions of Socrates (Grote) 46–7n7
Platonic Academy 10, 11, 13, 45
Platonic dialogue 9, 11–14, 38, 41–2, 46–7n7
pleasure(s) 163–202; insufficient 191–6; and itch to be seen 171–9; myths of 163–5; and phallus 181–91; purpose of 71–2; and shame and castration 179–81; and understanding of *jouissance* 165–71

pleasure principle 21–32
Plotinus 109, 110, 111
Poe, Edgar Allen 147
Poetics (Aristotle) 141–2
point of view: of gods vs humans 138–41; in psychoanalysis 137–8; and truth 130–1
Polybus 133
Polynices 146, 147, 149–50
pornography 184
Poros 82
post-structuralist thought 42
pre-Socratics 104–7, 112, 115, 154, 195
Preyer, Willhelm 96
Priapus 61
primal event 7, 114–15
primal fantasy 94
primal horde myth 95, 115, 188
primal scenes 94
primordial human 52–3, 55–6
primordial phenomena 55–6
Proclus 109
procreation 101, 148
Project for a Scientific Psychology (Freud) 57
Prolegomena (Kant) 136
Protagoras 14–15
Protozoa 64–5
Psyche (Rohde) 110
psychoanalysis: existential 113; and fate 125–9; as form of *orthe doxa* 17–18; as imposter 46; intellectual status of 2, 3; introduction of term 93; as kind of knowledge 11–21; against nature 21–6; object and end of 155–7; vs Platonic dialogue 9, 11–14, 38, 41–2, 46–7n7; re-engineering of 1–8; 'truth effect' of 127
psychoanalytic theory, anxiety over role of Greek myth in 6–7
publication, conflict over 32–42, 48n26
punishment, undeserved 141–2
Pythagoras 27–8

Q 57
Queneau, Raymond 35

Rabaté, Jean-Michel 83
Ragland, Ellie 77
Rapaport, David 24
Rat Man 143
the real 78, 83–4, 87n28, 117, 130–1
reality 105
reality principle 23
'recapitulation theory' 95, 119n6
reflection 109–10, 120n23, 151
repetition: of chain of signifiers 100; drive and 74; vs reminiscence 25, 47n20; as

response to event we cannot process 80; temporal and spatial 139–40; traumatic 115
repetition compulsion 63
The Republic (Plato) 20, 40, 45
return, instinct to 63
reunification 110, 111, 113
Richardson, N. J. 177–8
rigid designator 150
Rilke, Ranier Maria 56, 85n4
Rohde, Erwin 110
Romeo 126
Roudinesco, Elizabeth 4–5, 36, 45

Sade, Marquis de 173–4, 197n11
sadomasochism 175
Saint-Anne Hospital 11, 13, 41, 44–5
Sartre, Jean-Paul: on 'Actaeon Complex' 176, 180; critique of Freud by 113; on freedom 155, 159n30; on Papin sisters 186; on shame 177
'Saturnine complex' 111
Schelling, Friedrich Wilhelm von 55, 56, 141
Schickslatod 108
schools of antiquity 8
Schreber, Daniel Paul 101, 103, 148, 191
Schwärmerei 103, 119–20nn15–16
science: Aristotle against 129–32; seduction of 27–32; and truth 129–32
scientific quest 28
Scilicet 33, 48n28
scissiparous 86–7n16
scopophilia 181
The Second Sex (de Beauvoir) 31
secret speech 141–4
seduction of teaching 26–32
self-interest and death drive 22
self-love 59–60
self-preservation 59–60
Semele 109, 165, 185
seminar(s): attendance at 43, 48n31; disorientating form of 30–1; as exclusive event 31–2; importance of 30; Lacanian 2, 4, 5–6, 9–38; participation (dialogue) in 45–6
Seminar I (Lacan) 74, 177
Seminar II (Lacan): on anthropocentrism 101–2; crisis leading to 36; on dualism of Freud 112; on mirror-stage 96, 98–9; *Oedipus at Colonus in* 156; on origin of forces that move us 120n26; on Plato's *orthe doxa* 17; on psychoanalysis and Platonic dialogue 11, 12, 22–3, 45; on return of slave in Plato's *Meno* 6; on sexual reproduction 101; on symbolic vs physical death 147
Seminar VII: The Ethics of Psychoanalysis (Lacan) 5–6, 100, 146, 149–50, 169–70, 173
Seminar VIII (Lacan): on atopia 20; on discourse of Diotima 147; on elitism 39–40; on fundamental lack 68; on the 'good' 103; on initiation into mysteries 27–8; on love of gods vs human love 192; on myth of love 82–3; on Plato's Academy 10; on structure of seminar 31; on transference 26
Seminar X (Lacan): on cause 137; on first cause 104–5; on *jouissance* 192; on nature of love 27; on omnipotence and all seeingness 138; on placenta 174; on Tiresias 196n2
Seminar XI: The Four Fundamental Concepts of Psychoanalysis (Lacan): on Actaeon and Diana 176; of Aristophanes' myth of sexual reproduction 67; on chance 115; on knowledge 26; on libido and lamella 77; on masculine and feminine psychology 190; on primal loss 73–4; on the real 83–4, 117; on repetition 140; on Socrates vs Plato 41; as stand-alone introduction 5; transcription of 4, 37; on *tychic* 136, 137–8
Seminar XIII (Lacan) 196n2
Seminar XVII (Lacan) 35, 43–4, 194
Seminar XX: Encore (Lacan) 30, 37, 43, 168, 193, 195
sex act, witnessing by child of 94
sexual desire 53, 59–60, 84–5
sexual instinct 54
sexuality and epistemology 67, 180
sexual pleasure 163–202; insufficient 191–6; and itch to be seen 171–9; myths of 163–5; and phallus 181–91; prohibition regarding understanding of 165–71; purpose of 71–2; and shame and castration 179–81; in story of Jupiter and Juno 163–4; and understanding of *jouissance* 165–71
sexual reproduction myth 52–90; in *Beyond the Pleasure Principle* 61–7; dangers of Eros in 58–61; Freud's use of Aristophanes' 53–61; Lacan's use of 67–85; lamella as immortal desire in 67–78; problem with sex in 53–8; and truth of myths 78–85
SFP (Societé Française de Psychanalyse) 11, 36–7
shame: and castration 179–81; in myth of Actaeon and Diana 172–3, 178–9; in

myth of Daphne and Apollo 174; and phallus 182–3; Sartre on 177; and transference 198n25
Shepherdson, Charles 114–15
Shew, Melissa 131–2
sight and hunger for knowledge 180, 184
signifier(s): and absence 99–100; chain of 100; and creation 100; law of the pure 150; phallus as 181–91; that represent ourselves 100–1, 148
Silverstein, Eduard 62
simulacrum 181, 182–3, 189
snobbery about publication 33, 48n26
Societé Française de Psychanalyse (SFP) 11, 36–7
Societé Psychanalytique de Paris 11
Socrates: atopia of 20, 29, 30; on death 148–9; death sentence of 29; and the good 41; as hysteric 195; and *orthe doxa* 16, 17; Plato and 10, 41–2; vs Sophists 15; and teaching 11; wisdom vs knowledge of 26–7; and writing 32, 33, 38
Socratic dialogue 9, 11–14, 38, 41–2, 46–7n7
Socratism 20–1
somatic cells 64
Sophists 14–15
Sophocles: and innocent guilt 141; Oedipus myth of 12, 127, 129, 132, 153–4; and revival of Greek literature 157n3; Theban plays of 139
sparagmos 107–8, 157, 186
Spencer, Herbert 59, 86n8
Sphinx 80, 139
splitting: and *jouissance* 173; of primal people 67; reproduction by 86–7n16; of self into mortal and immortal parts 64
spontaneous universe 93–6
the stain 137
Strachey, James 154
Strasburger, Eduard 63
structuralism 28, 77, 97–8, 100, 119n10
structural linguistics 156
suicide 152–3, 159n29
Sulloway, Frank 3
superego 174, 193, 197n13
symbol(s) 98
symbolic 78
symbolic Father 187
symbolic order: attachment of subject to 78; and castration anxiety 99; and destiny 143; effects of existing within 140; entry into 97; and gaps 82; and object and end of analysis 155–6; and *orthe doxa* 17;

procreation in 101; and repetition 100; universal character of 98
Symposium (Plato): Aristophanes' myth of Eros in 7; on castration 69; on creation 92, 114; as frame narratives 40–1; and lamella 68; on love 52, 67; on music 25; on pleasure 72; sexual reproduction myth in 52–3, 55–6, 71, 73; Socratic dialogues in 38; on teaching 26–7, 31; tragedy in 5, 147, 148, 156; and truth of myths 78–9, 82, 84, 85

Tammuz 92
Taylor, A. E. 78
Taylor, John 182
teacher, wisdom of 26–7
teaching 9–38; and atopic academy 43–6; of *Beyond the Pleasure Principle* 21–32; in École Freudienne de Paris vs Plato's Academy 10–11, 46n2; meaning of 6; of psychoanalysis against nature 21–6; and psychoanalysis as kind of knowledge 11–21; and resistance to writing 32–42; science, surprise, and seduction of 26–32; of virtue 14–16
Television (Lacan) 114, 131, 193
Teresa (Saint) 168–9, 191, 197n5
Thanatos 86n11, 114
thaumasios / thaumezein 28, 29
Theaetetus (Plato) 28
theatre 176, 178, 197n15
Thebes 145–6
Themistocles 19
Theogonis 158n23
Theogony (Hesiod) 91, 108, 118n1
Theuth 32
Thomas Aquinas (Saint) 105–6, 120n18
Three Essays on the Theory of Sexuality (Freud) 12, 33, 53, 54–61
Timaeus (Plato) 45, 55, 104
time 139–40
Tiresias: and argument between Jupiter and Juno 7, 163–5, 166, 171, 193–4, 195, 196; blinding of 145–6, 163–4, 180; and Dionysus 184; Freud as 143; and Oedipus 133; transformation into woman of 145
Titans 107, 109, 186
Totem and Taboo (Freud) 94, 98, 107, 109
totemism 95
Tracy, David 157n8
tragedy 7, 125–62; in Aristotle against science 129–32; in *The Bacchae* 184–5; and causal gap 136–8; and chance 125–6, 129, 130; cultural specificity of 127; as cure 154–7; double-entendres in 134;

ending and beginnings in 92; and fate 125–9; god's eye view in 132, 138–41; humans vs gods in 132–5; and individual agency 132; and innocent guilt 141–54; and metamorphosis 144–54; origins of 184–5; and secret speech 141–4; women in 185–6, 198n29
Trakl, Georg 56
transference 26–7, 48n22, 147
Transformations and Symbols of the Libido (Jung) 61
transgender 7
transgression: creation and 91; gender and epistemological 184; and pleasure 165, 169, 171, 178; and shame 179; and tragedy 145, 155
transvestism 188–9
trauma: and chance 117–18; and death drive 114; and fear of castration 99; and guilt 155; and lamella 83; primal event at origins of 7; and repression 78
traumatic events 93–6, 115
traumatic repetition 21, 115, 116
Tristes Tropiques (Lévi-Strauss) 80
truth: being surprised by 30; forgotten 13, 15, 47n10; gendering of 180; and knowledge 16, 18, 26; Lacan on 131; language and 25; love of 180; of myths 78–85; nakedness and 180; point of view and 130–1, 137–8; and reality 105; science and 129–32; and sight 180; as subjective experience 106
'truth effect', of psychoanalysis 127
tuche: and accidental universe 115–16, 117; Aristotle on 130–1; definition of 7; and fate 129; and gaps in causality 136–7; and humans vs gods 132, 133; and secret speech 144
Tybalt 126
tychic 117–18, 130, 132, 136, 137–8, 144

unconscious: and chance 117–18; collective 101; and creation 93, 117; language of 22, 23, 30, 156; and sexual reproduction 74, 75, 77, 83; and tragedy 126, 127, 129, 135, 137, 140, 142, 144
understanding 29; dangers of premature 30
uniqueness, love as expression of 73, 86n15
unity: androgynous 85n4; and first cause 95; in mirror 96; non-relation vs 113; and original sin 107; Parmenides on 106, 109; vs strife 12, 112; and truth 26, 105
universal eye 138–41
universe: accidental 114–18; disrupted 28, 105, 112; flawed 106–14; spontaneous 93–6
university discourse 34–5
University of Vincennes 44, 48n32
unveiling, shame at 182–3
Uranism 85n3
Uranos 108
Urpflanze 55
Urphantasien 94

vacuousness 69
Van Beneden, Edouard 63
veil(s) 179–81, 183–4, 189–90
Venus 120n26
Vernant, Jean-Pierre 128–9, 132–5, 139, 142, 157–8n15
Villa of Pompeii, frescoes in 183–4
virtue 14–16
vis viva 57
voyeurism 171–2, 176–7

Waldeyer, Heinrich von 63
Wallon, Henri 97
The Wasteland (Eliot) 196n2
Weatherill, Rob 103
Webster, Richard 3
Weismann, August 63–4, 72, 84
Weismann barrier 64
Weltseele 55
Wilamowitz-Moellendorff, Ulrich von 81–2
Williams, Bernard 155
Williams, Linda 184
Winter, Sarah 127–8, 129, 153
Wolf Man 94
wonder created by teaching and science 28, 29
writing, resistance to 32–42, 48n26

Zeitlin, Froma 186, 188–9
Zeus: and creation myths 92, 108; and mystery cults 109; and myth of sexual reproduction 52–3, 55, 69–70, 114; and Semele 185, 191
Zeuxis 197n18
Zissos, Andrew 145
Zupančič, Alenka 148

Taylor & Francis eBooks

Helping you to choose the right eBooks for your Library

Add Routledge titles to your library's digital collection today. Taylor and Francis ebooks contains over 50,000 titles in the Humanities, Social Sciences, Behavioural Sciences, Built Environment and Law.

Choose from a range of subject packages or create your own!

Benefits for you
- Free MARC records
- COUNTER-compliant usage statistics
- Flexible purchase and pricing options
- All titles DRM-free.

Benefits for your user
- Off-site, anytime access via Athens or referring URL
- Print or copy pages or chapters
- Full content search
- Bookmark, highlight and annotate text
- Access to thousands of pages of quality research at the click of a button.

Free Trials Available
We offer free trials to qualifying academic, corporate and government customers.

eCollections – Choose from over 30 subject eCollections, including:

Archaeology	Language Learning
Architecture	Law
Asian Studies	Literature
Business & Management	Media & Communication
Classical Studies	Middle East Studies
Construction	Music
Creative & Media Arts	Philosophy
Criminology & Criminal Justice	Planning
Economics	Politics
Education	Psychology & Mental Health
Energy	Religion
Engineering	Security
English Language & Linguistics	Social Work
Environment & Sustainability	Sociology
Geography	Sport
Health Studies	Theatre & Performance
History	Tourism, Hospitality & Events

For more information, pricing enquiries or to order a free trial, please contact your local sales team:
www.tandfebooks.com/page/sales

 The home of Routledge books

www.tandfebooks.com